Caring

for Our
Parents

Caring

for Our

Parents

INSPIRING STORIES OF FAMILIES SEEKING
NEW SOLUTIONS TO AMERICA'S
MOST URGENT HEALTH CRISIS

Howard Gleckman

St. Martin's Press 📚 New York

www.stmartins.com

"My Rose Umbrella" used with permission
from the estate of Natalie Fenninger

Book design by Mspace / Maura Fadden Rosenthal

Library of Congress Cataloging-in-Publication Data

Gleckman, Howard.
    Caring for our parents : inspiring stories of families seeking new solutions to American's most urgent health crisis / Howard Gleckman. — 1st ed.
        p. cm.
    ISBN-13: 978-0-312-38099-1
    ISBN-10: 0-312-38099-2
    1. Older people—Long-term care—United States.   2. Older people—Home care—Social aspects—United States.   I. Title.
    HV1461.G56 2009
    362.6—dc22

                                                        2008046217

First Edition: June 2009

10   9   8   7   6   5   4   3   2   1

In loving memory of
Herb and Marilyn Gleckman
and
Al and Ida Kline

Contents

Introduction

This book tells the story of how we care for frail seniors and younger people with disabilities in America. It is a way to learn from the experiences of those who get this help, and from their families, who often make enormous personal sacrifices to give them the care they need.

Through their eyes, I discovered the irrational and disjointed ways we deliver and pay for this assistance, and how our dysfunctional system often drives people to get the wrong care, in the wrong place, at the wrong time. I saw firsthand the physical, emotional, and financial price families pay to help friends and relatives. I saw once-middle-class seniors who worked hard all of their lives end up destitute, forced to share tiny nursing home rooms with strangers or struggling to live at home.

I hope to give readers an inside look into today's failing long-term-care system, and also to provide some ideas for making it better. With all the talk about reforming health care in America, it would be a tragedy if we missed the opportunity to fix long-term-care services as well.

My first glimpse into this world came from personal experience. My wife and I cared for both her father and mine in the 1990s. But after spending as much as two years with the extraordinary people in this book, I quickly learned how lucky we were, and how hard it is for most long-term-care families.

I also learned this:

- More than 10 million Americans are getting long-term assistance today, either at home or in institutions. As many as 44 million relatives and friends are helping them.

- Nearly 70 percent of all sixty-five-year-olds will need some long-term care before they die. One out of every five will require this help for more than five years.

- The cost is staggering: more than $200 billion in paid care each year. The average annual price of a nursing home stay exceeds $78,000. The hourly cost of a home health aide approaches $20. Families contribute hundreds of billions of dollars more in informal help.

- Most paid long-term care in America comes from Medicaid, the welfare-like government health system that won't help unless you are impoverished, and which still forces many into nursing homes when they don't need to be there.

- Less than 10 percent of this assistance is paid by private long-term-care insurance, which remains too expensive and too complicated for most middle-class families.

- Medicare, the government's universal health system for seniors, does not provide long-term care. Under its perverse logic, if you suffer a major heart attack, Medicare will pay tens of thousands of dollars to treat you. If you suffer from Alzheimer's, it very likely will pay nothing for your care.

- More than eight of ten Americans who need personal assistance and other long-term care will get it at home, and not in nursing homes. Most is provided by family members who are often unprepared and untrained for this difficult work.

- New ways to deliver care, and for neighbors to help neighbors, are blossoming throughout the country. But we are still learning which work best and how to pay for them.

- As the Baby Boomers retire, today's long-term-care challenge will balloon into a full-blown social and financial crisis. Twenty million Boomers will need this assistance by mid-century. Most will have no way to pay for it on their own, even as the cost of providing care threatens to overwhelm government resources. If we don't act soon to fix the system, it will bankrupt us and our families, and then it will help bankrupt the government.

• There are solutions. Europe and Japan have already found them. So can we.

The story of long-term care is the mirror image, or perhaps the inevitable consequence, of what's become known as the Third Age. It is both wonderful and unprecedented in human history that so many seniors are living active and happy lives well into their eighties and beyond. But they are not immortal.

The British journalist Alistair Cooke once said, tongue firmly in cheek, "In America, death is optional." Of course, it isn't. A few of us will die suddenly, perhaps from a violent heart attack or massive stroke. Most of us, however, will suffer from multiple chronic diseases or dementia, as our bodies gradually fail. Or, at a much younger age, we may be struck down with a disease such as multiple sclerosis or suffer a crippling injury.

We like to say, "I'll never be like this. Just shoot me first." But that never happens. Today—or tomorrow—our parents will need help with their everyday lives. They will need the kind of assistance we have come to call long-term care. Perhaps it will be aid cooking or bathing, or help balancing a checkbook or getting to the doctor. Then, in not too many years, it will be our turn.

While there are many scandals in the world of long-term care— horrible nursing homes, incompetent or abusive family members, financial con men, and indifferent bureaucrats—that is not what this book is about. Instead, I focus on the lives of ordinary families. They are a little like front-line soldiers: What they do each day is often heroic, but it is also painfully commonplace. After learning their stories, I hope a reader will fairly say, "These are the struggles I will face unless we can find ways to do this better."

All of the stories in this book are true. The names are real, except that of one woman, who requested that I not use her name. The descriptions of all the events are based on what I saw or what was described to me by family members. When possible, I verified events I did not witness with documents or multiple interviews.

In many ways, of course, these accounts are deeply personal. But they are also universal. They are the story of long-term care in America.

Caring

for Our

Parents

ONE

The Phone Call

Ann was out with friends on the evening of February 21, 1996. I was sitting in my favorite chair, reading a book and listening to music, when the phone rang. I don't remember the book or the music, but I will never forget the call. With just a few words, my family was sent plummeting into a painful, mysterious, and all-consuming world for which we were completely unprepared.

A five-minute conversation turned an ordinary suburban couple into caregivers for an elderly parent—a role we would play without respite for the next year and a half. Within twenty-four hours, we would begin careening from crisis to crisis, grasping for solutions to problems we only half understood, all the while being undermined by a medical and financial system that was as woefully unprepared to manage long-term care as we were.

It would be, at once, the most difficult and the most rewarding thing I have done in my life.

What happened to us on that raw February evening is so common that elder-care professionals simply call it The Phone Call. If you have not received one yet, chances are you will. Nearly 70 percent of our parents will require personal care sometime during their old age. A typical senior will need it for three long years, and one out of every five will depend on it for five years or more.[1] More often than not, it will all begin with the ring of a telephone.

For us, the caller was my father-in-law, Albert Kline, a quiet retired government worker. He was calling from a pay phone at a hospital in Ft. Lauderdale, Florida. In a broken voice, Al tried to explain that his wife, Ida—my mother-in-law—had suffered a massive stroke. Al couldn't get the words out. "I can't believe this is happening," he said again and again. But the message was clear enough.

When my wife returned a few hours later, I broke the news as best as I could. Ann first called her father, then her brother, Ron. We arranged to get the first plane to Florida the next morning, and when we arrived at the hospital, we found Ida on life support in the intensive care unit. She was, by any reasonable definition, already dead. Still, we needed to make the decision to remove her from the ventilator that was pumping oxygen through her body.

I stood frozen in the doorway of her room, unable to decide whether to go in or not. Entering felt like an invasion of her privacy. Ida, who was not a small woman, seemed lost in the large hospital bed, her breathing maintained only by a gray metal machine, a plastic tube in her mouth. I struggled to capture an image of the warm and gregarious woman who had persevered despite a very difficult life. Yet, at just seventy-two, that Ida was gone.

But seeing my mother-in-law was only the first shock of that day. While Ann, Ron, and I struggled to absorb what was happening, Al had more news. Standing in the corner of a soulless waiting room, he broke it simply and quietly: "I have a tumor."

What Al had was advanced melanoma. He had suffered a bout of this skin cancer a half decade before, but it had been successfully treated and was half-forgotten. On our recent visits to Florida, he had complained of back pain. But, deep in denial, we all convinced ourselves that this was nothing more than normal discomfort for a seventy-four-year-old.

In fact, his melanoma had returned. It had gone undiagnosed for a long time, and now the cancer was aggressively attacking the rest of his body. Al and Ida had never told anyone that the disease was back— not their kids or their own brothers and sisters, who lived nearby. For months, Ida had been Al's sole caregiver. She'd done it with no one to talk to, or to help with rides or advice. She'd had no shoulder to cry on. The stress almost certainly had helped kill her.

Now that overwhelming responsibility was about to fall to Ann, a lawyer with the U.S. Environmental Protection Agency. Ron, a peripatetic college professor, couldn't do it. Besides, sons rarely care for aging parents.

The day Ida was removed from life support, we arranged her funeral. She'd be buried in her hometown of Wilkes-Barre, a grim little place in the coal country of central Pennsylvania. When Ida was a teenager, she couldn't wait to get out of Wilkes-Barre. But her parents were buried there, and Al felt this was where she should be laid to rest, too.

Al was much too sick to travel to the funeral, so Ron flew to Pennsylvania, where a brief graveside ceremony was held. Al, Ann, and I stayed in Florida and held a memorial service in Al and Ida's living room.

A few days later, we met with Al's oncologist, who talked about experimental treatments and drug trials. We listened, skeptical but too overwhelmed to ask him the probing questions we should have. We did ask if Al had much hope of survival, or if we should consider ending his debilitating chemotherapy and instead enroll him in hospice. An in-home hospice program would provide an aide for ten hours a week, a registered nurse who could check in on Al to be sure that his pain was being managed, and a social worker who could help us plan any additional care he might need.

But the oncologist rejected the idea out of hand. Government rules required that a doctor certify that a patient had less than six

months to live before Medicare paid for hospice, and he flatly refused. "Your father isn't there yet," he told Ann.

It took us a while to figure out that Al's melanoma was going to
kill him, and that all of this doctor's grand plans were little more than
a long-shot attempt to buy my father-in-law a couple of extra months.
Perhaps this doctor, like many oncologists, saw hospice as a kind of
surrender in his personal war with cancer. The doctor had no suggestions for what we *could* do, but whatever his reasons, hospice was, for
now, out of the question.

Still in shock from her mother's sudden death, Ann now had to
find a way to care for her very sick father—from a thousand miles
away. Al didn't make it easy. He wanted to stay in the apartment he
had shared with Ida for so many years, but he refused any help. He
wouldn't even consider a nursing home or assisted-living facility.
He would not move to the Washington, D.C., area to be with us or to
upstate New York, to be near Ron.

Yet Al was, in many ways, helpless. He could not cook. He had
no idea how to use a microwave, and in any event was too weak to
stand in the kitchen, so all his meals had to be made for him. He
couldn't do any housecleaning. The idea of his driving terrified us
all. We had no idea what to do.

Ann needed to get back to her job, and Ron needed to return
to his. So we decided to hire a part-time aide who would come in for
four hours a day, three days a week, to cook and clean for Al. We'd
try this while we attempted to return to our lives. Ann, feeling deeply
guilty about how little she was doing for her dad but not sure what
else she should do, flew back to Washington.

After a month, there was another phone call. This one was from
Al's brother, Jake, who had met Al for dinner and was stunned at
how much he had deteriorated.

Ann was back on a plane the next day, taking more time off from
work. She was not sure how sick Al was, but she knew she had to find
better arrangements for him. Ann began to think about taking a leave
from her job to stay in Florida with her dad.

She brought Al back to the doctor. This time, he concluded that further treatment was futile, so we turned to hospice to help keep Al comfortable in the days he had left. We all met with a hospice nurse in Al's living room. She explained how the program worked, how Medicare would pay for it, and how Al could remain at home. But this had to be Al's decision.

At first he seemed comfortable with the plan.

The nurse took us through pages of numbingly routine forms until we got to the question of whether Al was likely to live for less than a half-year, as Medicare regulations required. And for the first time, Al heard his death sentence. No one had ever told him just how sick he was.

"So, I am going to die in six months," he said, in what was at once a question and a statement.

"This doesn't mean you're going to die in six months," I told my father-in-law. "It just means a doctor says so to make you eligible for hospice. They don't really know."

And so they don't. But Al was going to die soon, and this was the first time any of us said it out loud.

We enrolled him in the home hospice program, but by now Al was so unsteady on his feet that he needed assistance getting to the bathroom at night. He wouldn't let Ann help him, so we had to hire aides on two twelve-hour shifts. The overnight aide mostly slept or watched TV, but she had to be there for those few minutes Al needed her.

While Medicare paid for hospice, it did not pay for those extra aides. Al paid their fees out of his pension. Ann stayed with her father for the first two weeks of his hospice care. But she had a job, and a life, back in Maryland.

Even with the aides, hospice, and Ann's help, the toll of the melanoma was too much. Al was having trouble eating, was deeply depressed, and was visibly failing. Despite all of our wishes, he could not stay at home.

So, after just a few more weeks, Ann brought her dad to be near us. We had no idea where he could live, so we first arranged to have him admitted to a large local nursing home until we could plan the next steps.

It is not always easy to get a patient into a good nursing home on such short notice. But we had one big advantage: We could "private-pay." That is, we were willing to write very large checks without relying on government assistance. About half the total cost of long-term care is paid by Medicaid, the welfare-like government health program for the poor. But Medicaid pays about 15 percent less than the retail rate, so nursing homes are always happier to have private-pay patients like Al.

The official price—a decade ago—was $5,000 a month. With add-ons, it was closer to $6,000. We learned that in a nursing home, you pay extra for just about everything, from adult diapers to snacks.

After a harrowing flight, which left Al extremely weak and disoriented, we brought him to the facility, a large multistory building that was part of a huge seniors' complex just a few miles from our house.

He was immediately taken to a small room. As I stood in a hallway watching the nurses struggle to stabilize him, I was convinced he would die within hours, and wondered if perhaps that might be a blessing.

But Al didn't die—and once he recovered from the trip and got his bearings, he had one wish: to get out of that sterile and impersonal nursing home.

He was wheelchair-bound by then, and struggling to manage his steadily increasing pain. There were good days. One warm early spring afternoon, Al munched hot dogs, his favorite food, on our patio. And there were bad: late-night calls from the nursing home telling us that Al had fallen, or half-coherent calls from Al himself, as he tried to grasp what was happening to him.

After one of those falls, Al was X-rayed, and we learned how widely the cancer had spread through his body. Ann and I knew we would lose him soon, but those extra weeks were a gift.

Al's goal of escaping the nursing home became ours, and after three weeks we did get him out. He refused to live with us, so we found him an apartment in a nearby assisted-living facility. We rented furniture, put up family photos, and hired a live-in aide to care for him.

Al moved in, but said it still didn't feel like home. The apartment needed, he decided, more artwork on the walls. So we found some paintings at a furniture rental store. Once we hung those, Al smiled for the first time in months. He was, in some way, home.

He lived there for one week.

One morning, a few days after we finally got him settled, the phone rang again. This time it was my mother, Marilyn. My dad, Herb, had been admitted overnight to their local hospital in Delray, Florida.

This time Ann stayed in Washington with Al while I caught the next available flight to Florida. I found my father in the intensive care unit, alert but ashen. All my mother could tell me was that he had suffered a heart attack and that, at two A.M., the local rescue squad had taken him to a nearby hospital emergency room.

After I saw my dad, I tried to find out what was wrong with him. It was almost impossible to get answers, but I finally cornered a cardiologist in a hallway. My father had not had a heart attack. His problem was congestive heart failure, an extremely common ailment among the elderly. His heart was literally wearing out, and was no longer able to pump enough blood to the organs in his body.

His cardiac disease was very bad. After eighty-one years, my dad's heart was pumping at less than 15 percent of its normal strength. The doctors were amazed he was still alive. Age, a long-ago heart attack, and an old three-pack-a-day cigarette habit had finally caught up with him.

After a couple of days he somehow stabilized, and my mother and I started to think about what would happen next. Then the phone rang again.

It was Ann. Al's regular aide had taken the day off, so Ann had gone to his apartment to check on things. When she arrived, she found Al barely responsive. She realized right away what was happening: Her father was about to die.

The fill-in aide was screaming and crying and clumsily trying to perform CPR. It was a nightmare. Ann tried to comfort her dad while hustling the hysterical aide out of the apartment. She kept thinking that she wanted her father, who even in the best of times loved the quiet, to die in peace and calmness.

While Ann and I were talking, Al stopped breathing. As he wished, Ann did not call 911. It was May 26, just three months after Ida's stroke.

Even today, it is hard for Ann to look back on the last months of her father's life without weeping. "Nothing," she says, "worked out the way I wanted it to."

Ann began making arrangements for her dad's funeral. I got a plane back to Washington and we prepared to bury Al next to his beloved Ida. Al's life had ended, but our long-term-care story was only beginning.

As soon as the doctors diagnosed my father's heart disease, they loaded him up with drugs: ACE inhibitors to help his blood flow more easily through his body, beta blockers to improve his heart's ability to pump, and diuretics to help remove the fluids that built up in his lungs and legs when his heart still could not do its job. At one point, he was taking a dozen different medications. Then they inserted a small device in his chest to regulate his heart rhythm and shock it back into a proper beat when necessary.

After the surgeon did his work, I asked him how much longer he thought my dad would live. "If it was me, I wouldn't sell him a six-month life insurance policy," replied this doctor, who knew everything—and nothing—about the human heart. That was how I learned my own father, like Al just days before, would soon die.

But this doctor was wrong. Stubborn, life-loving Herb lived another fourteen months. Only once in all that time did my father and I talk about his death.

My parents lived in a second-floor garden apartment in a build-ing with no elevator. After my dad became wheelchair bound, there was no way to get him to the street or to a car. So an outing for him became the few-hundred-foot trip to the end of the walkway out-side their door.

By then, I was visiting my parents every few weekends. Each morning I was in Florida, I would roll my dad down that walkway until we found a place to sit, either in the warm sun or, on those swel-teringly humid South Florida days, in some bit of shade. One morn-ing, as we were making small talk, my father said, "I guess this is the end of the line. I'm going to die."

I was speechless. It was an almost perfect echo of what had hap-pened with Al just a few months before. How do we talk about dy-ing with those we love so much?

It was the subject we each faced every single day, yet never men-tioned.

"Me too," I replied after a long silence. "We are all going to die. The difference is you know what is going to kill you." He smiled. I wasn't sure whether to laugh or cry. So I did a little of both.

We knew my dad did not have long to live, but despite the heart-less prediction of that cardiologist, we didn't know how long. Years before, Herb had made it very clear that he wanted no extraordi-nary measures used to prolong his life. But my father still had time, and we all wanted to make sure he lived his remaining days as fully and comfortably as possible. We also knew that we needed to protect my mother, who would shoulder most of the burden of caring for my dad.

Unfortunately, we had few clues about how to pull this off. We'd learned from our experience with Al, but Ann, my mother, and I still felt overwhelmed.

Herb was deeply religious, and the most optimistic man I ever knew. He loved life, but approached the world with a special stub-bornness. He was happiest listening to music, especially opera, and in the 1950s and early 1960s owned a record shop in Providence,

Rhode Island. He had a marvelous time. Over the years, players from the Rhode Island Philharmonic and even the Boston Symphony would stop in to listen to the latest recordings and debate the relative merits of the musicians who'd made them.

But my father refused to sell records he didn't like, or at least those that didn't meet his lofty artistic standards. So the Melody Shop may have been the only music store in 1950s America where you couldn't buy a record by Elvis Presley. To nobody's surprise, except perhaps my dad's, the venture failed. Later he owned a men's haberdashery, and after that flopped, he and my mother went on the road selling women's accessories such as scarves and belts to high-end boutiques.

They made quite a success of this. My father would breeze in, swap stories, tell jokes, and eventually display the merchandise. The shop owners loved him. But they bought from my mother. After an hour or so of Dad's chitchat, she was the one who'd say, "So we'll put you down for a dozen of the blue and two dozen of the yellow."

My dad could also be incredibly impulsive. Every few years, seemingly without giving it much thought, he'd pull into an auto dealership, leave our old car in trade, and drive off with a new one. He never did any research, never shopped for a good price, and never told my mother what he was about to do.

In the mid-1970s my parents took a rare vacation, visiting friends in Florida. In the midst of that trip, at age sixty, my impetuous father decided to sell their business and move from chilly Rhode Island to sunny Florida. So they bought a condo in a day and, a few months later, moved to a hideous retirement community in Delray, a few miles outside of a once-charming beach town midway between Ft. Lauderdale and Palm Beach.

My mother, Marilyn, was a tiny woman of old school dignity and great resolve. She suffered from ill health for many years, but kept active. After they retired to Florida, she volunteered as a receptionist at the local police headquarters. The cops all loved her, especially for her ability to steer unhappy visitors back out the door long be-fore they'd ever reach the desk sergeant.

For her part, my mother didn't so much love people as feel curi-ous about them. Marilyn collected stories like some people collect bird sightings. She'd go to a local park, sit down on a bench next to a stranger, and in half an hour add a new story to her collection.

She was a loyal friend, but she also kept her distance. She was never a nurturing mother or wife. But now, after fifty years of mar-riage, Marilyn had a new role: to care for her increasingly helpless husband.

After his May hospital stay, Herb came home. He seemed to man-age well for a few months, but before long suffered another episode of heart failure and was readmitted to the hospital. This time, it was clear he would never again be able to care for himself.

On August 21, our phone rang once again. It was my mother. She was near tears—the only time I'd ever heard her lose control. The hos-pital had called at 9:30 A.M. to tell her my dad would be discharged by the end of the day. But discharged to where? That, said the hospital social worker, was my mother's problem, and she had until one P.M. to make the arrangements.

The easiest thing to do, my mom was told, was to find a nursing home for him. The hospital discharge planner gave her a list. That's when my mother called me.

Dad was not going to a nursing home. He was going to come home. But my mother could no longer handle his care without help, so we needed to find a home health aide. My mother picked an agency at random from the local telephone book, and explained her problem. It was not the first time the agency heard this story.

An aide met my parents at the hospital, and within a few hours, Dad was home. Suddenly, a two-person household became a three-person family. Naressa Moore was from Jamaica, but was living in South Florida with her daughter, who was going to a local college. Naressa had the beautiful lilting accent of the islands, dark skin, a round face with expressive eyes, and a gentle smile. She had been a nurse at home, and hoped to earn a nursing license in the United States. While she studied, she worked as an aide.

Naressa was blessed with an extraordinary mix of no-nonsense competence and great kindness. Like many wives who become care-givers, my mother was deeply ambivalent about sharing her home with a stranger, especially another woman. She knew she needed the help, but for five decades, Marilyn had run my parents' house. She'd cooked and cleaned, chosen what to buy and where to store the dishes. Now all these decisions would be shared with a woman whose culture, language, religion, and outlook on life could not be more different from hers.

As we had done with Al, we enrolled my dad in hospice. That decision proved to be incredibly important, but not for the reasons any of us thought.

Somehow it all worked. Naressa, Herb, and Marilyn became, in their way, a family. Naressa provided the difficult physical care for Herb that my mother could not. The two women shared the job of providing companionship for my dad, who was gradually losing his ability to walk, speak, and eat. The hospice nurses visited once or twice a week.

Back in 1996, my parents paid Naressa $85 a day. But even that was not simple. In long-term care, nothing is.

A few years before my dad got sick, he'd bought a Medicare managed-care insurance policy from a major national carrier. It promised all sorts of extra benefits beyond traditional Medicare: eye and hearing exams, glasses, and, if you believed their advertising, long-term care. Big, bold, full-page ads compared their insurance with traditional Medicare.

Under the Medicare column, it listed home care, and the "no" box was checked. Under the private insurance column, the home-care box was checked "yes."

None of it was true. The insurance company refused to pay for Naressa's time, so my mother paid more than $21,000 out of her own pocket while we fought with the company. We wrote letters. We appealed. We hired a lawyer. Seventeen months after my dad died, the company finally paid.

While my mother and Naressa were my father's caregivers, my role was to provide respite for my mom and companionship for my father, and to serve as an advocate for them both. Every few weeks, early on Friday morning, I'd fly to Florida, where I'd stay until Sunday evening, when I'd get the last nonstop flight back to Washington. Ann joined me on every other trip.

At first my days there were spent busily calling doctors, checking with hospice, and helping my mother with chores. As time went on, I'd spend less time doing things and more hours just sitting with my dad, listening to music or watching TV, sometimes holding his hand or quietly chatting.

The busy work, I realized, was a kind of denial. The more I chased after doctors or complained to social workers about one thing or another, the more I could avoid thinking about what really mattered: that my father was going to die soon and that the remaining time we had together was to be savored.

So I stopped running around and just sat with him.

It was so hard. I'd arrive at their apartment from an exhausting plane trip, hug my mother, and sit next to my dad, who was usually in a recliner in their family room. I'd realize how much weaker he was—even from just a few weeks before. I didn't want him to see me cry, so I'd get up and go into the bathroom. And sob.

But those hours with him were precious, unlike any I'd ever had. That is the thing about someone dying in slow motion: As hard as it is, it gives you time.

Time to resolve old conflicts.

Time to balance the scales.

Some days, though, it was almost too much. Early one Sunday afternoon, after months of gradually fading away, my dad was in bed. We were alone, watching a football game, while my mother and Naressa were off shopping. Herb began to doze, as he often did, his breathing labored despite the oxygen he was getting through thin plastic tubes attached to his nose.

I watched him for what seemed like an hour but was probably only a few minutes.

And I thought, for just a moment, about suffocating him.

He wouldn't struggle. No one would ever know. It would end his suffering, and my mother's. And mine.

I got up and walked outside into the musky South Florida air— fetid and damp even on a winter's day. My mind emptied.

Then I returned to my dad's room. He was still sleeping. The football game—the Dolphins and somebody—was still on. I sat back down. And watched.

There was one more member of our caregiving team, a hospice chaplain named Paul. He was a sixty-something Lutheran minister from Long Island, New York, with natural charm, a ruddy complexion, and the square-jawed good looks of a 1940s movie star. My dad, who was an observant Jew, had probably never knowingly met a Lutheran minister in his life, and surely one had never visited his home. But Paul and Herb became quite a pair.

They shared a love for opera and would listen to my father's large music collection for hours at a time. Then, somehow re-creating my father's joyous days in the Melody Shop forty years earlier, they'd argue about whether Pavarotti or Domingo was the superior tenor, or whether Callas was a better soprano than Scotto. After a while, the music would stop and they'd just talk. Their conversations were private, and neither ever shared them with me or my mom. But I knew that, after a time, they'd talk about life, and God, and death.

As the months passed, there was less music. Toward the end, there was none.

Paul and I played another important role in Herb's life. Because his illness trapped him in his home, my dad found himself spending most of his time with two women, Naressa and my mother. Sometimes it drove him to distraction. Having a guy around was a very big deal to him.

My father and I had a complicated relationship, as most fathers and sons do. I was a rebellious only child. That I had been a sixties teenager made it even worse. For many of those years, my father and I could barely speak to each other. But I went off to college and made my own life. By the time I reached my thirties, we settled into a comfortable friendship. Neither of us was much for sharing deep thoughts, but I came to enjoy our visits, and I think he did, too. For twenty years, we were friends.

As he got progressively sicker, our relationship changed again. My father had been trained as an accountant and had always done the family finances. But his weakened heart not only sapped his energy; it was also failing to pump enough blood to his brain. His ability to think and make decisions was gradually draining away.

Fortunately, long before he became sick, my parents gave me the legal authority to manage their finances (the documents are called financial power of attorney). After a few months, I gently asked if I should start keeping their checkbook. My dad reluctantly agreed. At first I wrote the checks, but he signed them. After a time, his signature became less and less legible. Then the day came when he could no longer write his name at all. So I began signing the checks, too. This simple task became another small rite of our difficult passage.

This is what some people call parenting your parents. But it isn't, really. You can provide for them in some ways. You can even do intimate physical tasks, such as changing a diaper or bathing them—the things they did for you when you were a child. But you will never become their parent. That is the role they filled from the day you were born—and a child can never really take that away from a parent.

What is it like to die of heart failure? The pattern of my dad's illness was pretty typical. He slowly declined, week after week. Every once in a while he'd crash, then rebound; but like an exhausted climber fighting the gravity of a steep, rocky slope, he'd rarely recover all he'd lost.

"I'm not in any pain," my father would say throughout his illness. This amazed and pleased him. Still, his decline was hard.

At first he could no longer get around without a walker. Then, as his strength gradually ebbed, he struggled to stand. Finally, he needed help just getting from his bed to a wheelchair. At first my dad could make the few steps to the bathroom by holding on to a dresser, the wall, and a grab bar by the toilet. Then he could get there only with Naressa's help. Finally, he could not get there at all.

In one of his hospitalizations, he had a catheter inserted to drain away his urine. This was done, we later learned, more for the convenience of the hospital staff than for my father's comfort, and he should never have been discharged before the device was removed. He hated the catheter, and the humiliating bag of yellow liquid that hung down his leg. After we got him home, we tried several times to wean him off it. But it was not possible, and he was constantly plagued by the threat of a urinary tract infection. With the elderly, these are common and always uncomfortable. If untreated, they can be deadly.

The stress on my mother, who had her own physical problems, was terrible. She had lost the sight in one eye, and on some days her arthritis was so severe she could barely stand. Yet she persevered.

She rarely talked about it, but the pressure showed. For her, caring for my father was a full-time job. My father needed to be fed, given his medications, moved from his bed to his easy chair, and perhaps to the living room couch. On a nice day, he'd want to go outside. She constantly worried about him falling. And as he got sicker, my father would become angrier and more frustrated, and that would just magnify my mother's own stress. If she went out, he'd complain about being left alone, even though someone was always with him.

Marilyn couldn't sleep. She was exhausted and often overwhelmed. Naressa was her rock, but on those days when Naressa was off, my mother would come close to panic. It was clear she was reaching her limits.

About two months before Herb passed away, something extraordinary happened. Early one warm May morning, I called my parents just before I left for work, as I often did. But this conversation was unlike any other.

My father got on the phone and said simply and with great certainty, "I died last night."

I asked him what had happened, but he could not answer. Whatever it was, whatever he had dreamed or imagined or seen was beyond his ability to describe. The words did not come to him. He put the phone down.

A few days later, my dad took a turn for the worse. He began drifting in and out of awareness. He never quite lost consciousness, but he became increasingly less responsive. For periods of time, he couldn't speak. He lost control of his bowels, and was unable even to turn over in bed without help.

It was finally more than my mother could bear. So we found a nursing home a mile or so from their apartment. The morning we moved him, I drove to the facility to make sure everything was set up as promised. Herb came a few minutes later by ambulance. When we arrived at his room, he suddenly became alert and asked where he was. I tried to explain what was happening. It was the last real conversation we ever had.

We made another decision at the nursing home. My father was being kept alive by that cocktail of prescription drugs. We asked the doctor if he could wean my dad off the pills so nature could take its course. He readily agreed.

On the morning of July 8, my mother called.

"He's very low," she said. "You should come."

Ann and I took the next flight and got to Florida around noon. It was a stiflingly hot and humid day, the sort my father, a New Englander deep in his soul, loathed.

When I got to his room, he was barely responsive. I'm not sure he was aware I was with him, although I believe he knew. My mother, Ann, and I took turns sitting with him. Paul came for a last visit, and we prayed.

At about five-thirty in the afternoon, he seemed stable, so we took my exhausted mother home for a break. On the way, we stopped to get her dinner. While we were gone, at about seven P.M., Herb quietly died. He was three months short of his eighty-third birthday.

I am still haunted that he died alone.

When we became caregivers, my family unwillingly joined one of the least exclusive clubs in America. It is a silent society—one whose members rarely know one another and almost never discuss their struggles. They don't even see themselves as caregivers. They are just . . . helping. Many, in fact, are convinced they are alone, although this club has tens of millions of members.

Today, as many as 44 million Americans care for more than 10 million elderly and disabled friends and relatives.[2] Some are seniors caring for spouses. Others are adult children helping their elderly parents, or even teenagers caring for siblings with disabilities. They are all races. Some are rich. Some are very poor. No one is immune.

They quickly learn that love is wonderful, but when it comes to long-term care, love is not enough. Families are being crushed by the high cost of care. As they struggle every day with the needs of their loved ones, they must navigate a financial system that is staggeringly expensive for government, yet leaves millions of aged and disabled Americans without the means to obtain the basic assistance they need to live a dignified and comfortable life. This irrational payment system drives patients and their families into what is often the wrong care, at the wrong time, in the wrong place.

A typical frail senior has almost no money—less than $8,000 in financial assets. Most live alone.[3] As many as two million may have no one at all to care for them.[4] And without assistance, many go days without bathing or eating. They soil themselves. Some die with no one to comfort them in their last hours, their bodies left undiscovered for days. Others die in hospitals, connected to massively expensive— but ultimately useless—machines.

In 2007, we spent more than $200 billion on paid long-term

care.[5] These staggering costs are not paid by health insurance, and usually not covered by Medicare, the government health program for seniors. Private long-term-care insurance pays for less than 10 percent.[6] More than half is paid by Medicaid, a welfare-like government program. But in the United States, in contrast to most of the rest of the developed world, you must first impoverish yourself before getting any help.

Millions of American families are caught in the long-term-care trap. They have too much money to be eligible for Medicaid, but a typical nursing home costs more than $200 a day,[7] and they are not close to having the funds to pay these astronomical costs on their own. As a result, they are at risk of losing nearly everything they have—and still getting care that one daughter of a nursing home–bound mother describes as "not fit for an animal."

Think of it as a roll of the cosmic dice. Government provides near-universal basic health care for the old and for many younger people with disabilities. That means that if your dad is sixty-five and suffers a massive heart attack, Medicare will pay tens of thousands of dollars for surgery and the hospital stay he needs to fix the damage. But if, as with my father, his heart disease leaves him so sick that he can no longer care for himself, it will provide little or no coverage for the help he needs to get through each day. If he has Alzheimer's disease, there is a good chance that when it comes to paying the bills, your family will be entirely on its own.

Even worse, that $200 billion is only part of the cost. More than 80 percent of long-term care is informal, provided by family members and friends. Some estimate the value of that care at an additional $350 billion a year.[8] Add it up and, as a nation, we may be spending as much to assist our elderly and disabled as we do on national defense.

In many ways, my family was incredibly lucky. My father had a safe place to live and a wife who could provide emotional support and some physical care. Until the last month of his life, he was alert, although he needed assistance with activities such as eating and going to the bathroom. He had a loving and capable aide and the financial resources to pay for her help.

I had enough job flexibility to take days off so I could spend time with my parents. I had the skills to find people who could answer our questions, and tremendous support from my wife. I was an only child, so the burden of caring for Herb fell to my mom and me alone. On the other hand, I had no siblings to fight with.

Millions of American families are not so fortunate. They don't have the time or ability to help aging parents or disabled relatives. They have no idea how to navigate the extraordinarily complex world of long-term care. Old family wounds tear open under stress, and cooperation gives way to confrontation.

Still, there is some good news. Dozens of creative new housing options are blossoming, and traditional nursing homes are remaking themselves. Financial market gurus and government policymakers are exploring ways to make long-term care affordable for average families.

At the same time, policy experts and even some politicians are starting to think about better ways to finance care for the elderly. They are looking at experiments in countries such as Germany and Japan to see if they can somehow be adapted to the United States.

In many ways, caring for our parents was the most rewarding thing Ann and I have ever done. It was a special opportunity to give back some of the love and care they'd given us when we were kids. But it was also the toughest thing we've ever done.

This is the story of long-term care in twenty-first-century America. It is a blessing that many of us will have the opportunity to care for our parents or disabled relatives, that we can have precious time with them in their final months, and that we can give back for what they did for us. But it is a curse that the richest nation in the world has not learned to use its resources to provide that care in the best way possible.

TWO

Natalie

It is easy to imagine Natalie and Katherine as best pals. Absolutely comfortable with each other, long past the time when old arguments matter. Friends in a way young people can never be. In their own younger days, they'd call on each other often. But as they got older, visiting was no longer so easy. Still, when Katherine could, she'd travel across the Potomac River from Virginia to see Natalie, who'd been living for so many years in a rural Maryland retirement community. They'd spend gentle afternoons chatting and catching up on the news.

"We were so congenial," Natalie remembers. "Katherine would come and talk. Maybe we'd have a cup of coffee."

But Katherine was going blind and losing her hearing. Natalie, who had suffered a series of small strokes, could no longer speak clearly. The simple, comfortable chats they loved so much had become a struggle. So, one afternoon, as they finished their coffee,

Katherine put down her cup and made a practical, matter-of-fact suggestion: "Why don't we just say goodbye now?"

It was the last time they ever saw each other. "That was five years ago," says Natalie. "I don't know if she is still alive."

By the time I met Natalie Fenninger, she was ninety-three and had outlived nearly everyone in her life: her beloved brother, most of her friends, three husbands. Natalie seems amazed, and almost a little bemused, that she survived those three spouses. She married her first, Dick, when she was just seventeen. She married her last, Carl, when she was eighty and already living in the retirement home.

Natalie lives at Friends House, a community operated by the Quakers in Sandy Spring, Maryland. She's been there for thirty years. Most of that time, she had a nice apartment, which she eventually shared with Carl. Then, as her health failed, she moved to the complex's assisted-living unit. Now she is in the nursing home. "My last stop," she calls it.

Confined to a wheelchair, sharing a room with a stranger, rarely able to get outside, Natalie passes her days sleeping, taking comfort in her memories. For more than seventy years Natalie kept a journal, recounting her experiences in a simple, straightforward narrative. But she can't write anymore, so the volumes—some bound in red, others in blue—sit untouched on an old wooden bookcase that takes up one wall of her half of the small room. For a while she tried dictating to nurses or visitors, but it was not the same. So she put the journals away. She does not look at them now.

Natalie, the lifelong writer, still creates poetry, though. She dictates verses that describe what she hears and sees in the Friends House nursing home. Poems about the rain or her friend James, the maintenance man "who changes clean floors to mirrors."

A tiny woman with a weathered face and neat, straight gray hair cut in practical bangs, Natalie is extraordinarily comfortable with her life. She is unfailingly polite, and her blue eyes sparkle as she tells her stories and asks me questions.

Natalie has an unusual brain disease that causes temporary

amnesia, and she probably has also suffered a series of small strokes
in recent years. Her memory works like this: She can pick up a conversation where she left off a few weeks before. She can recall small
details from years ago, and often when I visit her, she remembers to
ask me about my wife. But then, abruptly, she asks, "Have you been
here before?"

Natalie is aware of what is happening to her, and baffled by her
hit-and-miss memory, but resigned to it all. "I can feel myself losing
strength," she says. But a few minutes later she'll add, "I don't feel
I have trouble getting through the day."

The kind of care Natalie receives is not medical treatment aimed
at helping her get healthy. It is, rather, the support that people with
long-term chronic illnesses need to maintain the best possible quality of life for their remaining days. This long-term care may be as
simple as assistance with cooking or eating, bathing or taking medicine, changing a lightbulb or balancing a checkbook. For many, it is
as basic as having a safe place to live.

Long-term care may mean a stay in a nursing home, as it does for
Natalie. Or it may be the help of a home health aide, as it was for my
dad. Either way, such assistance is extraordinarily expensive. Each
year, we spend three times as much on long-term care as we do on
college tuition.[1] It is not unusual for individual families to spend
$50,000 a year. Except for buying a house, it is the most costly thing
many of us will ever face in our lives. Some months, Natalie was
spending $16,000. (We look in more depth at the financing of care
for Natalie and others in Chapter 9.)

You don't need to be old to need long-term care. Millions of
younger people who were born with a physical or mental disability,
or who suffered a traumatic injury or illness in their young adult-
hood, also need this assistance. Autism, auto accidents, and multiple
sclerosis all push the young into the world of long-term care. Thanks
to extraordinary advances in medical technology, these people—who
once would have died at a young age—now live many years.

They, and their families, must deal with their often extreme physical limitations. Many younger people with disabilities, however, live productive and relatively active lives. For them, care means the personal assistance they need to get going each day. Perhaps it is help bathing or getting dressed, or the use of a wheelchair-accessible van to get them to and from work.

But many who require this care are aged, and Natalie Fenninger is the face of long-term care for the elderly in America. Like her, seniors receiving this assistance are typically widows in their eighties or older who live alone, have little income, and may be suffering from dementia or other mental impairment. For them, long-term care mostly means help confronting the growing frailty of old age.

Like millions of others, Natalie doesn't need much acute medical care. She takes prescription drugs, and once in a while she'll require the attention of a doctor. But mostly she just needs help bathing and getting around—whether it is to the dining hall, the activities center, or the bathroom. That is how it is with most elderly patients in long-term care.

Natalie is dying, but not in the way people died through most of human history.

Never before have we confronted this challenge of long-term care. Until just a few decades ago, there was no old age for most of us. Our great-grandparents worked hard, got sick, and died.

The idea of a long, relatively healthy old age followed by a period of disability and decline was unknown in human history. Before the mid-twentieth century, injury and infection did their work quickly. Pneumonia, once called the old man's friend, killed with rapid efficiency. Few of us lived very long with disabilities. Even a severely broken leg could be a speedy death sentence, as untreated infection ravaged the human body. A severe illness killed within days or weeks, a few months at the most. A hundred years ago, an adult hospitalized with diabetes could expect to die within a month.[2]

Today, thanks to extraordinary advances in medical technology, all that has changed. We not only survive serious illness and injury, but our doctors repair us so we are as good as new. We have an entire generation of seniors power-walking with new knees and hips and watching movies with eyes no longer dimmed by glaucoma. They are swimming laps at the local pool, energized by blood flowing smoothly through once-clogged arteries, now repaired by surgeries that could not have been imagined a century ago. Stroke, heart disease, and even many cancers have been turned from quick killers to treatable chronic illness.

Mostly, this is terrific news. Eighty-year-olds are thriving and productive. Some still work, many volunteer, others travel or play golf. Magazines are filled with advice on how to age well. "Active adult" communities sprout like weeds. Universities make big money offering summer programs to intellectually curious retirees.

It was not always this way. In 1900 the average American lived to just forty-seven. In the 1930s, when Social Security was created, life expectancy was barely sixty-five. It was neither an accident nor an actuarial joke that most Americans would die just as they retired and started collecting their government pensions. Now, a sixty-five-year-old getting her first Social Security check is likely to live for nearly twenty years in retirement, and to be healthy for most of that time.[3]

A baby born in the United States today can expect to live to at least seventy-eight, and perhaps much longer. And the fastest-growing age group in the nation is eighty-five-year-olds. In 2000 more than 4 million Americans reached that milestone. In a bit more than twenty years, as the 77-million-strong Baby Boomer generation ages, more than 9 million of us will be eighty-five or older.[4]

Eighty-five matters. In the early twenty-first century, that is the age at which the human body often breaks down, even for the healthiest among us. After eight and a half decades of hard use, our body parts simply cease to function. Our joints become arthritic. Our heart muscles weaken. Our memories fail. Medical science has not prevented physical decline; it has merely postponed it. As physician and author Atul Gawande puts it, "We wear down until we can't wear down anymore."[5]

Of those still living at home or with relatives, only about 3 percent of those aged sixty-five to seventy-four need help walking, but at eighty-five and older, nearly 17 percent need assistance. More than 40 percent of those older than eighty-four need help leaving their homes, and one quarter need assistance preparing meals, managing their money, or doing housework. More than 10 percent need help getting dressed, or moving from their bed to a chair.[6]

It is this growing disability that drives our parents to need the personal help that is called long-term care. Only about 5 percent of people in their sixties and about 15 percent of those aged seventy-five to seventy-nine will require this care. But then things change dramatically. By the time they reach their mid-eighties, more than 40 percent of seniors will be unable to manage their routine activities of daily life. By their nineties, like Natalie, nearly everyone will need some assistance.[7]

Age is also a major indicator of the group of diseases that most terrify the old: Alzheimer's and other forms of dementia. The chances of suffering from some form of severe memory problems are only about one in twenty for people in their seventies. But one out of every four people in their eighties will have one of these diseases. By the time they reach their nineties, almost 40 percent will have some form of dementia.[8]

Like my mother-in-law, Ida, a few of our parents will die suddenly from massive strokes, heart attacks, or accidents. However, sometime in their old age, two thirds of today's sixty-five-year-olds will need some help coping with disabling illnesses, injuries, or simple frailty. They'll need that assistance for an average of three years before they die.[9]

Dr. Joanne Lynn, who has written extensively and passionately about end-of-life care, has identified four groups of frail elderly. She estimates that about one in five die suddenly from strokes, heart attacks, or accidents. The rest suffer from often-severe illness but nonetheless live for a long period of time.[10]

Of the rest, about 20 percent manage relatively well for many years and need little assistance until their last days or weeks of life, when their health declines rapidly. Many are cancer patients, and for them, hospice care can play a potentially important role.

Another 20 percent have diseases such as heart and lung failure. These patients can also live with their illness for a very long time. But like my dad, they face a period of steady physical decline in their last years or months. Often they will be hit with severe, acute episodes of their disease, or struck by infection or pneumonia. They bounce back, but rarely to where they were before the crisis. Finally, they succumb, often to one of these complications.

The largest group, about 40 percent of the aged, are dying in slow motion. They suffer from dementia or severe strokes or simply become "frail" as their bodies wear out. Doctors often diagnose their condition as "failure to thrive," or what Lynn calls "prolonged dwindling." They are the people who most often need assistance with meals, transportation, and housecleaning, and who eventually may need home health aides or institutional long-term care.

Lynn describes them as living on the edge of a cliff. A common cold may be all it takes to push them over the precipice. Or they may live with their frailties for years. For them, medical science has changed the very definition of dying.[11]

Tragically, as skilled as it is at treating disease, modern American medicine is far less adept at caring for the frail elderly. While long-term care is not medical care, it is often the closest many of the frail elderly will come to the routine medical assistance they need.

For many seniors that's because just getting to the doctor is not easy. If you cannot drive or climb steps, a simple trip to a physician's office becomes an insurmountable challenge. It is one reason the frail elderly get so much of their medical treatment in expensive and inefficient hospital emergency rooms.

Even if a disabled senior can physically get to a doctor, finding one willing and able to provide proper treatment is even harder. Despite our rapidly aging population, the number of board-certified geriatricians is actually declining.[12] Amazingly, while there are more than

35 million Americans aged sixty-five or older in the United States today, there are just 7,128 board-certified geriatric medicine specialists to care for them, 20 percent fewer than a decade ago.[13] That is one specialist in senior medicine for every twenty-three thousand older adults.

And it isn't just doctors. Less than 1 percent of nurses, physician assistants, or pharmacists are certified as geriatric specialists, and fewer than one hundred psychiatrists are newly trained each year to specialize in the care of elderly patients, who face critical mental health issues ranging from dementia to depression.[14]

Why, when geriatric medicine should be booming to keep up with the rapidly increasing numbers of seniors, is it collapsing? Money, for one. Pay for these doctors is lower than for other specialties, a problem made worse because it takes more time to treat elderly patients. In an era of the eight-minute office visit, doctors don't get paid extra by either the government's Medicare program or private insurers for seeing these patients. In 2005 a typical geriatrician earned $163,000. By the standards of most of us, that's a lot of money, but it was barely half what a dermatologist could expect to make.[15]

And there is another reason: "Doctors don't like patients who don't get better," says Dr. David Greer, dean emeritus of the Brown University Medical School and a specialist in geriatric medicine.[16]

That is where my dad was, and where Natalie has been for the last year. She will not get better. She is on the edge of that cliff Lynn describes.

Long-term care is delivered in many different settings. Most get it at home. In fact, despite all the attention paid to nursing homes, the overwhelming majority of the elderly and disabled get their care in their own houses, or in those of their children, and most of it is provided by relatives, usually spouses or daughters. About three quarters, or 7.5 million, of the 10 million Americans in long-term care live at home. Another 1.4 million are in nursing homes, and 1 million reside in an ever-expanding selection of group housing arrangements.[17]

The costs of long-term care are staggering. Today, home health agencies charge up to $20 an hour for trained aides, or $200 a day for a live-in.[18] Assisted-living facilities cost an average of nearly $3,000 a month.[19]

Then there are nursing homes. There is the old story about the elderly widow who chooses to spend her last days sailing the world on a luxury cruise ship. She gets good food, a nice room, a house-keeper, and even the assistance of a doctor, all for less money than it would cost to stay in a nursing home. It is not a joke. In 2006 a nursing home stay cost an average of $213 a day.[20] The average per-person daily cost of a cruise: $200.[21] But don't kid yourself, a nursing home feels a lot more like a hospital than an ocean liner.

The past few years have seen a blossoming of new care options for those staying at home, including adult day centers, co-housing—where unrelated people of different generations live together—and the growing "village movement," where seniors who are neighbors make formal arrangements to share resources, information, and services.

But home care is not for everyone. Some seniors have no friend or relative to care for them, or are too sick to stay home. Others may have a spouse like my mother who, after months or years of caregiving, finally succumbs to the stress of managing a chronically ill loved one. In fact, the declining physical health of caregivers is the single most important indicator of when a patient will be admitted to a nursing home. Many times, it is more critical than the failing health of the patient.

For those who do need institutional care, a whole new universe of facilities is developing. There are high-end continuing-care retirement communities, with entry fees in the hundreds of thousands of dollars, which provide increasing levels of assistance as residents grow older and frailer. There are large formal assisted-living facilities, often operated by big corporations, which house hundreds of seniors in private rooms or modest apartments. And there are small family-owned group homes, sometimes called board-and-care homes, which provide housing and personal care to just a handful of residents.

Even nursing homes are changing in dramatic ways. These institutions, once considered humane alternatives to asylums, have come to be dreaded by most seniors and those with disabilities, many of whom insist they'd rather kill themselves than be forced to stay in one.

As the chronically ill are discharged faster from hospitals, and as technology makes it possible to provide more intensive treatment outside a full-blown medical center, nursing homes are caring for many different populations with widely varying needs.

These institutions are moving in two sharply divergent directions. Some are abandoning long-term care in favor of far more lucrative rehabilitation services or assisted living. At the same time, other facilities are looking for creative ways to make nursing centers feel less like hospitals and more like homes. Aggressive advocates for these changes, such as Dr. Bill Thomas, argue that nursing homes must completely remake themselves in the next few years.

Like Natalie, as many as half of nursing home residents suffer from some form of dementia. Among the rest, some are in the last weeks or days of life, as my father was. But there are many people residing in nursing homes only because they have nowhere else to live. They have no one to care for them at home, yet they cannot afford the $3,000 a month it costs to stay in an assisted-living facility.

These nursing home residents have spent all of their money on health care or long-term care in other settings, and they are now broke. After a lifetime of hard work and playing by the rules, all of their money is gone. So many—often widows like Natalie—have had to turn to Medicaid, the joint state-federal health-care system for the poor.

The problem is that Medicaid will usually pay for care only if it is provided in a nursing home. And while it is gradually beginning to offer some alternatives, the program often does not cover help at home or in an assisted-living facility. Three quarters of the program's long-term-care dollars for the elderly and physically disabled still go directly to nursing homes.[22] Hundreds of thousands of seniors who should be living elsewhere are being forced into these facilities, which are often the most expensive setting for the government and the least pleasant for many patients. That, too, is what happened to Natalie.

Natalie would be the first to tell you that she is very fortunate. She not only is in a high-quality nursing home, but she has family to watch over her. As many as one out of every three of the frail elderly and disabled have no one at all to care for them.

These people are at extremely high risk. They suffer from malnutrition, dehydration, and bedsores. Those over eighty-five are six times more likely to die in fires than those in the prime of life.[23]

Even those frail seniors who do live with family often fall victim to accidents, such as falls, burns, and, sadly, abuse. As many as one million are abused by their own caregivers—often other family members.[24]

In Natalie's complicated blended family, a stepdaughter and a grandson have taken on the difficult roles of managing her care. Gretchen, the daughter of Natalie's last husband, Carl, is her primary caregiver. At sixty-six, she has had a long career as a manager of computer systems for defense contractors. Gretchen is thinking about her own retirement. "I have a place to live in Phoenix. I am able to retire. I just have to wait until . . ." She doesn't finish the sentence.

Like many caregivers, Gretchen found herself in a role she never expected. She helped care for her own mother, who died in 1994 after a difficult illness. But Natalie was her stepmother and Gretchen, plainspoken and analytical, doesn't seem the sentimental type.

"It wasn't planned," she says. "You just get pulled in."

There was something else. In a way, it was an exchange of gifts.

Natalie and Carl had only five years together. But to Gretchen, they were her father's happiest. Gretchen was in her fifties when Carl and Natalie married, and had long since gone off on her own. But she remembers Carl as a cold and distant father and, later, as a lonely widower. Until he met Natalie.

"Natalie gave us back our father," Gretchen says. "He learned how to accept love."

So after Carl died in 1999, Gretchen became Natalie's friend, companion, and chief caregiver. She visits Natalie every week, and on Sunday afternoons leads the Friends House nursing residents in hymns.

"I don't know what I'd do without Gretchen," Natalie says. "She is so full of pizzazz and so intelligent. If there is a problem, she can solve it."

Richard Hanna, Natalie's grandson from her first marriage, manages the money for her. Or at least he did while there still was some left.

A New Mexico commercial real-estate developer, Rick is thin and balding, with a neatly clipped mustache that matches his sandy hair. He never really knew his grandfather Dick, who died when Rick was just three. But Natalie was the gentle, ladylike grandmother he'd visit two or three times a year and somehow fell in love with.

"She was a Norman Rockwell grandmother, quiet spoken, always nice," Rick remembers. "She was a very gracious lady."

For a long time they wrote letters back and forth. Rick would write seven or eight pages, always careful to use extra-large type so Natalie could read them. Natalie looked forward to his correspondence and was thrilled to reply. But like her diary, the letters ended when she could no longer write.

Rick banters easily with Natalie. "I'll take care of you, but I'm not coming to your funeral," he tells her, and he sounds almost convincing.

"That's okay with me," Natalie responds, eyes twinkling, smiling her impish grin.

Rick visits Natalie only about once a year now, but he and Gretchen work together to manage Natalie's life. Most of their choices have been driven by the cost of her care.

Since Natalie's body began to fail in 1999, she has burned through more than half a million dollars. For a time in 2006, she was spending as much as $16,000 per month for an assisted-living bed at Friends House, around-the-clock home health aides, medications, and other medical supplies. "We've done what we can to keep her comfortable, and to keep her from suffering," says Rick. "But the bills kept piling up."

Natalie, whose husbands invested well during their lives, and who always carefully saved for herself, was far better off financially than the typical senior. "Thank God," says Rick. "She is a Quaker and doesn't have high style with clothing."

Most seniors are far less fortunate. The average seventy-five-year-old has a net worth of about $115,000. But among eighty-five-year-olds who have no spouse but need some help with daily living, two thirds have assets of less than $5,000, and barely 15 percent have sufficient funds to pay for a year or more in a nursing home.[25]

But the future is not much better for younger and healthier seniors. They, too, are likely to fall far short of having the money they'll need to pay the cost of long-term care.

By now, most people have seen the retirement security tables published by brokerage firms and mutual funds. Each looks at whether people in various age groups have put away enough money for retirement. Those numbers are pretty grim. They generally show that about only one third of us are likely to have enough money to maintain our lifestyle in old age; another third may achieve that goal with a bit of good luck. The rest are facing a precipitous decline in their standard of living after retirement. And that is without having to bear the burden of long-term care.

Think of it another way: Most Americans have the bulk of their financial assets in one place, their 401(k) retirement plan. At the end of 2006, the average balance in these accounts was about $121,000. But that number doesn't tell the whole story. While roughly 7 percent of us had more than $200,000 in our retirement plans, almost 40 percent had less than $10,000—barely enough to pay for six weeks of nursing home care.[26] For most of us, these balances are currently far smaller in the wake of the 2008 stock market collapse.

Of course, many Americans will have other sources of income in retirement, such as Social Security, and more than two thirds of retirees own a house.

However, access to these assets masks a disturbing trend. When families must increasingly rely on their own resources to support their retirement, they are very vulnerable to unexpected shocks that occur late in their working life. Two thirds of adults suffer some negative event in their fifties and sixties, such as a divorce, a lay-off, or a major illness or accident. And when they do, they lose earnings, have higher out-of-pocket medical bills, and often dip into the savings they were relying on to support them as they aged. For instance, people who divorce in those years suffer a 44 percent decline in their wealth, widows see their assets fall by 13 percent, and those who are laid off see their wealth fall by as much as one third.[27]

Whether they suffer such a shock or not, retirees also face added expenses as they age. For instance, as more and more retirees lose health benefits from their jobs, and as Medicare costs steadily increase, out-of-pocket medical expenses explode as people get older. A typical sixty-five-year-old couple will need to put aside at least $250,000 for acute medical care before they die, and perhaps more than $700,000—a sum that also excludes any long-term-care costs.[28]

That's why, like Natalie, many middle-class seniors are likely to run out of money long before they become old and frail. A few— less than 10 percent—have purchased long-term-care insurance to help finance their care. Others may turn to their children for financial support. But many who spend through their assets will have only one option: Medicaid.

This joint state-federal health program for the poor is much less well known than its bureaucratic sibling, Medicare. But Medicare pays for almost no personal care, while Medicaid spends more than $100 billion a year on this assistance, financing almost half of all paid long-term care in the United States. Medicaid was created in the 1960s to provide health care for low-income women and their children. But now more than sixty-five cents of every Medicaid dollar is spent on seniors and the disabled.

That's what is paying for Natalie's care.

She now lives in a tiny double room with two hospital-type beds. Her roommate, Helen, has the bed closest to the door. Helen's side of the room has a TV and an end table, and is decorated with her original artwork. She was once a very talented painter.

Natalie has her hospital bed, a desk, and her bookcase. There is a small window and a shared bathroom. A few family photos adorn the walls on her half of the room.

Helen and Natalie get along pretty well, except for the TV.

"She is a very nice person," Natalie says, "but Helen likes to have the radio on more than I do."

Natalie means the TV, and, in truth, she hates to have it on at all. But once she became a Medicaid patient, she had no choice but to share a room. She grumbled, uncharacteristically, when she had to move.

"I miss my privacy," she says.

Who pays for her care doesn't matter much to Natalie, who isn't very aware of her financial situation. It matters a lot to Friends House, however, which receives only about two thirds of the $264 a day it would get if Natalie were still paying herself. Overall, the nursing home industry says it loses about $13 a day for each Medicaid resident.[29]

Because Friends House is a nonprofit that receives a large amount of charity each year, it can afford to keep residents such as Natalie. For many months, while Rick and Gretchen struggled to sort out the Medicaid paperwork, Friends House got no money at all for Natalie's care. Once Medicaid agreed to cover her, the government reimbursed the home for those costs.

In part, Friends House has helped Natalie out in big and small ways because she has been there for so long. For the staff and for many residents, she is woven deeply into their community.

Darryl Clemmer has been executive director of Friends House for two decades, an extraordinarily long time in an industry where staff turnover is a chronic problem. For all the years Darryl has been at Friends House, Natalie has been a fixture there.

"She is a character," he says. His wary smile tells me that for all her charm, Natalie has also been more than a little demanding over the years.

Natalie's story (and that of Rick and Gretchen) is just one of 10 million in the United States. Many are tales of love and compassion in the most difficult circumstances and, in their own ways, examples of what is wrong with long-term care in America. Some, like Natalie's, may help provide guideposts for those who want to fix our troubled system.

As Natalie and her family learned, our system of long-term care in the United States is what the nursing home reformer Bill Thomas calls "a jumbled, institutionalized, regulated system that bears no resemblance to the kind of care we all want."

It was never planned. It somehow evolved. And, sadly, it took a lot of wrong turns along the way.

Many frail elderly are alone, homebound, without friends, family, or regular access to food or medical care. Too many die too soon.

While some nursing homes, such as Friends House, do provide capable, loving care, too many do not. These institutions, which began in the twentieth century as a well-intentioned attempt to replace the scandalous asylums of the nineteenth century, instead turned into nightmares themselves. Massively expensive, with highly regimented and impersonal services delivered by overworked and underpaid staff, many nursing homes are the antithesis of the loving care we all want for our parents.

Home care, which the aged overwhelmingly prefer, is often given with love, and in a familiar setting. But it can also be dangerous because most family members have never learned the skills they need to manage someone who is frail or disabled. Elderly spouses, who often suffer with their own physical problems, struggle to help their loved ones, and frequently fail. Adult children, who may live many miles away, try to juggle jobs and the needs of their own children even as they do what they can for their parents.

And for most families, the money to pay for it all is far out of reach. Even wealthy families such as Natalie's can easily run through a lifetime of savings to provide the help their loved ones need. Then, finally, when they are completely impoverished, the government steps in with what is often inappropriate care. Is this system worthy of the wealthiest country in the history of the world?

Bill Thomas believes that the image of long-term care that most of us keep in our hearts is from the biblical tale of Ruth, who selflessly cares for her widowed mother-in-law, Naomi. In that story, Ruth, herself a widow, tells Naomi, "Wherever you go, I shall go. Wherever you lodge, I shall lodge."[30]

Eventually, Ruth gets the financial support she needs from the community, remarries, and has a son of her own. Naomi is "sustained in her old age."

It is a lovely story, and it is what we want for our own families. But it is far from the modern reality of nursing homes, medical indifference, and staggeringly expensive bills that we have created as a society. Says Thomas, "Our deep-seated cultural narrative is that old age sucks, and then you die."

The question is: Can we somehow change that narrative? Can we re-create at least some of the spirit of Ruth and Naomi in modern American society?

On some days, Natalie says she is ready to die. Often now she dreams about being with her brother, Jack, who was killed by a land mine on Guam on August 1, 1944, or with Dick, her first husband. "Isn't that funny," she says.

But there is something about Natalie that tells me she is not yet ready to go. In her modest room, on a late winter afternoon, I see a small branch with seven small leaves, still green, sitting on her windowsill. The branch is in water, in a tiny cobalt blue vase. She points to it proudly and tells me she hopes it will take root. We look at it together and she says, yes, there may be something there, a hint of green life. I say it is important to be optimistic. "Yes, it is," Natalie replies. And she smiles again.

THREE

"This Is What I Do, 24/7"

May Barrett, seventy, grew up in Hawaii and now lives in the Virginia suburbs of Washington, D.C. Her daughter, Michelle, is a thirty-seven-year-old Air Force lieutenant colonel. Cheryl Fears, fifty-seven, is a dynamo of a woman from northwest Arkansas, where she lives with her husband, two twenty-something sons, four dogs, and two cats. Judy Dow, fifty-three, is a Native American educator and artist who lives in a suburban ranch house with her husband, Steve, a local contractor.

At first glance, they have almost nothing in common. Except that May, Michelle, Cheryl, Judy, and Steve are, like more than 40 million other Americans, giving up a big part of their lives to care for a parent or spouse. They are all reluctant, but deeply committed, caregivers.

Who are they? Ordinary people who are thrown, usually without warning, into an extraordinary yet unfamiliar role for which they are unprepared. They are the caregivers who provide a high level of physical and emotional assistance to their loved ones.

If you were to paint a picture of the typical family caregiver in America, she would be a forty-six-year-old woman who is assisting a parent (or two) while trying to hold down a job outside her home.[1] Often, she must balance the demands of children with those of aging parents. On average, she spends fifteen to twenty hours a week helping an elderly or disabled relative.

About 40 percent of caregivers are adult children, and another 40 percent are spouses. The rest are neighbors, friends, or other relatives. Most are women, though increasingly men are providing assistance to parents or wives.[2]

In 1989, about two thirds of caregivers had some help assisting their loved ones, usually from relatives and sometimes from paid aides. But by 1999, more than half were on their own—a trend that is even more troubling given that both the caregivers and those they are helping are getting older. Only about one quarter of families have any help at all from paid aides, and fewer than 10 percent of the aged and disabled have aides as their primary caregivers.

What do these family caregivers do? Nearly all help with shopping, transportation, and household chores such as cleaning or cooking. Half make sure bills are paid and checkbooks balanced. And nearly half do the physically and emotionally difficult work of helping their parents or other disabled relatives with bathing or going to the bathroom.[3]

Unless you have been there, it is hard to imagine what it is like to care for an elderly parent or child with disabilities. It defines your life. There is nothing you do without first thinking about how it will affect your role as caregiver. It is all-consuming.

And many pay a huge price for taking on this responsibility. Sometimes that cost can be measured in dollars. Often, however, it is physical, and nearly all these caregivers are under tremendous emotional stress.

MAY AND WALT

This is May Barrett's day: Every morning, she struggles to get her husband, Walt, up and out of bed and into the bathroom, where she tries to get him washed and shaved. This would be difficult for most wives, but it is especially so for May, who weighs just ninety pounds. Walt, who is ninety, suffers from severe dementia and Parkinson's disease. He can no longer follow simple instructions, such as "Stand up" or "Turn to the right." And he weighs 190 pounds.

Eventually, May, who took early retirement from her government job to care for her husband, moves Walter into his comfortable brown recliner in their sunny family room. If it is a good day, Walt will stay in his chair, watching TV or tossing a soft pink ball with a visitor. If it is not, Walt tries to get up and walk across the room.

That's when he falls. It happens once a week or so, and when it does, May cannot pick him up. So he crawls from the family room, through the dining room, and into the bedroom. There, he grabs hold of the box spring on their bed and, with his still-powerful upper body, pulls himself up. From there, May gets him back into his wheelchair and, eventually, into his recliner.

If that doesn't work, she calls their daughter, Michelle. Trim and athletic, Michelle gets her dark hair and almond-shaped eyes from her Japanese-American mother and her square jaw and lean athleticism from her Midwestern dad.

Michelle is an Air Force lieutenant colonel who had a distinguished career as a pilot, a prized role still rare among women. But in 2006 she gave up flying for a job at the Pentagon, so she could return to Virginia to help care for her dad. "I fly a desk now," she says with just the smallest trace of regret.

In the time I have known her, May seems to have become visibly frail. In just the past couple of years, she has developed diabetes and lost more than thirty pounds. Most frightening, May, who is just seventy, is beginning to have her own memory problems.

One afternoon, I ask her about her government career. She

reaches for the words, but they do not come. She looks at Michelle, who cues her. "You were a budget analyst."

Yet May does all she can to keep Walt at home. "This is what I do," she says, "twenty-four/seven."

Behind her kind eyes and old-fashioned courtesy, May is a very tenacious woman. She is well connected to local advocacy groups, and knows better than many caregivers whom to call for advice. But like many wives, she will not accept an aide in her home. Caring for her husband of thirty-eight years is her job, and she will not easily relinquish it. "We are on our own speed this way," she says. "We do things the way we want. . . . We are not at the stage where I need help."

Michelle is resigned and can only laugh. "You are a stubborn Asian lady," she tells her mom.

May doesn't eat well, and doesn't have the time or energy to exercise.

"I'm sad for my mom, that this is her life," Michelle says.

Caregivers such as May are less likely to get their own proper medical care, and are more likely to die than those of the same age who are not helping parents or spouses.[4] Like my mother-in-law, Ida, thousands of spouses and adult children are literally killing themselves caring for their relatives at home.

May has not only Michelle's help, but also assistance from the four adult children from Walter's first marriage, three of whom live near the Barretts. Everyone pitches in. Walt's son Lee has dinner with May and his dad once a week. His son-in-law Kenny helps with the yard work.

But more than anything, May needs the kind of help she can't get from Michelle or the other children. Several times each day, she must move Walt from his chair or bed to a wheelchair and to the bathroom. She could use some equipment to make this easier, and someone to come by and teach her how a 90-pound wife can help her 190-pound husband get to the bathroom.

But May and Walt can't get that help. They don't have long-term-care insurance. They are far from rich, but have too much money to qualify for Medicaid. Walter does have Medicare, of course, which will pay for a wheelchair. It will also pay for a commode. But it won't pay for a single device that includes both. Why not? Well, says a government official, "It is not approved. It is considered a convenience item."[5]

Every few days, there is another crisis. Maybe it is a fall or trouble getting Walt in and out of the car. Although Michelle's half-siblings from Walter's first marriage do what they can, May mostly calls Michelle, her daughter. "I dread those calls," Michelle admits. But, she adds, "I want to help out."

When May's calls come during the day, Michelle tries to duck out of work. If they come at night, Michelle drops whatever she is doing at home, or pulls herself out of a fitful sleep, and heads for her parents' house, just a few miles away. Now she is thinking about taking a morning off each week to help her dad get started.

Walt does not know who Michelle is anymore.

When the handsome young woman comes to visit, he often tells her about his daughter and about the planes she flies. A veteran of the old Army Air Corps, Walter is immensely proud of the daughter who has achieved a rank far beyond his own. But he doesn't know that the woman whose success so delights him is the same person sitting across the room.

"Is that hard?" I ask Michelle.

"That's just the way it is," she replies.

Three days a week, Walt goes to the adult day-care center just a few miles away. For about a year, he was going to a county facility. But when he could no longer walk, the center told May that Walt couldn't stay. Now he goes to a different place, where three-day-a-week care costs more than a thousand dollars per month.

Increasingly now, May and Michelle worry about what will happen next. May desperately wants Walt to stay at home. But she knows that as his dementia gets progressively worse, even this new center will no longer take him. A nursing home would cost $90,000 a year—"all we have left," says May. Hiring home health aides is a possibility, but they'll cost close to $20 an hour.

Gently, Michelle pushes her mom to get some help. But she knows are limits. "It is not my house," Michelle says. "I have to remember it's still my parents' home."

It has been almost a decade since Walt got sick, and eight years since he could no longer fend for himself. All May does these days is care for her husband. When he is home, she is home. When he is at day care, she shops, goes to support groups, or worries about making ends meet. She quit her government job eight years ago, long before she was ready.

The weight on her shoulders grows daily. For now, planning for the future is beyond her. Michelle, meanwhile, spends most of her free time helping her mom and dad cope with one crisis after another.

She spent weeks figuring out how to make it easier for her mom to move Walt. By trolling Web sites, she discovered that combination wheelchair/commode. But it costs nearly $1,000. And after weeks of calls to Medicare, to their Medicare supplemental insurance company, to the firm that sells the device, to Walt's doctor, to a local insurance counselor, and to the local chapter of the Alzheimer's Association, they still can't figure out how to pay for it.

May and Michelle did get a doctor to prescribe a visit by a physical therapist, who will try to teach May how to move Walt, and perhaps give her some tips about how to keep him from falling. But their unspoken fear is this: One day, Walt will fall on top of May, and they will both be seriously hurt and end up in a nursing home. One elder-care specialist says it is a familiar story. "I'm afraid I know how this will end," she says.

Putting a monetary value on the kind of unpaid assistance May and Michelle give Walt is not simple. If they had to pay aides for the work they do, the cost would be staggering. Let's say they hired an aide for ten hours a day, just five days a week. Even with a typical discount for the additional hours, a paid assistant would likely charge $140 a day. That is $700 a week, or more than $36,000 a year. "Who has that?" asks May.

If all families had to pay aides to do this work, the price would far exceed $100 billion a year. Add lost wages and benefits, as well as out-of-pocket costs, and the price tag explodes. The seniors' group AARP figures the total value of care provided by friends and relatives topped $354 billion in 2006.[6]

A quarter of these family caregivers, or nearly 7 million people, have a special challenge. They are trying to help their loved ones from long distance, often from hundreds of miles away. I did.

So did Michelle, who helped as best she could while she was stationed in Texas, and eventually took a transfer to Virginia so she could be closer to her mom and dad.

Jack Fredine was a distance caregiver, too. For nearly a decade, his dad, Gordon, suffered from dementia. His mom, Edith, tried to care for Gordon in their home in Maryland, mostly alone. For most of that time, Jack lived in New Orleans with his wife and two sons. His sister, Pat, lived in Hawaii with her husband and daughters.

That is the way it is in America today. We move great distances to pursue our dreams. Sometimes our parents move to follow warm weather or the promise of a low-cost retirement in Florida or Arizona. Then someone suddenly gets old or has a stroke. Or, like Gordon, slowly, inexorably loses his memory.

Usually daughters take on the burden of helping care for a frail parent. But because Pat lived so far away, the task of managing the never-ending crises fell to Jack, a big, plainspoken engineer who looked and even talked exactly like his dad. "I used to answer the phone, and people thought it was him," Jack remembers.

One year, Edith fell and broke both her wrists. Jack dropped everything to help out.

A few years later, just before Christmas, Edith suffered a severe bout of sciatica and arthritis. Once again, she could not take care of

Gordon, or even herself. Once again, Jack put his life on hold. "I got the hell up here, stayed over the holidays, then my wife came up to help."

When Katrina hit the Gulf Coast in 2005, Jack, his wife, Susan, and the boys were lucky. They were not flooded out. But they couldn't stay. So they picked up and moved to Austin, Texas, just as Gordon was beginning to fail. Jack was struggling to balance the move even as he was making repeated trips to Maryland.

"I was coming back every few months," Jack remembers. "Some goddamned red flag was always flying. It was getting old."

These distance caregivers face their own special challenges. Nearly 40 percent regularly rearrange their work schedules, and one third miss workdays.[7] They also struggle with time spent away from their spouses and children, as well as added travel costs. In the year and a half I was making my regular visits to help my mother care for my dad, I spent close to $10,000 on airfare, hotels, and rental cars. It turns out that is pretty typical. One recent study reports that relatives living at a distance spend an average of nearly $9,000 a year caring for loved ones.[8]

—————————— CHERYL ——————————

having a spell with my mom now and thought i'd write. i think she has gout. have done all i know for now until i can take her to a foot dr. in am. the adult day care that she was attending had to shut down due to lack of funding. not another one in the area yet. hopefully in july a new one will open that is medicaid approved. we have a new one but it is private and would charge 75.00/day. more than we can afford, ... my mom's [dementia] doesn't seem to be progressing and i'm told that she looks great.

she and my father celebrated their 61st anniversary. had lots of family for a drop in reception on a sun. early afternoon. they both

had so much fun that my dad wants to do it again next year. caregiving for parents is a lot of work!!! do you think they said that about
raising children? i can tell that i'm not taking care of myself as i
know i should. hard to keep up with the household chores and
entertain her. she can't stand very long and i have to be with her
when she is standing or walking.

—E-mail from Cheryl Fears, April 14, 2008, 2:50 A.M.

Cheryl Fears, who cares for her parents in Springdale, Arkansas,
puts it simply: "You just pretty much have to give up your life if you
are doing this."

It was the time stamp on her e-mail I noticed first: 2:50 A.M.

That's when May e-mails, too. When you are a caregiver, sleep
does not come easily, even on good nights. Cheryl was having a
tough one.

A vivacious natural saleswoman, Cheryl worked part-time for
years in an antique and gift shop. When the owner wanted to sell,
Cheryl happily bought the business. It did well, and she had a ball.
While her husband, Roy, was a successful insurance agent, her shop
provided some much-needed extra income to help raise their family
of four boys.

Then Cheryl's mother, Katy, was diagnosed with Alzheimer's
disease. Her dad, Charles, already suffered from macular degenera-
tion, a progressive eye disease that leads to blindness. It didn't take
long before it all became too much. "We need to rethink what's going on here," Cheryl told Roy.

"We were killing ourselves," she remembers now. "Maintaining
the business, his work, and caring for and shopping for my mom. It
was too much."

So Cheryl sold the gift shop. She moved her parents from their
home a few miles away and into her own house. To make things a
little easier, she built an addition for them, with a kitchen, bathroom,
bedroom, living room, and small dining area. Cheryl now spends her

days caring for her parents and managing Allen, a paid aide who helps out on weekends and some weekdays.

Cheryl is not alone. More than half of family caregivers report that they take time off from work to provide long-term care, and one out of every six says they have had to take a leave of absence from their job.

Not surprisingly, the sicker their loved one gets, the more caregivers suffer at work. For example, 40 percent of those providing the least intensive level of care report having to leave work early or go in late, 17 percent say they have had to take a leave of absence, and 6 percent quit their jobs. But by the time they are providing very intense care, 83 percent say they have to miss work, and 41 percent take a formal leave. More than a third, like May and Cheryl, quit work entirely.[9]

According to one study, women aged fifty-five to sixty-seven who care for frail parents have to cut back on at least seven hours of work a week. This translates into $6,300 in lost wages every year, plus $2,300 in foregone benefits, such as health insurance and retirement savings.[10]

When caregivers reduce their work hours, they suffer more than an immediate loss of income. There are hidden costs that may prove more catastrophic over the long run. Working fewer hours means they are reducing both what they can contribute to their 401(k) retirement plans and what they'll get in Social Security benefits. Twenty years from now, when they are aged and frail, today's caregivers will themselves be more likely to become impoverished and end up on Medicaid.

And they are not just losing future earnings. Caregivers report spending more than $5,000 of their own money annually to help pay for a frail parent's medical care, transportation, and other costs.[11]

The emotional price is hardest to measure, although nearly all caregivers pay it. These children, spouses, and friends measure their days from crisis to crisis. There is always another emergency, another unexpected bill to be paid. There is always another phone call. The stresses can be highest when a loved one is at home, but they hardly disappear when Mom is in a nursing home.

The problem is especially severe when only one caregiver is trying to handle everything herself. That is very common, especially when an elderly wife is caring for her husband. She often must do the work alone, without the help of children or paid aides.[12] Imagine for a moment being eighty and frail and trying to take care of a husband who is bedridden and suffering from such severe memory loss that he doesn't know who you are.

Faced with that pressure every day, it is no surprise that up to 40 percent of those caring for dementia patients report suffering from depression.[13] Others go along, trying to ignore the stress, until they crash.

──────────── THE MELTDOWN ────────────

Steve and Judy Dow live in Essex Junction, a growing suburb of Burlington, Vermont. While Steve ran his construction and electrical business, Judy tried to manage two teenage kids, care for her own frail parents, Robert and Marguerite, and provide daily assistance to her mother-in-law, Beverly, who was suffering from increasingly severe dementia and lived alone about a half hour away.

A skilled basket maker, historian, teacher, and ethnologist, Judy now finds herself caring for her parents and her mother-in-law. She juggles their medical care, financial issues, shopping, personal care, and never-ending paperwork. She calls herself "the tour director," as she describes a typical day. "This doesn't come with a how-to manual," she says.

At first, the family hired aides to help Beverly at home, but they'd frequently call in sick at the last minute. Judy would frantically call the home health agency to persuade them to send a fill-in. Trouble was, these replacement aides often had no idea what to do, so Judy would have to give them a crash course in dementia care. Then she'd rush off to work.

One evening, Judy Dow had a meltdown. She had spent the day dealing with yet another crisis with her mother-in-law, and she was trying to help her daughter finish college applications. Steve came home after his own hard day at work, and Judy simply could not find the energy to make dinner. She broke down in tears. "I can't care for your mom and my parents, and our kids, and give you the care you need," Judy told Steve. "I just can't."

It happens a lot. The more family members try to do, the more likely they will wear down. Often it is their emotional stress and poor health that drive the relative they are caring for into a nursing home or other institution. One new study concludes that the frail elderly are three times more likely to enter a nursing home within a year after their caregivers begin to suffer from high stress.[14]

That's exactly what happened to Judy. First she gave up a steady job with the local school system for the extra flexibility she got as a consultant.

"You can't do this," she says, "and keep a nine-to-five job."

Then, after a year of trying to care for Beverly at home, she and Steve finally decided to move his mom into a nearby assisted-living facility.

As Judy found, the number of hours family caregivers must give grows steadily as their loved ones become more frail. Half of those getting personal care require less than about two hours of care a day. But as they become more disabled, their needs increase dramatically. Fully 20 percent require nine hours of help every day.[15]

Despite the Dows' frequent problems with aides, at least Beverly, who had long-term-care insurance, had the financial resources to hire paid assistance.

ON THE FRONT LINES

Today about 2 million paid aides care for the aged and disabled in the United States.[16] Some, called certified nurse assistants (CNAs) or geriatric nurse assistants (GNAs), have learned basic first aid and special skills such as how to bathe or feed the frail elderly, or help them go to the bathroom. Others, with less training, are homemakers or companions. Still others are licensed to administer medications. Many work in nursing homes or assisted-living facilities; others, directly in private homes. But wherever they are, these often underappreciated health-care workers do some of the most difficult work imaginable for little money and few benefits.

These aides provide the backbone to our system of personal assistance. Yet they are paid an average of $9.60 an hour, about what they could make bagging groceries. We pay people who wash our cars and tend our lawns more than we pay the aides who care for our parents.[17]

While an agency may be paid $20 an hour for a CNA's time, after it takes out taxes, overhead, and profit, an aide may only see half of that. A CNA who works on her own may get $12 or $15 an hour, but must pay taxes, gasoline, and other costs from that. Less-skilled aides, of course, make even more modest incomes.

As a result, it is not uncommon for aides to work two or three jobs. Often they will take a full shift in a nursing home, then another eight or ten hours in a private home, and weekends with yet another family.

These front-line workers have among the most dangerous jobs in the United States. Largely because of back injuries they suffer lifting patients, aides are far more likely to be hurt on the job than coal miners. Yet nearly 60 percent of nursing home aides and 75 percent of home health workers have no health insurance of their own.[18] Few receive sick leave or disability insurance. That means if they become ill or are injured on the job and cannot work, they do not get paid.

Allen Wood is a tall and trim forty-five-year-old, a former GI with wavy black hair, black-framed glasses, and a gentle manner. He juggles five clients. From nine A.M. to eight P.M. on weekends, and on some weekdays, he cares for Cheryl Fears's parents, Charles and Katy.

Allen is paid $14 a hour, and during a good week may work as many as sixty hours. But he works on his own. He must pay taxes, has no insurance, and gets no paid vacation.

Before he became a home health worker, Allen had been working as a toolmaker. After his own father got sick, he says he started to learn about aides. "I was seeing my dad and realizing so many people need care." And he learned something else: "To get good care in homes is hard for people."

Like many aides, Allen says he enjoys his work, but admits it is not easy. "It is such a giving job. It's really rewarding." But, he adds, "I get really tired. It can be exhausting. I've got to have some downtime."

He takes off two Wednesdays a month.

Allen says he has sometimes struggled with depression, and he is not alone. Nearly 11 percent of personal care workers say they have faced bouts of depression in the past year, the highest rate of any occupation in the United States.[19]

By contrast, Marybelle Kamara has a plum job. Marybelle is a CNA and a program assistant at Braddock Glen, an adult day-care center in Annandale, Virginia. For a year, she helped Walter Barrett with his meals, and with some of the games and exercises available to the seniors who come to the center.

Marybelle has a big, welcoming smile and a bubbly personality. A single mom at thirty-six, she lives with her thirteen-year-old daughter, Ashley.

She was born in Sierra Leone, grew up in England, and came to the United States at eighteen. Marybelle has been an aide since she was twenty-one. She has toiled at twelve-hour shifts in the home of a stroke victim, and worked in a nursing home and in the lockup unit of a facility for mentally ill criminals.

Except for the nursing home, she found all her jobs rewarding. "I kept moving because I wanted to learn," she says.

At Braddock Glen, she is an employee of Fairfax County, Virginia, which is not only one of the wealthiest jurisdictions in the United States but also one with a deep commitment to caring for its seniors. A program assistant such as Marybelle earns about $30,000 a year to start, but, with experience, can make as much as $50,000. She is also eligible for benefits, such as vacation pay, health insurance, and retirement.

But, for Marybelle, as with many like her, the real satisfaction is psychic. "My grandmother passed three years ago," she says. "Here it is like I have not lost her. There are so many grandmothers here. It makes you feel like you are part of them."

About one third of aides are, like Marybelle, immigrants. They not only have the same challenging work, but must also bridge massive language and cultural gaps.

In many cities on the East and West Coasts, aides are overwhelmingly from other countries. In the Washington, D.C., area, most are from West Africa, the Carribbean, and the Philippines. In New York, most are from the Caribbean, while some are from Russia or Ireland. Very few are native-born Americans. By contrast, in northwest Arkansas, most are, like Allen, white and native-born.

Marybelle and Allen are the aides without whom our system of long-term care would collapse. They provide the physical skills and emotional support essential to family caregivers. Like my dad's aide, Naressa, they are indispensable.

Despite their struggles, most caregivers—those who are paid as well as family members are driven by their deep affection for the people they are helping. It is not always so. The elderly and disabled are frequently victims of abuse, incompetence, and, most often, neglect. As many as one third have no one at all to care for them.

Each year, there are as many as three hundred thousand reported cases of elder abuse in the United States. But studies suggest that as many as one million people over age sixty are victims of abuse or neglect by someone upon whom they depend for care. Another one million are unable to meet their own needs, and suffer from malnutrition, an inability to keep themselves clean, and improper use of medications.[20]

Often, abuse by caregivers is driven by incompetence. For example, the frail elderly frequently get bedsores, in part because their caregivers don't know how to prevent them. Similarly, the aged become dangerously dehydrated because their caregivers don't know to provide them with enough liquids and don't recognize the danger signs of extreme fluid loss.

In other cases, abuse is more overt. Sometimes seniors are tied to beds or chairs, or otherwise restrained. Often they are threatened, or subjected to emotional abuse. In about 12 percent of cases, their money is stolen. Most victims are women, but increasingly, so are the abusers. In 1990, 42 percent were women. By 1996, 49 percent were female—frequently adult daughters.[21]

Why does it happen? Experts say caregiver stress and frustration are big reasons. Another related cause is isolation. Imagine an elderly couple unable to leave their home, with no friends or visitors, and one spouse almost entirely dependent on the other.[22]

Despite these dangers, seniors and the disabled increasingly want to stay at home rather than move to a nursing home or other institutional setting. Both Medicaid and long-term-care insurance policies are becoming more flexible, so there is at least some chance the funds will be there to provide this care.

As the Baby Boomers and their parents age, the demands for home care will only grow. New laws, social pressures, and the staggering costs of nursing homes will increase the need for care, from either family members or paid aides.

The push to keep the frail elderly and disabled out of nursing homes and in community settings will only increase the need for these helpers. After all, in a nursing home, one aide may care for a dozen patients. But when visiting homes, as Allen does, an aide may be able to care for only one or two clients during the course of a day. By one estimate, the demand for aides will triple in less than three decades.[23]

Where will they come from? As opportunities for women to make more money in the workplace grow, will daughters continue to give up their own careers to care for elderly parents? As parents age into their nineties, will seventy-year-olds be willing or able to spend their own retirement years helping them?

Maybe they'll want to turn to paid aides. But even if children and spouses can afford to hire them, who will do the work? Who will be willing to clean bedpans and do the backbreaking job of moving the demented for low pay and few benefits? In an era when the United States is working so hard to close its borders to immigrants, will native-born health workers fill the gap?

The need for caregivers will grow rapidly, far into the foreseeable future. But where will the Mays and Michelles and Marybelles and Allens come from?

FOUR

The Champion

In September 2004, Peggy Ingles, a champion breeder and rider, was working out a retired racehorse at her farm in northern Maryland. It was routine morning exercise—something she had done thousands of times before. But on this day, the animal spooked. Maybe it heard an unexpected noise or saw a shadow. No one knows. But in a few horrifying seconds, the animal stumbled and fell backward, its massive weight crushing Peggy's neck against a fence railing. Instantly, her badly bruised spinal cord swelled and cut off nearly all her mobility. "I could move one bicep," she remembers. "That was it."

Amazingly, in a lifetime of working horses, Peggy had never had a serious fall. She kept thirty horses at her stables, called Starstruck Farm, and she was at the peak of her career. In 2002 and 2003, she won national championships with two of her half-Arabians, the chestnut Post Exchange and the striking all-white Sohn. She was already starting to train Post Exchange's son, Mission Accomplished, to be her next champion. But in just moments on that warm September day, Peggy's life changed profoundly.

"At first I couldn't feel a thing," she remembers. "Then it hurt, but only for a while."

In that instant, Peggy began an odyssey of perseverance and recovery, and of frustration and disability. Against all odds and the belief of many medical experts, Peggy has regained some of her mobility. But she remains unable to care for herself without help. And much of her day is spent struggling with the mundane details of life that the rest of us take for granted: getting out of bed in the morning, eating a snack, tracking down a piece of lost mail.

Most of us do these things with barely a thought. Peggy can't.

In the photographs that line the walls of her small apartment in a nondescript suburb of Baltimore, Peggy sits tall and strong on her horses. But now, on a cool spring afternoon, she almost disappears in the seat of her huge electric wheelchair. Her brown hair is gathered up in a practical ponytail, the same style she used to wear on the farm. She is dressed in black sweat pants and a black top, and has on a pair of oversize plastic-framed glasses. Like many paraplegics, she has lost so much muscle mass that she is rail-thin. Her face is gaunt. Her legs are attached to the chair with Velcro straps.

But Peggy, who is now forty-nine, greets me with a huge smile, a strong voice, and a powerful will. Thanks to intense physical therapy, she has made near-miraculous progress in her rehabilitation.

Still, improvement has sometimes been frustratingly slow. It was a month before she could raise a hand to her face. Then she could move one arm and a few fingers. The trouble was she had use of her left arm but only the fingers of her right hand, so there was still almost nothing she could do for herself. "It was," Peggy says, "a kind of joke."

Now she can use both arms and her right hand. With the help of her "old-lady walker," she can even take some steps on her own, and she can ride a stationary bike.

Peggy accomplished all of this with a combination of hard work and a cutting-edge physical therapy program at the Kennedy Krieger Institute in Baltimore.

Designed by Dr. John McDonald, Kennedy Krieger's rehabilitation program uses electrical impulses to simulate the signals the brain normally sends to muscles to initiate movement. It works like this: When we want to walk, our brain sends a complex set of messages to our leg that say, "Take a step." But when someone has an injury like Peggy's, the damaged spinal cord blocks those signals, and the leg won't move, even though the brain is trying to tell it to.

But with the right jolt of electricity at the proper time, a leg or an arm gets the message to move, much as it did before the injury. With repeated exercise, muscle memory can sometimes return so that, eventually, limbs function again. So, patients like Peggy succeed by tough, sweaty exercise, working those muscles over and over again until, eventually, they begin to remember what they are supposed to do. That's why the atmosphere at Kennedy Krieger is more like a gym than a hospital.

For months Peggy went at it four hours a day, three days a week. She exercised on a stationary bicycle and on an elliptical machine, working her arms, legs, and abs. She also did other, more routine physical exercises, using a treadmill, tossing a ball, building her strength, all the things she was not supposed to be able to do.

On good days and bad, she battled through those intense physical therapy sessions. Despite the challenges of even getting to the institute, she missed only one appointment—on the day her sister got married. Now she goes to Kennedy Krieger once a week for four hours of therapy, which she supplements with workouts at home and regular electrical stimulation of her damaged muscles.

"You have to be very motivated," says Kennedy Krieger's Elise Babbitt. "You have to not listen to what everybody else tells you."

Before Peggy got to Kennedy Krieger, she didn't listen a lot. That meant ignoring medical experts who constantly told her what she would no longer be able to do. It also meant battling a long-term-care system that threw up endless roadblocks to her rehabilitation.

For Peggy, "We can't do that" was never the end of the conversation. It was always just the beginning.

All this work not only helped remake those broken connections between Peggy's brain, arms, and legs, but it also greatly improved her overall health. Her heart, skin, and bones are all healthier, making it more likely she'll live a long life without the infections and other side effects that often plague the wheelchair-bound.

For all of its well-documented problems, the U.S. health-care system has great success treating severe, traumatic illnesses and injuries such as Peggy's. Not many years ago, she would have died from her injuries. Now we have the skills and technology to save Peggy's life. But we don't know how to help her manage what will be decades of chronic disability.

Peggy is just one of 3.5 million Americans between the ages of eighteen and sixty-four who need some level of personal assistance to help manage their disabilities.[1] She is one of the quarter million living with the terrible consequences of sports or auto accidents, gunshot wounds, or falls that cause severe spinal cord injuries. Almost two thirds of them are under age thirty.[2] More than 1.5 million Americans suffer traumatic brain injuries. Four hundred thousand have multiple sclerosis, a debilitating disease of the central nervous system. Most are under fifty.[3] Each year, one out of every thirty-three children in the United States is born with a developmental disability, such as autism, Down syndrome, or cerebral palsy.[4]

While these younger people with disabilities share with the elderly a need for long-term care, their circumstances are often very different. Those over sixty-five require personal care for a relatively short period of time—on average about three years. Younger people with disabilities often need assistance for decades. Some are even living into old age, which creates a whole new set of complex medical and long-term-care issues.

While many of those with disabilities need only limited assistance—for instance, help showering and dressing or transportation to work—those with severe brain or spinal cord injuries need very intensive care, often around the clock. Their families must not only provide basic personal assistance, but often also operate costly and sophisticated medical equipment. However, since only half of the severely disabled aged twenty-one to sixty-four are married, this very difficult care must be provided by parents or friends.[5]

The financial situation of these younger disabled is often very different, too. Only about 13 percent of those who are severely disabled work full time, and they make an average of less than $13,000 a year.[6] While many seniors have built a modest nest egg, with some savings and perhaps a home, younger people may never have had the opportunity. Peggy, for example, saved very little, instead pouring most of her income back into her farm.

If a family's principal breadwinner becomes ill, their money can dry up almost overnight. As a result, one quarter of the disabled live in poverty and have no resources at all to pay for long-term care.[7] Given the staggering costs of both acute medical care and long-term care, many end up on Medicaid.

That's what happened to Peggy. Immediately after her fall, she was airlifted to the University of Maryland's Shock Trauma Center, one of the nation's most sophisticated centers for treating catastrophic injuries. There, she was quickly stabilized by a team of skilled doctors and nurses.

She spent three weeks at Shock Trauma. Like many small-business people, she had no health insurance. So, as she was being discharged, Peggy was presented with a bill. It was for $1.75 million. She could not pay any of it.

As a result of her medical debts and her inability to work, Peggy had to go on government assistance, including Maryland's state health insurance plan for the poor and uninsurable. She also became eligible for Medicaid, the joint state/federal medical program that pays for her personal care.

After Shock Trauma, Peggy's next stop was a local rehabilitation hospital, where she stayed for three months. She was still helpless and needed assistance with eating, going to the bathroom—everything. "It is hard," she says, "to be trapped in your body."

Her time there was awful, she remembers. She'd call for help, but no one would come. Worst of all, she was told she'd never regain the use of her arms and legs. She received limited physical and occupational therapy, aimed only at helping her live with the disabilities she had. No one was interested in helping her get better.

"They told me this is how you are going to be. Deal with it. . . . It was the worst thing they could do."

Tough, and a perfectionist in all she does, Peggy talks about that rehab hospital with disdain. "They are the people who gave up hope. I said, 'I'm afraid not.'"

Finally, she was transferred to a nursing home, where she stayed another three months. She says she got good care, but only because she was young and gregarious and developed a good relationship with the nurses and therapists. Sometimes, she says, "you learn to smile even when you're angry."

Still, she saw terrible things there. Once she learned to use a wheelchair, she'd travel around the nursing home chatting up the staff or visiting other patients. One day, she rolled into another resident's room to find that the patient, an elderly woman, had died. She told the nurses, but hours later, when she returned to the room, the woman's body was still there.

Peggy was convinced that if she did not get out, she would die, too. She focused all of her formidable will and physical ability on achieving two goals: regaining the use of her limbs and going home. It was an aim she shared with my father-in-law, Al, and so many others.

Living at home is a priority for many disabled, especially adults who have suffered injuries or accidents. Unlike many frail elderly, who are nearing the end of their lives, these younger disabled feel they have decades of productive living ahead of them. For them, long-term care is not the assistance they need to stay alive. It is of-

ten the personal care they need to lead busy lives. It is help showering and dressing in the morning before they go off to work.

People with disabilities have become a well-organized and aggressive political movement. One of their demands has been to get
long-term care out of nursing homes and back to private homes and
communities. It isn't always easy, but their advocates have helped
change the way America thinks about long-term care.

Like many people with disabilities, Peggy knew she could not go
back to the place that had been home for her. After her accident,
she lost everything. She had to give up her beloved Starstruck Farm,
which she was leasing. She sold her pickup and whatever other equipment she could. Her horses were gone, shipped off to other stables.

She was able to find a small apartment, for which her rent is subsidized, so she pays only $196 a month, but she has to cover utilities
and the phone, too. Anything extra her family chips in is deducted
from the $600 a month she gets in federal cash assistance.

In the long run, Peggy wants to be back on a farm with her
horses—maybe working with at-risk kids. But she has a long way
to go.

That she has recovered so much is a triumph. For now, though,
she is still unable to get out of bed, shower, or go to the bathroom
on her own. She can eat without assistance, but she cannot cook. To
open a cup of yogurt, she must grasp the container with her one
good hand and rip the foil top off with her teeth. "I don't even want
to think about where it has been," she says, snorting.

In one way, Peggy is very lucky. Medicaid would normally pay
only for her to stay in a nursing home. However, under a special
program, she can live in her apartment. Medicaid pays for an aide
for nine hours each day, and the government pays for Peggy's health-
care supplies and drugs, and sometimes—after weeks of arguing—
for some of her medical equipment.

That daily nine hours of personal assistance is a great help, but it
is not enough. So, in January 2007, Peggy's twenty-year-old daughter, Cassie, moved into the apartment to help out.

Peggy didn't ask her to, and only reluctantly agreed to Cassie's decision. "I wanted her to have a real life and not be bothered with me."

Now Cassie is trying to juggle college, the Army Reserve, and caring for her mom. She witnessed her mother's accident, and afterward, at just seventeen, ran the farm herself for six months. She is a talented artist; her sketches of horses line the walls of Peggy's apartment. But she's had little time for her art since her mom was hurt.

In truth, right now Peggy could not get along without Cassie. While Peggy has hired a succession of home health aides to assist her, some work out and some don't. Some are unreliable or inattentive when they do show up. Some have only limited personal care skills. A few are caring and capable, but they don't stay long. That doesn't surprise Peggy. After all, they are paid only about $10.50 an hour, equal to about $21,000 a year for a forty-hour week. That is roughly the poverty rate in Maryland for a mother with three kids.

For a while, Peggy had a live-in for extra help. In return for free rent, the young woman agreed to care for Peggy at night, when her paid daytime aides had gone home. Instead, her helper went out on dates. Many nights, she wouldn't return until dawn. In September 2007, Peggy fell out of bed. She lay on the floor for six hours, until her companion finally came home and helped her get up.

Peggy fired her on the spot. Not longer after, Cassie moved in.

Still, during the day, Cassie is at school and Peggy needs help. It is especially important for her as she gets started each morning. She needs assistance getting to the bathroom and bathing, and she needs someone to make breakfast for her.

One morning before Cassie moved in, Peggy's regular aide failed to show up. Without help, she couldn't get out of bed to go to the bathroom. You haven't lived, Peggy says, unless you've started your day lying in your own urine while you try to persuade someone at the home health agency to send a substitute.

Eventually, the agency sent a replacement. He was a nice guy, but had no skills working with someone with limited mobility. "I think his last job was as a gardener," Peggy says with a laugh.

Many of her aides come from African countries. They are caring, reliable, and hard workers. But often language and culture get in the way. "You ask about your elbow; they think it is your knee," Peggy says. Then there are the peanut butter and tomato sandwiches she sometimes gets for lunch. Tasty enough, but unexpected. Peggy just shrugs. "I don't know where that comes from."

She is remarkably philosophical about her accident. "You ride long enough and these things happen," she says. But she is not so sanguine about much of her care. Her anger flashes as she talks about her incontinence wipes. At first, she got them for about three cents each. Then the insurance company changed suppliers, and the cost increased by more than ten fold. Peggy doesn't pay out of her own pocket, but still she is furious at the waste. "They say that's the way it is," she fumes. "I was dumbstruck. I never had enough money that I could burn it like that."

At the same time the insurance company was wasting money on the wipes, it battled her for months when she tried to replace the worn-out seat cushions for her wheelchair. They frayed in six months, but the policy is to replace them every two years. Those are the rules.

Dealing with health-care agencies, government bureaucrats, and insurance companies wears Peggy down in a way grueling physical therapy does not. "It is," she says, "exhausting."

One afternoon, she gets a call from the sales rep for Lifeline, the company that sells emergency notification devices that allow someone who falls to signal for help. The caller asks if Peggy has moved. "No," she replies, with a mordant laugh, "I haven't gone anywhere for a while."

He is asking because her new contract has been returned to the company by the post office, marked Addressee Unknown. Peggy can only sigh. Another stupid mistake. More hours lost sorting it out.

If this happened to you or me, it would be a minor annoyance. We'd grumble, drive to the post office, fill out a form, and fix the problem. For Peggy, there are no minor annoyances.

Peggy keeps her personal care ship from sinking only because she has Cassie and at least four aggressive advocates to help her navigate the mind-numbingly complex long-term-care system. Her father, seventy-two, a retired corporate executive, has taken it upon himself to bust through the bureaucratic roadblocks that stymie Peggy's recovery.

She wanted to get an air mattress to prevent bedsores, a common, dangerous, and potentially deadly consequence of being immobile for long periods of time. But the insurance company would not get her one. Instead, it insisted it would pay for the special mattress only after she'd begun suffering from the dangerous skin ulcers. Peggy's dad went ballistic. She got the mattress.

"He is a force of nature," Peggy says. "He is napalm dad."

Peggy also has the help of a nonprofit firm called the Coordinating Center, which manages all of her care under a contract with the state. The center provides her with a case manager, who helps guide her through arcane and often illogical Medicaid rules. Despite the center's slightly Orwellian name, staffers there know whom to call, and they know the magic words that get things done. "The Coordinating Center is amazing," Peggy says.

She also has Aaron, the representative for the private health insurance company that provides coverage through Maryland Medicaid. Peggy calls Aaron "my guy."

And then there is Peggy herself. As a businesswoman who is no wallflower, she has the ability to work the immensely complex long-term-care system in ways that an eighty-five-year-old widow with dementia could not even dream of.

Still, Peggy knows that without her powerful support system, even she might not be able to live independently. She also knows that she is in some ways trapped. It will be nearly impossible for her ever to get off Medicaid. There are many reasons, but the biggest may be that taking a job would require her to buy her own health insurance. That might be possible if she went to work for a big company with a comprehensive group policy. But if she tried to work at a small company, or tried to buy insurance in the individual market, no private policy would ever cover her.

If she went back to work, she wouldn't just lose her state health insurance. All the rest of her formal support structure—Medicaid's personal-care benefits, her subsidized apartment, and the help of the Coordinating Center—would also disappear. While politicians love to talk about the value of independence and self-reliance, Peggy knows the system they have created makes that impossible.

"I want to be financially independent, but if I make too much money, I lose everything."

So, to feel useful and relieve the boredom of long days in her apartment, Peggy helps run several nonprofits for no pay. Some are for owners of the Anglo-Arabian horses she loves so much. The one most special to her, however, is the Maryland Network for Injured Equestrians. It helps raise funds for wheelchairs and other medical equipment for others who've suffered riding accidents.

As part of her rehab, Peggy got back on a horse for the first time in the spring of 2007. In a way, she loved it. But, she says, it was just a pony. What she really wants is to ride her champion, Post Exchange, again. She's going to do it, she says. And when she does, "I don't want it to be therapy. I want it to be fun."

LISA

For all of the challenges Peggy faces trying to live independently in her apartment, she is far happier than she was in the nursing home. But others who are disabled have no choice. Despite major efforts to find alternatives, at least two hundred thousand young people with disabilities still live in nursing homes or other institutions.[8]

Lisa, who asked me to not use her real name, is never going to get back on her horse again. And unlike Peggy, she may very well spend the rest of her days in a nursing home.

"I never thought my life would be like this," Lisa says.

For nearly forty years, from the time she was twenty, Lisa has lived with multiple sclerosis, a debilitating and poorly understood disease of the central nervous system. Gradually, MS stole her eyesight and her ability to walk. She struggles to speak, and it is sometimes very difficult to understand her. Lisa's mind remains mostly sharp, she is fully engaged in the world, and she is a voracious listener of audiobooks. But in recent months, the MS has begun to affect her memory. Sometimes now, especially when she is tired, Lisa becomes confused and can't remember things she's said just a few minutes before.

For four decades, though, she has found a way to live a full life, despite her MS.

When Lisa was first diagnosed with the disease, she was engaged to a college classmate. She was a beautiful, smart young woman, and before she got sick, attracted herds of suitors. But soon after her boyfriend learned about her disease, he left her.

Lisa kept dating, and eventually married Jack. It wasn't an easy marriage. Jack had trouble holding down jobs; he suffered from depression and sometimes abused alcohol and drugs. Despite Lisa's own health problems, she took care of Jack as much as he helped her. But it was mostly Lisa's kids who provided the personal care she needed.

About those kids: After her diagnosis, the doctors told Lisa she could never have children. It would put far too much stress on her body and could even jeopardize her life, they insisted. She ignored them, and had two babies five years apart. Those kids she was not supposed to have are both college graduates now.

"I'm stubborn," Lisa says with more than a bit of pride.

Until about five years ago, Lisa stayed active, working part time, going on cross-country trips, and even taking vacation cruises. As it became harder to get around, she'd use a walker. Sometimes she'd rely on a motorized cart. Her MS slowed her down, but it never stopped her.

One morning in 2006, she woke up and her legs wouldn't work. In the past, she'd suffered episodes where she'd lose her ability to walk, but it would always come back. This time it didn't.

Despite their struggles, Lisa and Jack had stayed together—until the day she could no longer walk.

"I can't do this anymore," he told her. A few weeks later, Lisa moved to a nursing home.

The facility, operated by a major chain, has a good reputation. It is located in a wealthy suburb, and is surrounded by nice gardens. The common areas are warm and comfortable. The aides are usually polite and mostly competent.

Like most nursing homes, this one has a rehab wing. That's where the company makes its profits. The patients there are younger, and usually recovering from major surgeries, injuries, or strokes.

But that is not where Lisa lives. She shares a room in the long-term-care wing. Most other residents there are in their eighties or nineties, and nearly all suffer from dementia. It is no place for a fifty-something woman. For Lisa, just being in that environment is deeply depressing. "It is disconcerting," she says, "when the people you eat dinner with are dropping like flies."

She has had many roommates in the time she's been in the nursing home. These days, she is sharing a room with a woman who is ninety-three and very ill. She has dementia, and wakes Lisa up long before dawn most mornings with her pleas for breakfast. "When she starts crying," Lisa says, "I put on my headphones and listen to a book. What else can I do?"

Late one night, her roommate, who was sleeping on her back, began to vomit. Lisa, whose own long years of illness had given her a sophisticated layman's knowledge of medicine, knew that unless the woman was rolled on to her side, she was in danger of choking to death. Lisa pressed her Call button. No one came. She pressed it again. Finally, an aide arrived.

"She had no idea what to do. She seemed more interested in

cleaning her up than turning the patient so she wouldn't choke. I kept telling her, but she wasn't listening."

On other days, Lisa has received her roommate's medication. This is never supposed to happen in a nursing home, where drugs are distributed in "blister packs," sealed packages with prepared doses for each individual patient. But just as false teeth, eyeglasses, and even clothing regularly get mixed up in nursing homes, so do prescriptions for medications.

On many mornings, Lisa is awakened at 7:30 A.M. by an aide taking her out of bed and putting her in a wheelchair so she can be brought to the shower. If she protests, they tell her that this is the only chance she has to be bathed. If she refuses, she won't get another chance until tomorrow. "They ruin a lot of dreams," Lisa says.

One day, I join Lisa for lunch. We are at a table in one corner of the dining room. This, Lisa says, is where the younger patients sit, where those who still have their minds eat.

"We are the—what do they call us? The high-functioning ones," Lisa says. "The others sit over there."

An aide brings me a sandwich, which may be tuna fish or chicken salad. I can't tell. Lisa gets a sandwich, too. It is on a china plate. This is a nice place, after all. But it is wrapped in plastic. So is her drink; and her straw is wrapped in paper.

Lisa has the use of only one hand, so she can't unwrap her lunch. She tears open the straw with her teeth. Aides are lingering in the dining room. One group is laughing and joking in the corner. No one offers to help Lisa with the plastic wrap. I ask if I can help. I don't know what she does if there is no visitor to assist her.

It costs Lisa almost $9,000 a month to live here.

Like so many other nursing home residents, Lisa will soon run out of money. When she does, she'll go on Medicaid. And for all of her problems at this facility, she is terrified that when she can no longer pay out of her own pocket, she'll end up in a place that is much worse.

That won't happen, but only if she manages the system carefully.

If she makes a mistake, she could end up in a Medicaid mill, or in a facility miles from her friends and family, which would make their visits even less frequent than they are today.

Lisa is why advocates for the disabled have battled so aggressively to keep young people with disabilities out of nursing homes. Like frail seniors, most younger disabled people rely entirely on informal care from relatives or friends. However, the most severely disabled, such as Peggy or Lisa, frequently end up on Medicaid, which too often still forces them into institutional care.

Until the 1980s, those with disabilities commonly lived in institutions: nursing homes or even asylums. Children with Down syndrome or other developmental disabilities were written off as "retarded" or even insane, and often locked away for the rest of their lives. Not surprisingly, they didn't live long.

But over the last twenty years, the disabled have become aggressive advocates for themselves. Their biggest demand has been for a system of community care that would allow them to stay at home, or perhaps in a group home, but out of a nursing facility.

Their biggest victory came in the 1990s, when lawyers for two mentally disabled Atlanta women, Lois Curtis and Elaine Wilson, argued that they should be cared for in a community home rather than in a state psychiatric hospital. Their case eventually ended up in the U.S. Supreme Court, which ruled in June 1999 that states must make "reasonable" efforts to find community care for people with disabilities.[9] Ever since, many legal and legislative battles have been fought to define what "reasonable" means, but the decision revolutionized the way government cares for those with disabilities.

Now the community-care movement is slowly beginning to spread to the frail elderly. Medicaid long-term care is finally paying for assistance in people's own homes.

Still, many cash-strapped states remain reluctant to support home care, even though it is often the least expensive alternative. Georgia was paying nearly twice as much to keep Lois Curtis and Elaine Wilson confined in a psychiatric hospital than it spent to care for them in the small group home where they lived after they won their case. Yet almost a decade after this landmark lawsuit was decided, states and the federal government prefer to pay more to keep the aged and disabled in nursing homes—the very places so many people dread.

FIVE

The Claws of the Dragon

Bill Thomas is the sort of man who would kick off a Middle East peace conference by announcing that it might not be a bad idea to turn the Old City of Jerusalem into a parking lot. He is one of those larger-than-life characters who simultaneously provokes and infuriates. A physician, author, actor, and prolific speaker, Thomas wants nothing less than to fundamentally remake the way we think of old people. His goal is to "bring elders back to the heart of society."

He'd like to start by abolishing nursing homes as we know them.

On the stage of a packed ballroom in a downtown Chicago hotel, Thomas can hardly sit still. The room is filled with advocates for the aged and disabled, nursing home operators, and promoters of alternative housing for seniors. These people already don't like one another very much. The advocates think the nursing home operators are greedy and incompetent. The nursing home owners think the advocates are hopelessly naïve. The alternative housing people are convinced they have found the only true answer to the difficult question of how to provide care for those who cannot stay at home.

Thomas wants all of them to rethink their deeply held beliefs about long-term care. He questions. He challenges. He pushes people to doubt.

With his thick, curly black hair, bushy beard, casual slacks and shirt, and Birkenstocks, it is easy to write Thomas off as a character who dropped out of the 1960s—the Jerry Rubin of nursing homes. Indeed, he happily calls himself a social revolutionary.

Nursing homes, he says, haunt us. "We fear and dread institutionalization above all else. The system is abhorrent," Thomas fairly shouts.

A man sitting next to me is furiously taking notes, his sweet roll half eaten and forgotten. He does not laugh at Thomas's one-liners. I learn later that he is an executive of a Midwestern nursing home company.

But if the anti–nursing home crowd thinks they have an ally, they, too, are about to be disappointed. Thomas's fury at traditional institutions doesn't mean he is about to embrace the folks who have come to this conference to promote "aging in place"—the idea that, with the right help, millions more frail seniors can live at home. These advocates are supremely confident in the moral superiority of their view. And Thomas can't wait to burst their comfortable bubble.

"Aging in place is a negative vision," he bellows. "It is a vision of escaping the claws of the dragon." Thomas tells these advocates they are peddling a false choice. Of course, if you ask someone whether she'd prefer to stay in her own comfortable home or be confined to a nursing facility, she'll vote for home every time. But, he adds, that doesn't mean she's getting good care there. Her choice merely reflects her terror of the alternative.

Thomas, who has two disabled daughters himself, is a powerful advocate for the elderly and disabled. But he also recognizes their enormous physical needs and what it would cost to allow them all to stay at home. It would take hundreds of thousands more home health aides, and tens of billions of dollars in home renovations and medical equipment. And even after all that, there is no assurance they'd truly get better care.

"There isn't enough money in America to finance the illusion of independence for seventy million aging Boomers," he insists.

Besides, says Thomas, who as a kid couldn't wait to leave his own small town, Americans suffer from an innocent nostalgia for communities and families that may never have existed outside of an Andy Hardy movie. In reality, home is often a lot less happy than we like to think it is. And the truth is that many seniors have no one to care for them as they age. It is not uncommon for a ninety-year-old widow to outlive not only her husband but also her children.

So, in Thomas's world, many of us will inevitably find ourselves living out our days with groups of other seniors. The right question, he insists, is how can we make these facilities as caring and home-like as possible?

In 1991, as a newly minted physician, Thomas was hired as the medical director of Chase Memorial Nursing Home in rural New Berlin, New York. He remembers the eighty-bed facility as "a small-town nursing home with a fine quality record." But it was still a traditional facility. And the unbending structure and deep institutionalization of nursing homes made Thomas crazy. Every resident was expected to wake up at the same time, eat the same meal at the same time, play bingo and go to bed at the same time. Thomas was convinced that this regimented life had to be utterly demeaning to both the residents and the staff.

It is, he repeats like a mantra, a life of "loneliness, boredom, and helplessness."

So Thomas rounded up some grant money and remade the place. He brought in parakeets and dug up the lawn and turned it into an organic garden. He arranged for children's programs so residents could have regular contact with kids. His idea was to make the place as much like a home as possible.

Just as important, Thomas wanted to change the relationships between the aides who provided the day-to-day care and the facility's management. In traditional nursing homes, which are almost military-like in their rigid top-down organization, aides are expected to do what their supervisors tell them, without question. The atmosphere is often extremely tense. Morale is low. At a typical nursing home, it is not unusual for 100 percent of the staff to leave within a year.

Thomas believed that if the nurse assistants had more flexibility in the way they did their jobs, they'd be happier and more responsive to the needs of residents. In the hierarchical world of nursing homes, this was considered not only radical, but dangerous. Left on their own, would aides care for their patients? Turns out, they would.

Eventually, Thomas's ideas became what he called the Eden Alternative, the model for hundreds of similar facilities that have since sprung up around the country.

At dinner at a trendy Capitol Hill restaurant, a few months after that Chicago conference, Thomas is at his most provocative. He is comparing traditional nursing homes to prison.

"In prison," he says, "every inmate is treated exactly the same. That same logic applies in the nursing home. It is the definition of a repressive environment."

He tells me about Erving Goffman, who in 1961 dubbed nursing homes, hospitals for the mentally ill, prisons, and similar facilities as "total institutions." In his book *Asylums*, Goffman described them this way: "All aspects of life are conducted in the same place and under the same single authority. . . . Each . . . activity . . . is carried out in the immediate company of a large batch of others, all of whom are treated alike and required to do the same thing together. . . . All phases of the day's activity are tightly scheduled, with one activity leading at a prearranged time to the next, the whole sequence of events being imposed from above."[1]

Although Goffman was studying primarily psychiatric hospitals, it seemed to Thomas that the author had perfectly described nursing homes. Profoundly affected by both Goffman and his own personal experiences, Thomas makes no secret of his future vision of these traditional nursing homes. He wants nothing less than to shutter them all.

But even corporate nursing home owners concede he is on to something. When I ask a Washington lobbyist for the nursing home industry if Thomas is an outrageous self-promoter or a visionary, he replies simply, "Yes."

The lobbyist puts it this way: "When you get past the birds and dogs, he is dead-on when he talks about the isolation and loneliness of old age and disability and how important it is to give families and patients greater autonomy."

Thomas's solution: new communities where seniors can live out their lives in skilled nursing homes, but in a way that is as comfortable and noninstitutional as possible. He is trying to expand the Eden concept by making even more radical changes in the relationships between residents and staff, and between aides and management. He also wants to make profound physical changes in nursing facilities. He calls these new institutions Green Houses, small group homes clustered together on larger campuses.

Thomas and others like him may be taking the first steps in a movement that will revolutionize the way we care for elders. Maybe.

Bill Thomas is just the latest in a long line of social reformers who have tried to transform the way we provide long-term care in the United States. We have struggled with this challenge for our entire history. Sadly, it has too often been a tale straight out of Charles Dickens: a story of high-minded social reforms twisted into a hellish world of poorhouses, insane asylums, and old-age homes.[2]

THE AFTERTHOUGHT

For most of human history, a family or clan took care of its own frail or sick as best it could. If it could not, or would not, the person simply died. Medical treatment for the elderly (who might have been no older than forty) or severely disabled did not exist. Community care, beyond the extended family, was largely unknown.

In the America of 250 years ago, most of these responsibilities still rested with families. A widowed mother, blind uncle, or "feeble-minded" young adult lived with relatives, who provided what financial and personal support they could. But communities were beginning to take on some collective responsibility, too. When family members could not help, neighbors and churches provided assistance, including food and shelter.

Even in those earliest colonial days, however, local governments often provided help when no one else would. In Massachusetts, for example, a law was passed in 1742 that required towns to care for "any person . . . uncapable to provide for him or herself."[3] And by the 1760s, Boston was spending a substantial share of its budget on public assistance for the poor.

However, most needy people were taken into the homes of local families, who were paid a small government stipend for accepting these borders. This came to be known as "outdoor" relief, in contrast to "indoor," or institutional, care. In return for this help, recipients were expected to do what work they could to help the host families, perhaps by sewing or cleaning.

For most of American history, this public assistance was based not on age or medical need, but simply on economic status. Thus, government provided the same relief to anyone who was poor and had no family help. Frail widows were treated the same way as orphaned children, or adults who suffered from mental illness or alcoholism, even though the kind of care they needed was very different. As a result, from its earliest days, publicly supported long-term care for the disabled or the frail elderly was what former Medicaid administrator Bruce Vladeck calls "an afterthought, a side effect of decisions directed at other problems."[4]

It took until the last half of the twentieth century before policymakers began to realize that a frail widow had very different needs from, say, an unmarried low-income mother with children. And, even today, government programs such as Medicaid still struggle to come to grips with those differences.

In early-eighteenth-century rural and small-town America, where everyone knew everyone else, this system of outdoor relief came naturally, although some communities were more generous than others. Caring for the poor was considered a religious obligation, although this assistance was often extended only to local residents. People without community ties were "warned out," the polite term of the day for being run out of town.

Boston built America's first public institution for the care of the poor in 1664.[5] But it was not until the 1730s, as towns such as Boston and New York began to grow, that public almshouses became commonplace. In these booming seaports, where sailors and other indigent transients often needed help, people were less likely to have the close ties that made it possible for neighbors to care for one another.

At first these institutions were small, housing only a dozen people or so, and they were built to look and feel like family homes. While in the early eighteenth century these almshouses were considered residences of last resort for the poor and sick, their home-like atmosphere was much like what Thomas and other reformers are trying to re-create today. In the early days, at least, the care provided in these institutions was relatively generous.

At first, perhaps because of the long-standing personal relationships that developed in small-town America, the idea that some members of every community would inevitably become frail or chronically ill and need communal help was simply accepted. But by the 1820s, that began to change. Poverty, and its many causes, came to be considered a sign of personal moral failure. And with that change in attitude came a profound rethinking of the purpose of institutional care.

No longer were the indigent simply to be provided with food and shelter. Now they were to be reformed. Poverty or illness were character flaws that could be corrected, the reasoning went. And the place to save these lost souls was the poorhouse.

By 1840, there were 180 almshouses in Massachusetts,[6] and government began to actively discourage community care for the poor, sick, and old. Of course, many people were still cared for by their own families. But by the end of the Civil War, 80 percent of those who needed long-term government relief got it in an institution.[7] It would be another 130 years before that attitude began to change.

Dickens was not exaggerating much when he described these poorhouses in his classic 1837 novel, *Oliver Twist*. In his workhouse, the orphan Oliver receives "three meals of thin gruel a day with an onion twice a week, and half a roll on Sundays."[8] The almshouses of mid-nineteenth-century America were little different. Harsh conditions and brutality were the norm. Indeed, this abuse was often seen as a necessary incentive for inmates to change their sinful ways.

This cruel system was not initially aimed at the old and sick, but inevitably, still lumped in with all other indigents, they suffered the same fate. After all, if insanity and drunkenness were symptoms of moral failure, so was a frail old age: If you had been a better, more God-fearing person, you would not be infirm.

It is hard to imagine, but important to remember, that these institutions were created by social reformers of the time. As with penitentiaries (whose name came from the word *penitent*) and insane asylums, their aim was to provide an environment that would bring "order, regularity, industry and temperance" to the lives of residents, and cure them of their moral failings.[9]

By the end of the Civil War, economic pressures in these public institutions grew and conditions worsened. At the same time, the population changed. Criminals were sent to the penitentiaries, the mentally ill to the asylums, and children to orphanages. By default, the chronically ill elderly became the last residents of almshouses. By the early twentieth century, the institutions even began to be called homes for the aged.[10]

At the same time, another kind of long-term care was quietly developing along the fringes of mainstream society. Jews and blacks, who were often barred from public asylums, began creating mutual aid societies to care for their elderly. Later, other ethnic and religious groups did the same. Sometimes these organizations helped support community assistance. But they also established more than one thousand private homes for the aged.

They also brought a sea change in community attitudes. To them, the aged and disabled were not examples of individual moral failure. Instead, they were simply people who needed help.

By the late nineteenth and early twentieth centuries, as Americans came to realize that illness and frailty had medical and not moral causes, institutions such as tuberculosis sanatoriums evolved into hospital-like environments. Later, as private nursing homes began to replace public homes for the aged, this medical model would become the dominant structure for long-term institutional care. In many ways, these homes were a vast improvement over the brutality of the public poorhouses, but they also set the stage for some of the problems of institutionalization against which Thomas and others rail today. Once again, what began as social reform would become the very cause of future problems.

The 1930s brought two powerful changes to the nation's insurance system. Either might have created a financing mechanism for long-term care. But as it happened, neither did.

The first was the establishment of private health insurance, which began in earnest with the Depression-era Blue Cross plans. But these policies, and those that followed, covered medical care only, and not long-term personal assistance.[11] At the same time, President Franklin Roosevelt established Social Security, which would eventually do more to pull the elderly out of poverty than any other program in history. But Roosevelt, always a pragmatist, chose not to include health care in his plan, perhaps remembering the powerful opposition of the labor movement to an earlier effort to provide national medical insurance.[12] Unions wanted to bargain for health benefits; they didn't want them made freely available by government.

FDR did, however, create Old Age Assistance, which funneled federal cash to those states that gave financial assistance to the low-income elderly. However, that money would be available only to those living at home or in a private institution, not in a public facility such as an almshouse.[13] It would be the death knell of the nineteenth-century poorhouse.

Beginning in the 1950s, Congress approved a raft of new programs that provided a huge financial boost to the private long-term-care institutions we now know as nursing homes. First, government made it far easier to build facilities by making cheap loans available through agencies such as the U.S. Small Business Administration.

At the same time, Washington increased direct assistance to the elderly. In 1965, President Lyndon B. Johnson finally did what Roosevelt could not, and created the landmark federal health-care programs for seniors (Medicare) and the poor (Medicaid). Oddly, it was Medicaid, the program for the poor, that would come to finance care for more than 60 percent of nursing home residents. Still, for the first time, the federal government was paying directly for care in private long-term institutions—a guaranteed stream of revenue that made nursing homes a lucrative business indeed.

The result was an explosion of facilities run by both commercial operators and not-for-profit organizations such as churches. By 1970, 72 percent of all institutional care was provided by nursing homes.[14] The use of other facilities, such as small board-and-care homes, fell precipitously.

────────── **BINGO, BIRTHDAYS, AND BIBLE** ──────────

Today there are more than sixteen thousand nursing homes in the United States,[15] more nursing facilities than McDonald's franchises. Some are for-profits owned by large public corporations, such as Kindred Health Care, or by secretive private equity firms. Others are small mom-and-pop facilities. About one in four are run by nonprofit organizations. Nursing homes have become a $128-billion-a-year business.[16]

Like their predecessors, these facilities were first seen as a vast improvement over what existed before. Yet somehow many became, as Thomas says, "the definition of a repressive environment."

Now Americans are likely to say, "Just shoot me," when confronted with the possibility of life in a nursing home. In some surveys, as many as 98 percent of seniors say they'd prefer to get care anyplace else, especially if they need only moderate assistance.[17] What happened?

It is not a simple story. In part, it is a tale of abuse, corruption, and greed, and of the sometimes mindless government regulation created in response. But like the history of asylums before them, the nursing home story is also one of good intentions gone awry.

It bears remembering that the evil nursing home is largely an urban myth. Many provide good-quality care. While plenty have profound problems, most are not nearly as bad as their reputations suggest. And some are not so much the creation of evil and greedy operators as they are the last stop in a system that is simply not capable of caring for its aged and disabled.

Asked to do too much for those who are gravely ill, even as they are the target of anger and frustration by overwhelmed and sometimes guilt-ridden relatives, nursing homes have become the whipping boy for a flawed long-term-care system in which they play only a relatively small part.

If we can just keep people out of them, say their harshest critics, our long-term-care problems will disappear. In fact, most of the frail elderly never spend more than a few days in nursing homes. More than 85 percent of those receiving long-term care already get their assistance in some other setting.

Still, about 1.4 million frail elderly and younger disabled live in skilled nursing facilities today. They are often the most helpless in our society. Nine out of every ten residents are sixty-five or older, and nearly half are eighty-five or older.[18] Roughly half are suffering from dementia, and more than half are confined to a bed or a wheelchair.[19] Many are there only because they have nowhere else to live, or because it is the only place where their state Medicaid program will support their care. The costs are staggeringly expensive. A "private-pay" resident will be charged an average of nearly $66,000 a year for a shared room or more than $78,000 for a private room.[20]

The price of the bed is only the beginning, however. Here is the 2008 price list for Friends House, where Natalie Fenninger lives:

Amenity/Service	Cost
Semi-private room	$264 per day
Private room with private bath	$303 per day
Incontinence care	$179 per month
Hand-feeding	$156 per month
Turning and positioning	$79 per month

For a very ill resident in a private room, that comes to more than $115,000 a year.

But most long-term-care residents don't pay on their own. Nearly two thirds receive financial assistance from Medicaid. Another 13 percent—mostly those in rehabilitation after a hospitalization—have their stay paid by Medicare.

Nursing homes are filled with residents who have essentially been abandoned. Some are elderly widows or widowers who have outlived spouses, siblings, and even children. For others, children live great distances away or have, for whatever reason, lost interest in their frail and ailing parents. Perhaps they have been estranged for decades, still feuding over some half-remembered slight. Maybe they were abused by the parent who now so badly needs their help.

Steven Horowitz, the CEO of a group of senior living communities in Rhode Island, figures that as many as one third of his residents have no family members involved in their care at all. They are entirely alone. "They have nobody in the picture," Horowitz says.

Sometimes adult children say, "I just can't face Mom when she is like this," or "I don't want my kids to remember their grandpa this way." Often, there are other, even less pleasant motives involved. When Mom insists on staying home and her adult child wants her to move into a nursing home, or if siblings are fighting among themselves over where Dad should live, these disputes can often end up in court in what are called guardianship cases. They can get very ugly, and too often are about children who resent that their parents are spending their legacy on long-term care. One elder-care lawyer who often represents the frail elderly in these legal battles says grimly, "It is almost always about money."

Sadly, it is about money for nursing home operators, too. About two thirds of their facilities' operating costs go toward aides, nurses, housekeepers, and other staff. When nursing homes feel financially squeezed, as they often do, those are the first expenses that are cut. As a result, aides are often overworked and underpaid. Their average salary is less than ten dollars an hour.[21] Many work double shifts, or they follow their eight hours at the nursing home with a second job providing home care to private patients.

Many feel they get no respect from managers, residents, or their families. It is not uncommon for aides be insulted or even physically assaulted by difficult patients. They injure their backs lifting patients. Racial tensions often run deep in homes where aides are African American or immigrants and managers are white or native-born.

According to official nursing home reports to the government, a registered nurse spends an average of twelve minutes per eight-hour shift caring for each resident. Nurse's aides spend about forty-five minutes.[22]

But in the real world, this care is much more variable. There is less at night, when fewer aides are on duty. In the mornings, when assistance is far more intensive, it can be almost like an assembly line in its lack of humanity and dignity for both residents and aides.

In a harrowing first-person account of life as a nurse's aide, Thomas Edward Gass figured he spent 17.3 minutes per day with each resident. He described his morning shift routine this way: "There are twenty-six residents on my hall. Seventeen are incontinent. I and another aide have three hours to get them all ready for breakfast in the morning. On average, we are allowed fifteen minutes to get each resident out of bed, toileted, dressed, coiffed, and wheeled or walked to breakfast. Every morning is a head-on collision against time."[23]

On the best days, harried aides have little time for more than a hello. A resident who is grumpy or combative throws the aide behind schedule; she gets more impatient, and the process becomes even more unpleasant for everyone.

It all happens again at lunch. After that, it is all hands on deck to assist residents to their rooms for a nap. Then everyone returns to the dayroom for their afternoon activity ("bingo, birthdays, and Bible," in nursing home parlance). Finally, dinner and bed. With such a schedule, it is no wonder the biggest complaint of residents who still have their memories is boredom.

Robert Kane, a physician and highly respected long-term-care researcher, and his sister, Joan C. West, write about what it was like for their mother, Ruth, a resident of a generally high-quality facility. "Just across from the (nurse's) station, was an open area with a television set. . . . About a dozen wheelchairs were always lined up in front of this set, with people staring vacantly at it, including our mother, who long ago seemed to lose all interest in television."[24]

Nursing homes have dramatically improved over the past two decades. Most provide safe and responsible care for their residents under extremely difficult circumstances. Still, in the worst, residents get bedsores. They fall. They lie for hours in their own urine or feces. They are dehydrated or malnourished. Almost as bad, because nursing homes can get in trouble if patients lose too much weight, residents are stuffed with high-carbohydrate diets. In the very worst places, the stench of human waste permeates the building.

In 2008, the federal agency that regulates most nursing homes, the Centers for Medicare and Medicaid Services, identified 4,037 facilities where many residents either are physically restrained with special chairs, vests, or belts, or suffer from painful and potentially deadly pressure sores. At the same time, it listed 124 nursing homes, euphemistically called Special Focus Facilities, that were the worst of the worst. Six were either barred from accepting Medicare or Medicaid patients or voluntarily withdrew from the programs.

One was Evergreen Foothills Health and Rehabilitation Center in Phoenix, Arizona. In January 2008, after years of patient neglect, it was stripped of its Medicare license. A few weeks later, the state barred the home from caring for Medicaid patients.

At the eighty-bed facility, one dementia patient was found to have an untreated broken arm. A resident with severe osteoporosis had three untreated fractured ribs. Another dementia patient had been burned on the neck by a hair dryer, had not been bathed in weeks, and suffered from multiple bedsores. Still another had been given the powerful antipsychotic drug Haldol, although no medical evaluation had ever called for it.[25]

The government's list of abuses and mistreatment went on for 122 pages. However, just a month after the center's Medicare and Medicaid licenses were revoked, the owners were once again allowed to take these patients. Later in 2008, they sold out to a group of new investors. The facility is now operating under new management and a new name.

The problems of short-staffed nursing homes are not confined to the worst facilities. I have visited hospital emergency rooms that, on Friday afternoons, are routinely filled with frail elderly who have been dumped by these nursing facilities. Why? Because it is often easier to ship residents off to the closest ER than to find enough aides to care for them.

But even good facilities struggle. They work hard to provide a safe environment and prevent most of the bedsores and the falls. A new voluntary industry effort is under way to encourage both safety and high-quality care. Still, many facilities are not so good at maintaining the basic human dignity of their residents.

Two thirds of all nursing home residents receive psychoactive drugs such as antidepressants,[26] and one third are given even more powerful antipsychotics. The federal government estimates that 20 percent of those who get these medications have never been diagnosed with any form of psychosis.[27]

Why? Because the drugs make patients drowsy, and a sleeping patient is less trouble than one who is awake. Similarly, it is easier and faster to feed a patient through a feeding tube than to carefully hand-feed him a spoonful at a time. So, in the worst places, many residents are unnecessarily fed this way.

Both the federal government and the states heavily regulate nursing homes and require facilities to report major problems, such as falls or bedsores. But the spirits of many residents are crushed not by major medical mistakes, but by the small day-to-day events that often go unnoticed: an aide's unwillingness to take the plastic wrap off Lisa's sandwich; a resident forced to eat dinner at four-thirty in the afternoon, even though he is not hungry; a woman whose favorite dress gets mixed up in the laundry or who loses her false teeth and, thus, can't enjoy food until her dentures are replaced, weeks later.

These things happen because, in many nursing homes, the environment is modeled on a hospital (or, as Bill Thomas would say, a prison). The goal is to reduce risk by creating a heavily structured environment. Thus, Lisa's lunch is covered by plastic to cut the chances of infection. Even though the wrapping makes it impossible for her to eat, Lisa's food is wrapped because everyone's food is wrapped. It is a tiny symptom of Goffman's "total institution."

"How much medical risk are we willing to take to provide someone with a comfortable living environment?" Bill Thomas asks. "Risk is an essential element of life, and it is the very definition of a repressive environment to say that you may not take risks."

Balancing risk with the desire to preserve comfort and dignity has become even more difficult in recent years as the nursing home population has become sicker. That change has been driven by two powerful trends.

First, starting in the 1980s, the government changed the way it paid for hospital care. In an effort to save money, Medicare, the federal health program for seniors, began paying hospitals a fixed amount to treat each specific illness or injury. So, for instance, a typical hospital is paid between $5,400 and $6,400 to treat a patient with pneumonia, no matter how long he stays.[28] Of course, with such a payment system, the longer a patient remains hospitalized, the less money the institution will make. This drives hospitals to discharge patients faster.

Often it is to a nursing home—either for long-term care or for rehabilitation. Initially Medicare still foots the bill, but even steep nursing home rates are far lower than hospital costs. In the hospital business, this is known as discharging patients "quicker and sicker."

At the same time, nursing homes are losing less seriously ill long-term-care patients to assisted-living facilities. By 2007, nearly one million seniors were living in these institutions, which provide some personal care, but far less than a nursing home.

As a result, nursing home residents are sicker than ever before. Infection control and fall prevention are even more important, the need for care is more intense, and staff shortages are more severe. So staff and residents lose ever more autonomy in exchange for perceived increases in safety.

Even when nursing homes try to humanize their care, they are often stymied. The executive director of one nonprofit facility says he started a "happy hour" during which residents could enjoy snacks and even a sip of wine or beer every Friday. The idea was a big hit with residents, but was canceled after a few months because some of their adult children complained.

"I told them not to worry; we take the keys away from the residents who have electric wheelchairs," he remembers. "No one laughed."

The economics of these facilities makes nursing home care even more challenging. Nursing homes manage their beds in the same way airlines control seats. They usually are only about 85 percent full, but still want to fill as many slots as possible with the highest-paying customers, usually those who pay full price out of pocket. Only if they think a bed will be empty will they take the discount customers, who are the Medicaid patients.

Take, for instance, Kindred Healthcare, a for-profit company that operates more than two hundred nursing homes in twenty-eight states. The amount Medicaid pays varies dramatically from state to state and depends on how sick each patient is. But on average, Medicaid pays Kindred $155 a day to care for each impoverished resident. By contrast, a typical patient paying out of pocket or with long-term-care insurance is charged $236 a day. But a Medicare patient who is, say, recovering from a stroke, is where the real money is: for such a patient, Medicare pays Kindred an average of $447 a day, two and a half times the Medicaid rate.[29] It is true that nursing homes provide some additional services for a rehab patient, but not that many more.

Kindred's experience is very common. Across the country, Medicaid pays between $140 and $175 a day for long-term care; "private-pay" costs average about $213 a day for a single room and $189 for a double;[30] while Medicare will pay an average of up to $370 a day for a rehab or other short-term patient.[31]

Industry executives routinely talk about a "cross-subsidy," where Medicaid underpays and Medicare overpays. In the short run, the trick for nursing home operators is to find a way to balance these beds. But in the future, the trend is unmistakable: Many nursing homes are getting out of the long-term-care business.

For some states, cut-rate Medicaid reimbursements are not enough. To speed the process of scaling back institutional care, they are actually paying operators a bounty for every long-term-care bed they eliminate. In Pennsylvania, for instance, a nursing home that agrees to reduce its total number of licensed beds from 270 to 200, and its Medicaid beds from 162 to 128, can earn millions of dollars in extra state payments.[32]

Why would Pennsylvania pay a nursing home to stop caring for indigent patients? Because state officials believe the nursing homes can provide better care, and still save money, even after collecting the higher payments. Here's why: In the bizarre economics of long-term care, if nursing homes have empty beds, they will find ways to fill them, even if it means bringing in residents who are not very sick. In industry jargon, these relatively healthy are called the walkie-talkies. While these people would not normally need nursing home care, the institutions identify them by aggressively trolling hospitals for patients about to be discharged. As a result, the state pays millions of unnecessary dollars. When Pennsylvania surveyed 55,000 nursing home residents, it found 3,500 who were on Medicaid but not sick enough to be in the facilities.[33]

So the state is working out deals to share its cost savings with homes that agree to eliminate beds. It then turns around and uses its portion of those dollars to increase state subsidies for senior housing, expand adult day-care programs, and provide more money to families caring for loved ones at home. The goal is both to redesign nursing homes and encourage more frail elderly to stay at home.

This crazy system of nursing home financing has also removed from nursing homes a key link in the chain of care. Walk into a facility today and you'll see aides and housekeepers. You may see a nurse or two, usually sitting behind a high counter filling out endless paperwork. You won't see doctors, who are mostly irrelevant to nursing home residents.

Because the pay is so low and the work so grinding and unsatisfying, it is hard to get capable doctors to work in these facilities. Bill Thomas, who did this work himself for years, puts it like this: "Physicians realize that making a full-time career out of caring for these people is a loser's game. You have to be economically foolish and willing to sacrifice prestige if that's what you want to do."

So, many nursing facilities are chronically understaffed, or must make do with physicians who are barely competent. The government requires that a doctor visit a nursing home patient only once every sixty days. If a resident gets sick between visits, it is easy enough to ship him off to the local hospital emergency room, where Medicare will pay for his treatment.

All of these trends—growing regulatory and reimbursement challenges, staffing problems, and pressures to cut costs—are creating a race to the bottom: Will families find new long-term-care options before the nursing homes abandon this kind of care?

In some ways, it is already happening. Over the past decade, the number of nursing home residents has barely changed, even though ten million more Americans are aged sixty-five or older, and one million more are eighty-five or older.[34]

Faced with an irrational payment system, it is no wonder operators are scaling back their long-term-care nursing home beds. This is especially true of for-profits, which comprise about three quarters of all nursing facilities. Some are selling out to private equity firms, who see them as real estate opportunities, not businesses to provide care to the frail elderly. In a separate trend the industry calls "right-sizing," facilities are redesigning their buildings to include assisted-living and dementia care, as well as more lucrative rehab and very highly specialized skilled nursing services. These changes are easier for the big for-profit chains, which have access to Wall Street capital, and for large nonprofits, which can raise money through sophisticated fund-raising campaigns.

Smaller mom-and-pop facilities, however, find themselves squeezed between the higher costs of government regulation and consumer demands for better-quality care, on one hand, and their inability to finance costly upgrades and retooling of their services on the other. For much of the nursing home industry, says one insider, "it is evolve or die."

While old-style nursing homes struggle to survive, those frail seniors with the financial resources have more choices for institutional care than ever before. Assisted-living facilities, small group homes, and continuing-care retirement communities are sprouting all over the United States, all hoping to tap into the newfound financial resources of the elderly.

ASSISTED LIVING

Assisted-living facilities can be more comfortable than nursing homes, and far more appropriate for those seniors who require some level of personal assistance but don't need skilled nursing. They can also be less expensive, although that is not always the case.

Nearly one million Americans live in assisted-living facilities, with their rapidly growing population nearly rivaling that of nursing homes. These facilities—sometimes called adult care homes, personal care homes, residential care facilities, homes for the aged, or board-and-care homes—are a hybrid. They inhabit the world between nursing homes and independent senior living. Assisted-living facilities barely existed two decades ago. Now there are more than thirty-eight thousand of them in the United States.[35]

At first glance, the largest institutions look a lot like independent-living communities. Residents usually have their own one-room apartment with a private bath. Meals are served in formal-looking dining rooms rather than in sterile nursing home–type eating areas.

But just as nursing home patients are sicker than ever, so, too, are residents at assisted-living facilities. Increasingly, these places house more and more of those with severe chronic illness, including dementia.

"Now a lot of assisted-living facilities feel like hospitals with pretty wallpaper," says Nancy Fiedelman, a McLean, Virginia, geriatric care manager.

Residents are usually classified by the level of care they need, measured from, say, Level 1 through Level 4. The healthiest Level 1 residents may only need help bathing or daily reminders to take their medication, but otherwise can care for themselves. At the other extreme, the amount of care a Level 4 dementia resident in an assisted-living facility requires is nearly the same as she would need in a nursing home. And since the price often increases with each level, these very ill are paying close to what they would in a nursing facility.

Often a resident will move in with relatively few care needs. But the longer she stays, the sicker she'll get and the more assistance she'll need. The typical assisted-living resident is an eighty-six-year-old woman. Nearly 90 percent need help managing their medications, two thirds need help bathing, and nearly half need assistance getting dressed. They will live in the community for an average of twenty-seven months. One third will die there, while another third will eventually move to a nursing home.[36]

These facilities charge an average of nearly $3,000 a month,[37] but in large metropolitan areas, the price can easily be twice that. One new luxury facility in the Washington, D.C., area, operated by the giant Sunrise Senior Living chain, plans to charge $11,000 per month when it opens in 2009.

Nearly all these costs are paid directly by residents and their families. Overall, only about 12 percent of assisted-living residents receive Medicaid benefits, compared to more than half of nursing home patients. Sunrise, for instance, reports that it receives only 1 percent of its revenue from the federal program.[38] Medicare will not pay at all for assisted living. Long-term-care insurance may pay, but only if the resident is frail enough to meet strict claims standards. Usually, this means the resident must be unable to manage daily activities, such as bathing or feeding herself, without help.

Assisted-living facilities are also much less heavily regulated than nursing homes. Because the government rarely pays for care, there are few federal rules for how an assisted-living institution is run. State regulations vary dramatically, and licensing standards, consumer disclosure, and requirements for the competency of staff vary widely from one jurisdiction to another. There is not even agreement, from state to state, about what assisted living is.[39]

A quarter of the nation's assisted-living beds are owned by just thirty major multistate chains. Sunrise is the biggest, with a capacity of more than thirty-two thousand residents in nearly four hundred different facilities in thirty-eight states.[40]

Not all are large corporate institutions. Some are almost throwbacks to the old board-and-care homes first created in the eighteenth century, where frail elderly are living in small groups in private homes. But the twenty-first-century version comes with some interesting twists.

SIX

Changing the Culture

In the tony Washington, D.C., suburb of Potomac, Maryland, eight women share a stone-and-brick home in a suburban cul-de-sac. From the outside, the house appears to be no different from the others on an affluent street of oversize homes. Only when you walk up to the wooden door and see extra locks and a small sign warning people with infections not to enter are you aware that this house is not quite like its neighbors.

Its residents all suffer from dementia. Most are incontinent. The home where they live, called Cedar Glen, is an assisted-living facility. But it is as different from a two hundred–resident chain institution as Tony's Italian Café is from the Olive Garden.

Cedar Glen feels like a home. Walk in the front door and you enter a comfortable living room. It is late morning, and two elderly women are sitting on a sofa chatting and quietly watching television.

To the left are a dining room and an open kitchen. Behind the living room is an airy sunroom with an entry to a fenced yard. To the right, along a light-filled hallway, are the residents' private rooms.

Each room is a little different. Doors have locks for privacy, and on the outside of each entry is a large picture frame with photos of the resident and her family. The rooms are filled with personal furniture and mementos. Bathrooms are shared.

During the day, two aides care for the eight residents. In a traditional nursing home, the ratio might be two aides for twenty to thirty patients. Each morning, residents get up when they want, and have breakfast when they choose. Because the atmosphere is so much more relaxed, the aides have time to get to know them and their families.

Residents at Cedar Glen can participate in an exercise program in the morning and another activity in midafternoon, but they don't have a lot of other structured events. Some may help set the table for dinner, or fold laundry. Many dementia experts say this kind of activity, which mimics the chores patients used to do at home, before they were sick, helps make them feel comfortable.

Mimi Noamassi, who has been an aide at Cedar Glen for two years, is almost apologetic as she describes how long it takes newcomers to settle in. "When people first come, sometimes they don't like the place," she says. "Sometimes it takes a week. Sometimes two weeks."

That residents adjust so quickly is a near-miracle, according to dementia experts. At a traditional nursing home, it commonly takes three months before such patients begin to feel comfortable in their new surroundings.

Cedar Glen is one of five small group homes for dementia patients run by two couples, Terry and Bob Sitz and Karin and Craig Lakin.

"We want this to be very noninstitutional," says Terry. "We want residents to feel like this is their home."

Small group homes such as Cedar Glen are usually less expensive than large assisted-living facilities in the same communities, but they are by no means cheap. Cedar Glen costs about $5,000 a month.

And it has one big disadvantage when compared with a nursing home or a large assisted-living complex. Because each home is so small, it is not cost-effective to have a doctor, nurse practitioner, or even a registered nurse available in an emergency.

The company that owns Cedar Glen contracts with two local doctors and RNs to visit regularly. Mobile vans come by routinely to provide dental care and diagnostic exams, such as X-rays or blood tests. The aides know first aid, but if a patient suffers a fall, the aides can't do much more than call 911. That is the trade-off for a comfortable, homelike atmosphere. Is it worth it? For many it is.

Just a half hour from Cedar Glen, Harry and Nancy Weil have found a very different kind of community where they can live out their days. When they were in their sixties, Nancy and Harry, a newly retired corporate lawyer, moved to Riderwood Village from Pittsburgh to be close to Nancy's sister. Now in their early seventies, they are active and healthy, exactly the kind of residents their community is looking for.

With plenty of money and good health, they chose a continuing-care retirement community (CCRC). It is senior living that would have been unimaginable to their parents. In essence, these communities try to combine on one campus all of the care seniors will need for the rest of their lives: independent living, assisted living, and a nursing home.

Riderwood is a leafy complex complete with clubhouse, five restaurants, swimming pools, putting greens, and tennis courts. Grim dayrooms with blaring televisions are nowhere to be seen.

But retiring in such comfort is extraordinarily expensive. At a complex such as Riderwood, which is considered mid-priced in the CCRC world, a new resident would have to put up an entry fee of $400,000 just to move in to a two-bedroom apartment. While they are able to live independently, the Weils also pay a monthly charge of about $2,000.

Should they become sick, they might be able to stay in their apartment, but they'd have to pay the extra costs of a nurse's aide. If they need even more care and have to move to assisted living, they can stay on the same campus. This will be a great benefit, especially if, say, Harry gets sick and Nancy does not. She could remain in the apartment and, without having to drive, could easily visit Harry whenever she wanted.

But this would just add to the cost. Nancy would continue to pay the rent in their apartment and, for as long as Harry needed assisted living, they would have to pay for his care, too. At Riderwood, an assisted-living apartment costs $6,500 a month. If the time comes when he needs skilled care, he could move to the on-site nursing home. The cost: $250 a day, or nearly $8,000 a month.

CCRCs operate on several different financial models. Like Friends House, where Natalie lives, some are strictly monthly rentals, without the big entry fee. Others allow residents, or their heirs, to get back a fraction of their initial fee when they leave or die. Riderwood, owned by the Erickson Retirement Communities, returns the whole fee once a unit is reoccupied. In effect, residents are making the company an interest-free loan for all the years they live on the campus. That's why Riderwood markets to healthy young retirees such as the Weils. They are likely to stay for many years, and their no-interest loan is a lucrative source of income for Erickson.

The company vows it will never evict residents should they run out of the money they need to pay their monthly fees. Instead, it promises that a benevolent fund will pick up their costs once they become impoverished. As large numbers of once-young residents age and begin to suffer from chronic illnesses that require high-cost, long-term care, whether it will stay true to its word remains to be seen.

"A NICE CULT, BUT A CULT"

While small group homes and large continuing-care communities are the answer for some, it is hard to imagine a time without institutional skilled nursing care. What will these new facilities look like? Perhaps like Bill Thomas's Green House, which in many ways resembles the Cedar Glen group home.

Thomas wanted the Green House to be the next step beyond his Eden Alternative. That, he concluded, would require a change not just in attitudes, but also in management structure, architecture, and even language. His idea, like those of Cedar Glen's Terry Sitz and others, is to make institutional long-term care as much like home, and as little like a hospital, as possible.

In the nursing home world, Thomas is not alone. In the past few years an entire movement, which calls itself "culture change," has grown up around the belief that life in a care facility does not have to be miserable and can be vastly improved for both residents and staff. Thomas's idea is already becoming a reality. By mid-2008, Green Houses were operating at fifteen sites in ten states.

"We are a bit like a cult," admits Allen Power, a geriatrician, assistant medical director at St. John's Home in Rochester, New York, and Eden Alternative trainer, who is now looking closely at the Green House model. "A nice cult, but a cult."

The Village of Redford, located in a blue-collar western suburb of Detroit, opened two Green House buildings in August 2006. They share a thirty-three-acre campus with a traditional nursing home, assisted living, and independent living—all operated by the nonprofit Presbyterian Villages of Michigan, one of the state's largest elder-care providers.

Each building houses ten residents, and is built according to the same design. They look a lot like Cedar Glen, with a living room surrounding a fireplace, a dining area, and an open kitchen. Private rooms with private baths are located around the perimeter of these common areas.

One chilly December afternoon, two Green House residents are sitting at the dining room table playing a board game. Another relaxes on a sofa, in front of the fireplace, listening to Christmas music. Freshly baked cookies sit on a counter, awaiting snackers.

As at Cedar Glen, all of these residents have dementia, but they are quiet and comfortable. If you walk in without knowing what this building is, you would immediately realize it is some sort of group home for seniors. You'd never imagine it is a nursing home.

Emma, one of the two aides on duty, is also relaxed. She has plenty of time to chat with me, and with the residents. Linda, the other aide, is puttering around the kitchen, cleaning up and putting away dishes.

Neither Linda nor Emma is rushing from task to task. Nor are they standing behind a nurse's station grumbling about a resident or a manager—a common sight in a traditional nursing home. In fact, there is no nurse's station. The aides spend their shift among the residents.

In an attempt to break down the hierarchies of nursing homes, Thomas decided he had to give the aides a new name. So he calls them shahbazim, which he says is Persian for "royal falcons."

They are all certified nurse assistants who have taken an extra 120 hours of training in first aid, cooking skills and food handling, dementia care, and management.

The shahbazim act more like home health aides than institutional staff. They not only provide personal assistance, such as helping residents bathe, dress, or get to the bathroom, but they also cook, clean, and do laundry. And they are companions—maybe even friends.

This means more work and what some aides would consider more menial chores. At Redford, the shahbazim are paid $13.98 an hour, about 3 percent more than CNAs working in the traditional nursing home on the complex.

Most important, they have far more autonomy than traditional aides. They act as advocates for residents, almost as if they are their surrogate adult children. With their help, residents plan their own menus. If problems arise, the aides are responsible for working them out with residents and their families.

The biggest difference is that the aides and residents get the opportunity to build a relationship with one another, something that is almost impossible in a traditional nursing home. The shahbazim learn what the residents do and do not like, when they prefer to eat breakfast, and when they are likely to have to go to the bathroom.

"They know each other as people," says Ruta Kadonoff, deputy director of the Green House project. "A resident is not 'the stroke in 202.'"

Because the two Green Houses, with a combined twenty residents, share a campus with an old-style nursing home, they also have the services of a nurse, who can be at a patient's bedside in a matter of minutes. That is one big advantage these residents have over those in a stand-alone assisted-living facility such as Cedar Glen, which does not have the population to support the cost of such a medical professional.

Residents such as Glorine Reinhard are the reason Presbyterian Villages of Michigan spent nearly $3.5 million to build the two Green Houses. Glorine, ninety-four, welcomes me with a polite smile and a firm handshake. She is in her wheelchair, dressed in a blue-and-white top, blue slacks, and sensible shoes. She and her daughter-in-law, Barbara, are working on Glorine's Christmas cards.

We are in Glorine's comfortable room, which is furnished with a bed, chair, table, dresser, and an armoire, most of which she brought from home. There is a pink comforter at the foot of her bed—a gift from a group of volunteers. The walls are covered with art and family photos.

Glorine lived in assisted living at Redford for twelve years, but her increasing troubles with walking and her worsening memory problems required more care. So when the Green Houses opened in August 2006, Glorine was one of the first residents.

I ask her how she likes it.

She brightens and says, "I love it."

Why?

"We like being our own bosses. Before, we had to get up at the crack of dawn for breakfast. Now we get up when we want."

The ability of residents to sit at a comfortable dining table, eat when they want, and choose their own menus has had an extraordinary effect on their eating habits.

Nursing home residents are often given pureed food, which is easier to swallow, and also faster for aides to feed to them. Imagine having your lunch run through a blender until it is the consistency of baby food. It isn't very appetizing. Not surprisingly, few willingly eat it.

At Redford, all of the twenty Green House residents eat regular food, although a few remain on "soft" diets. Some who were on pureed meals at Redford's traditional nursing home were able to resume a normal diet once they moved to the Green House.

Glorine says that at first she and the other residents were losing track of days—a very common problem in nursing homes. So they asked the shahbazim to start each morning by telling everyone the date and day of the week and reporting on the morning's news.

"That was our idea," Glorine says proudly. "They weren't doing that, but we asked them to, and now they do."

Barbara says the staff is friendly and usually responsive to her requests. Still, she wishes there were more activities. "There's not much going on to keep their minds sharp," she says.

What activities are there? The morning I visit, a minister is chatting with a few residents. And, says Glorine, "we have a holiday party and monthly birthday parties." It seems, even at the Green House, it is hard to get away from Bible and birthdays.

But there is no bingo. Instead, residents create their own activities. Rather than participating in organized events, aides and residents work out chores to be done during the day. At Redford, for instance, one resident likes to help with the cooking. She can't actually do the work, but she can—and does—offer advice. Another vacuums. A third likes to help push a cart around the house.

Not every resident favors such chores. One said that she was paying $244 a day and had absolutely no intention of working. The staff quickly found other things for her to do.

There are two big unanswered questions about the Green Houses. One is whether they can be financially viable. The other is whether medical outcomes are better than they are at traditional nursing homes. The numbers for Redford are promising, but it is too soon to answer either question definitively.

The Redford Green Houses are not self-supporting now, in part because they have too many Medicaid patients and too few residents who pay their own way. Michigan reimburses Redford an average of $150 a day, nearly $100 a day less than the facility charges private-pay residents. As a result, the Redford Green Houses expected to lose about $277,000 in 2007.[1]

On the other hand, there are some indications that the Green House system can work financially, in part because costs are dramatically different than they are for a traditional nursing home. For example, Redford spends about seven dollars a day on food for each Green House resident, compared to a typical cost of almost thirteen dollars. That's because less is wasted and because food is purchased from local stores, where the staff can take advantage of sales, rather than from a large institutional vendor.

Labor costs are also lower. While Redford pays its shahbazim more than nurse's aides, it saves money because the Green House staff does more. Because the aides cook, clean, and do laundry, Redford does not need to pay separate staff for that work. Also, since the shahbazim coordinate their own schedules and do other administrative work, the nursing home saves on management costs.[2]

But the Green House concept won't catch on until operators are convinced they can make money or, in the case of nonprofits, be financially self-sustaining. So far only one for-profit home is adopting the model.

The most important question is whether Green House residents are getting better care. And, on that, the jury is also still out. No doubt, residents and their families seem happier and more satisfied. In one survey, Green House residents reported that they were better able to maintain their privacy, dignity, and individuality.[3] And the

Green House managers at Redford also say they have been able to sharply reduce the use of antipsychotic drugs. They don't have enough experience to know for sure if this is a long-term benefit.

Are Green House residents healthier than those who live in traditional nursing homes? It is too soon to know. And it is far from clear if Bill Thomas and the other believers in changing the culture of nursing homes have found a magic bullet. What they have done is begin to profoundly rethink the very idea of nursing homes. The operators of these facilities are starting to come to grips with the belief that a big part of their job is to maintain the dignity and self-respect of their residents. Preventing falls and bedsores is still critically important, but it is not enough.

The Green House idea is already catching on as a marketing concept. Go to almost any nursing home Web site and you'll read about "patient-centered care." But whether these buzzwords ever translate into widely accepted reality will be driven less by Thomas and the culture change movement than by residents and their families who insist on real reforms, not just words.

Nursing homes are a business, and in the end they will deliver the kind of care their customers demand and will pay for. That is true for institutions, and it is also true for people who get assistance at home.

SEVEN

Everyone Wants to Stay at Home

Gordon Fredine was a great storyteller. And he had stories to tell. A biologist by training, over a long career with the National Park Service, the sturdy, squared-jawed naturalist traveled far from his hometown of St. Paul, Minnesota. He was an early leader in the movement to maintain renewable resources—work that took him to destinations as far-flung as Uruguay and Ethiopia. After he retired in 1973, Gordon maintained his interest in preserving wild places, volunteering for years at the Scottish National Trust.

Whereas Gordon was a powerfully built, gregarious outdoorsman, his wife, Edith, was a petite, quiet homebody. She was tough, make no mistake, and knew her own mind. But unlike Gordon, who loved to spend time with friends, Edith was happy enough sitting at home reading, sewing, or knitting.

Edith was from tiny Long Prairie, about 125 miles northwest of St. Paul. When they first met, at Hamline University in 1929, Gordon must have seemed like quite the go-getter to this shy small-town girl.

They sat next to each other in classes, but Edith wasn't so sure about Gordon. Besides, it was the depths of the Great Depression, and the always-practical Edith had her doubts about Gordon's prospects. It took six years before she agreed to marry him.

In the end, it was a pretty good match. Edith and Gordon Fredine were married for seventy-two years.

In their younger days, Edith and Gordon moved around a lot. They spent their honeymoon in a fourteen-by-sixteen-foot tent in Yellowstone Park, where Gordon worked as a ranger. Gordon's academic career took him to the University of Minnesota and, later, Purdue University. After spending the war years with the navy in the South Pacific, he took a job with the U.S. Fish and Wildlife Service in Atlanta. Then, in 1952, he accepted a post at the National Park Service headquarters, in Washington, D.C.

By then, Gordon and Edith had two children. Jack, who was the spitting image of his dad, was born in 1939. Pat, small and fair like her mom, came along in 1948. So it wasn't any surprise that Edith was looking to settle down.

It didn't take long for her to find the modest rambler on Anniston Road in the leafy suburb of Bethesda, Maryland. She still remembers the day she first saw it: February 22, 1952. "It was the second or third one we looked at," Edith recalls. "It was a little five-room house, but we liked it. We liked the yard."

The couple never left.

On a gray autumn afternoon, Edith is reminiscing about her early days with Gordon—about Yellowstone and his exotic journeys, and about the cross-country train trip they took in 1963. We are sitting in their tidy living room. There are lots of magazines and books. One table is covered with family photos: of Gordon and Edith, Pat and Jack, their spouses, and the grandkids. On an end table next to the sofa is a gold-colored paper angel that Pat made when she was a kid.

Gordon died in this room.

Near the end, they moved a hospital bed into the living room.

Pat and Jack made it back in time and were with their parents on the steamy August day when Gordon passed away. He was ninety-six, and it was cancer of his larynx that probably killed him.

The last few weeks were rough. Gordon was incontinent and very weak. But almost to the end, the old outdoorsman was still able to get up and walk around the house. A local hospice helped, providing nursing care and other assistance during Gordon's last days.

But Gordon's decline, like that of so many elderly, began years before he died. He'd been forgetting things since the early 1990s. At first, driving was a challenge. He would get lost and have to call Edith so she could remind him how to get home. Then she began riding along to navigate, giving him the directions he needed to go places he'd been a thousand times before. Finally, he stopped driving entirely. By 1998, when Gordon was eighty-nine, his memory loss was severe.

"You can draw a line in 'ninety-seven or 'ninety-eight," says Jack. "After Pa's dementia kicked in, it was a very different life."

Gradually, Gordon lost the ability to care for himself. He could no longer bathe or shave on his own. He'd get confused outside the house.

For all that time, Edith took care of him at home. Mostly she did it alone, although she hired aides for the last few years. Despite a succession of illnesses and injuries of her own, nothing stopped her. Throughout their marriage, Edith says, Gordon worked hard to support her and the children. In those days, she says, "I did the things I wanted to do." Now that Gordon was sick and needed help, Edith felt deeply that it was her turn. "I was determined that I was going to live longer than Gordon and take care of him," she says. And so she did.

Gordon Fredine lived his last years the way most people do, and the way long-term-care experts say they should: at home. The idea is that they are cared for by their loved ones, in comfortable and familiar surroundings. Remember that biblical story of Ruth and Naomi. There were no nursing homes for them.

As difficult as Gordon's last years were, he came as close to that ideal as anyone could expect. Money was not a big problem. Gordon and Edith each had some long-term-care insurance. He had a good government pension, and they had been careful savers. They had loving, attentive kids and grandchildren, although Pat and Jack lived in distant cities. They had friends and neighbors—at least at the beginning. And unlike many dementia patients, Gordon was not combative or abusive.

"He just accepted an awful lot of things," Edith says. "I can't ever remember him getting mad at me."

But for all of that, caring for Gordon took a tremendous toll on Edith—just as it does on May Barrett, who cares for her husband, Walt, in Virginia; on Cheryl Fears, who does the same for her parents in Arkansas; and on millions of other spouses and adult children aiding frail seniors or younger family members with disabilities.

For almost a decade—all the time she was caring for Gordon—Edith hardly left the house, except to shop. Even when they had paid caregivers, she could not bring herself to take a break. "I'd leave, and he'd ask, 'Where's Edie? When's she coming back?' I just didn't want to leave him. I did not have a social life of my own."

It was not until a few months after Gordon died that Edith finally spent her first voluntary night away from home. She went to Texas to visit Jack.

But Gordon's illness had begun wearing on Edith years before. Just before Christmas 1998, she fell in the backyard and broke both wrists. The doctors put in pins and had to immobilize her arms. Jack and Pat brought in a paid home health aide for a few months, but Edith hated the arrangement.

Then, in 2004, just before another Christmas, Edith suffered a severe bout of sciatica and arthritis. She could barely move. Jack, who was living in New Orleans, dropped everything and came back to help both his mom and dad. His wife, Susan, joined him. Once again, Edith recovered and took control of Gordon's care.

Just three months later, on March 31, 2005, Edith went outside to pick up the newspaper. She stumbled and fell and broke her leg just below the hip. This time, she was hospitalized for several days and had to spend two weeks in a rehab facility.

Still, as soon as she could get home, Edith insisted on resuming her care for Gordon in their cozy house on Anniston Road. Jack and Pat thought about assisted living, but neither even suggested the idea to Edith. They knew what she'd say.

They did hire a professional geriatric-care manager, who helped put together a home care plan for them, helped them hire aides, and oversaw all of Gordon's needs. But she charged $100 an hour, and Edith, who bluntly describes herself as frugal, just didn't want to pay.

For a while they had aides 24/7, but Edith cut them back to part-time, five days a week. During the last months of Gordon's life, he was getting about thirty-five hours a week of paid care.

What happened to Edith is not uncommon. The physical and psychological stresses are so great that it is often the caregivers themselves, and not those they are assisting, who break down.

Like Gordon, three out of every four frail seniors and disabled younger adults live at home. It is where we want to live, and for those without the financial resources to pay for nursing homes or assisted-living facilities, it is where we must live.

As Edith and her family learned, however, caring for a loved one at home is complicated and demanding. It means preparing meals and arranging transportation, administering medications, struggling with the physical and emotional challenges of personal care, and even providing respite for caregivers who, like Edith, are often frail themselves. For adult children trying to provide this care, it often means changing a mother's diapers or bathing a father. It also means taking time off from work, neglecting spouses and children, and giving up vacations. Sadly, it sometimes results in care that may be loving, but can also be poor and sometimes even dangerous.

Edith learned that home care can be terribly lonely, both for those who are ill and for the spouses and children trying to help them. Because caring for a frail relative is so all-consuming, and because people become less and less comfortable visiting someone with severe physical disabilities or dementia, these families often find themselves isolated from neighbors, friends, and relatives.

Despite these tremendous challenges, expanding the use of home care has become a goal of advocates for the elderly, and recently even for the government. Both Medicaid and private long-term-care insurance are making it easier for those who stay at home to get benefits. Supporters of this concept believe firmly in two axioms: Care is better at home, and it is less expensive than living in a nursing home.

There is little doubt that people are happier at home than in a nursing home. All sorts of surveys show this.[1] But that does not mean they are getting higher-quality care, or even less expensive assistance.

Done properly, and for some patients, care at home is by far the best choice. But not always. And while the daily cost can be lower for some, it is not so for the very sick, who may need extensive assistance. For example, a home health aide may charge $150 for a twelve-hour shift, and a live-in aide can cost $180 to $200 a day. Add in the cost of rent or a mortgage, utilities, food, medical equipment, transportation, and the like, and the cost of staying at home can approach or even exceed that of a nursing home.

Even with limited help, the Fredines were paying $4,000 a month for Gordon's aides, a cost far beyond the reach of most Americans. Urban Institute researcher Richard Johnson finds that only about six out of ten frail seniors receive any help at all, even from family members. And only about 14 percent use paid aides.[2]

In the past few years, Medicaid, which once paid only for nursing home care, has become somewhat more flexible, and most states now offer some home-care benefits. In the mid-1990s, Medicaid spent only about 20 percent of its long-term-care funds on home and community care, and 80 percent on nursing homes. By 2006, almost 40 percent was going to home care and assisted living.[3]

But much of that money is targeted to the developmentally disabled, including those with diseases such as autism. For the frail elderly, by contrast, only 25 percent of Medicaid funding is used for home care.[4] In many states, this assistance is still very limited—only a few hundred dollars a month—comes with lots of restrictions, or is available to relatively few families. And just four states spend more Medicaid dollars on home care than on nursing facilities.[5] As a result, Medicaid often pays much more to keep a resident in a nursing home than it would to support the assistance she needs at home. It may not make much sense, but it is the system.

Private long-term-care insurance is also gradually becoming more flexible in the way it pays benefits. Newer policies offer comprehensive coverage for assistance at home as well as in nursing homes, and some give policyholders lots of choices in the way they use their benefits. However, older policies can still be extremely restrictive when it comes to paying home-care benefits. And any private long-term-care insurance is still financially out of reach for most families. Fewer than seven million Americans have any coverage at all.[6] These policies finance only about 7 percent of paid long-term-care costs.[7]

Home care isn't just about money. It is about skill, too. Caring for a frail adult is hard work, and it takes special knowledge that few family members have. Even many home health aides have limited training. Those with certified nurse assistant (CNA) certificates have learned basic care techniques. But as Peggy Ingles and the Fredines and so many others have learned, many aides don't know enough to provide the best-quality assistance.

When caring for the frail elderly, the simplest tasks become a challenge. It is not easy to turn a fragile patient in bed, or move someone who is unable to help himself from a wheelchair to a sofa. Bathing or even feeding an adult in a way that preserves her dignity takes time, patience, and skill.

Even when aides are willing, government rules often drive frail seniors out of their homes and into institutions. For example, in many states it is against the law for an aide to administer medicine to a patient, unless the care worker gets special extra training or is directly supervised by a nurse.[8] The rules are vague and often ignored, but sometimes seniors who could otherwise live at home end up in an assisted-living facility simply so someone can give them their prescription drugs.

The shortage of skilled personal care aides is getting worse, as the number of seniors needing help grows. There is already a dearth of care workers—as many as 52,000, according to one study.[9] Because the pay is low and the work emotionally and physically difficult, it is not easy to find skilled nurses, aides, or social workers willing to care for the frail elderly and those with disabilities.[10]

As with nursing homes, new ways to improve the quality of home care are on the horizon: creative new living arrangements for seniors and methods for them to work together to make aging easier, better training both for aides and families, expanded options for adult day care, improved medical care for the homebound, and—for the dying—greater acceptance of hospice.

Many of the most creative programs are still small experiments. They often struggle to find the money they need to thrive, and in a creative time of trial and error, some are likely to fail. However, just as Bill Thomas's Green Houses have the potential to transform the way seniors and the disabled get care in nursing homes, so these efforts have the chance to do the same for those trying to stay at home.

Pawpaw and Granny

Like Edith Fredine, Cheryl Fears is consumed by the effort it takes to care for her parents, Charles, whom she calls Pawpaw, and Katy, whom everyone calls Granny. A couple of years ago, Cheryl and her husband, Roy, built an addition to their own Arkansas home for her parents. Moving them in, it turned out, was the easy part.

Granny has dementia, and can sometimes be difficult to care for. Pawpaw is losing his eyesight and is starting to have trouble getting around. After years of caring for Granny on his own, the strain has taken its toll. So Cheryl, Roy, and their boys have accepted the task of caring for Cheryl's parents.

But unlike Edith, Cheryl and her family are extremely fortunate. It is Cheryl's good luck to be living in the largely rural northwest corner of Arkansas, where she is benefiting from the frustration of a very wealthy produce broker named Lawrence H. Schmieding.

Schmieding had a brother who suffered from dementia. Like so many others, Lawrence could not bear the thought of his brother in a nursing home, so he tried to arrange for home care. He quickly learned that even his vast sums of money couldn't buy good assistance. There simply were no local aides adequately trained to provide the level of care his brother needed.

So, Schmieding gave the University of Arkansas $20 million and told them to create a state-of-the-art elder-care program. What they came up with is a potential model for the rest of the country.

The Schmieding Center—what else would it be called?—is a one-story brick building along a nondescript industrial strip in Springdale. It is, in fact, right next door to Schmieding's produce company.

In one wing, there is a health center and rehabilitation facility. In the other, a library, a handful of classrooms, and a mock-up of a small apartment where students can get hands-on training in how to care for frail or disabled clients. What happens here is unusual, if not unique: a full-blown training program for both family and paid caregivers.

More than 700 people have been taught at the center since it opened in 2002. Aides and other paraprofessionals are offered up to 115 hours of coursework, substantially more than they need to get a CNA certificate in Arkansas. Family members can take courses, too, supplemented by an extensive video. The basic family caregiving training program takes two to four hours. If they choose, they can even take the same extensive coursework that paid aides get.

Both Cheryl and Allen Wood, Granny and Pawpaw's home health aide, were trained at Schmieding. Allen, who had been working at a local nursing home, already had his CNA certificate when he heard about the program back in 2001. He got additional skills training, but something else about Schmieding stays with him. "They teach compassion," he says.

I see it one summer evening as I watch an aide named Bernice manage a catheter on a life-size male manikin. A trained aide who already has her CNA certificate in North Carolina, Bernice knows the technique, but under the watchful eye of registered nurse Barbara Vaughan, she takes an extra small step. While she does her work she carefully moves a sheet around the model to keep as much of it covered as possible—a procedure often forgotten in the assembly-line rush of many nursing homes or even by poorly trained home care aides.

After she's finished, I ask Bernice what is the most important thing she's learned at Schmieding. She answers right away: "Respect."

Cheryl didn't need to be taught to respect her parents, but she desperately needed to learn the basics of caregiving: how to help Granny get up from her chair, how to feed and bathe her, and help her to the bathroom.

"The first time I had to give Granny a bath, I just couldn't," Cheryl says. "You learn about their basic needs, and how to respect their modesty. There are a lot of things I didn't know."

Barbara Vaughan is like all the teachers at Schmieding. Not only does she have years of clinical practice, but she's also had personal experience caring for a family member—in her case it was her dying mother. "I remember giving my mom a bath. It is so much easier to teach than it is to do," Barbara says. "We teach the skills, but the reality is just overwhelming."

Unfortunately, many family members are so overwhelmed managing each day's crisis that they don't have time to take courses. So the Schmieding Center has adjusted by cutting down class time, producing the video, and even setting up remote training programs in small towns around the state.

The shortage of skilled caregivers—either family members or

professionals—is not just a problem in the foothills of the Ozarks. It can be just as serious in Boston or San Francisco. Sadly, few programs like the one at the Schmieding Center exist today, and without the assistance of a wealthy benefactor, few communities have the resources to create them.

The problem is compounded by what happens—or, more accurately, what does not happen—just before a patient leaves a hospital or rehab center. Even though family members are often required to provide personal assistance or even medical care to a loved one returning home, few have any idea what to do. According to one national survey, nearly six out of every ten family members said they never received any instructions from a doctor or hospital in how to care for their loved ones. Almost a third said they were never shown how to change bandages or dressings, which is critical training, since small mistakes can easily lead to deadly infections. A third acknowledged they did not feel comfortable doing these tasks.[11]

In most medical facilities, a nurse or social worker called a discharge planner is supposed to advise a patient about the care she'll need once she gets home, or suggest alternative living arrangements such as a nursing home or assisted-living facility. This transition is critical to making sure that the ten million seniors discharged every year get the best possible care after they leave the hospital. It is especially important because people are sent home so much more quickly than they were a decade ago.

It almost never happens the way it should. Instead, a patient is more likely to have a hurried meeting with an overworked social worker, often only a few hours before discharge. She may be handed a fistful of papers with complicated instructions about which medications to take, what exercises to do, and when to see the doctor again.

If the patient needs home care, or requires a stay in a nursing home, the discharge planner will rarely give advice about which agencies or facilities are best. Instead, she may distribute little more than a sheet listing all the nursing homes in the area.

Says one hospital executive, "It's true. You get one of these pieces of paper that's been Xeroxed about twenty times. You know what I mean: It's too blurry to read, and the paper wasn't straight so half of the words go off the edge of the page."

The system breaks down in part due to money and, like so much else in medicine, from fear of legal liability. Because Medicare doesn't pay hospitals or nursing homes any extra for comprehensive discharge planning, there is little incentive for these institutions to hire and train more staff. Because patients are discharged so quickly, planners rarely get the opportunity to get to know them or their needs. Hospitals that do spend money on social workers are more likely to use them as advocates for patients while they are in the hospital, not as advisers for those about to leave.

At the same time, Medicare rules limit the kind of advice a hospital planner is allowed to give. And hospital lawyers, who worry about their institutions being sued if a family is not pleased with a home-care agency or nursing home, discourage staff from making specific suggestions. The bottom line: Medicare patients and their families are often on their own as soon as they are wheeled out the front door. Many are discharged to nursing homes even when they are likely to do better at home.[12]

Medicaid, on paper at least, does provide some counseling for beneficiaries and their families, but in most states little hands-on advice is actually available. Similarly, some private long-term-care insurance will provide care management, but this assistance is scanty at best.

Those who have the resources can hire private care managers on their own, as Edith did. These professional advisors, usually social workers or nurses, can build a plan for caring for the frail elderly, help hire home-care aides, and arrange for transportation and other services. But they are costly—often $100 an hour or more—and thus beyond the reach of many.

For those who don't have these resources, more centers such as Schmieding could make caring for an aging spouse or parent much easier and safer, save families money, and perhaps keep more people home for longer.

NATURALLY OCCURRING RETIREMENT COMMUNITIES

Marge and Ron Fenster have lived in the same western St. Louis suburban neighborhood for thirty-four years. They are both in their early seventies now, and Ron, who had a major stroke ten years ago, is pretty much wheelchair-bound.

Still, they want to remain in their home for as long as possible. It helps that Marge still drives and that they have a daughter who lives just ten minutes away. But things come up—small things—that Marge and Ron can't handle as easily as they once could.

Without help, the accumulation of those little crises could drive the Fensters out of their home and into formal senior housing. Maybe it is help with a leaky faucet or access to the advice of an attorney who specializes in elder law, or someone who can come by to help with yard work. Sometimes it is just the opportunity to meet new friends.

For most seniors, this kind of help is not easy to come by. Aging can be isolating. Old friends move away, have trouble getting out themselves, or die. Arthritis or a stroke can make routine chores impossible. And no one wants to ask strangers for assistance.

Thanks to the Jewish Federation of St. Louis, seniors such as the Fensters do have access to some of these services. Elderly residents of the area around the town of Creve Coeur, Missouri, can get transportation, home repairs, activities at local churches or the Jewish Community Center, and even a discount card for an ice-cream cone at the local Ben & Jerry's.

The nonsectarian project is being operated through something called a NORC. It may sound like the villain in a bad science-fiction movie, but NORCs could become one channel through which we deliver needed services to millions of seniors.

The name was invented years ago by social scientists who wanted to give a formal description to apartment buildings or neighborhoods with large numbers of aging residents. They called them Naturally Occurring Retirement Communities, which regrettably has been shortened to its dreadful acronym. Unlike formal senior living developments, such as assisted-living facilities or continuing-care communities, these simply evolved, more or less, by accident. The idea is to bring services to people where they live, rather than making them move to senior-living facilities in order to get help.

Today as many as a quarter of seniors may live in these informal communities. Some, such as Marge and Ron, moved in decades ago, raised a family, became empty-nesters, and eventually retired—all in the same house or apartment. Others arrived more recently. Like the Fensters, they live in suburban developments, or are among dozens of elderly couples, widows, or widowers quietly living in a single large apartment building.

The NORC in St. Louis covers a three-square-mile area. About 3,100 people, or one third of all the residents in the community, are sixty-five or older. With a staff of only five, the project has been able to put about half of them on its mailing list.

For many of these seniors, just a little bit of assistance may make the difference between being able to stay at home or having to move in with their adult children or into an institution. But the NORC is more than a ride, counseling, or a volunteer to fix a leaky faucet. The biggest benefit may be the opportunity to meet neighbors, or to have someone to call for help, or for company.

For Ron and Marge, it is chair yoga.

Every Tuesday night, a couple of dozen seniors gather for the class. Ron gets much-needed exercise. Marge takes care of registration.

"It is a chance to get out and get together," says Marge.

And it is more than that. If someone misses class for a week or two, a NORC staffer will call to see if everything is okay and ask if there is anything he can do to help.

"Absolutely the most important thing we've done is connecting people together," says Karen Berry-Elbert, who manages the NORC. "We help them find new friends, a place to go, and a reason to get out of the house. They feel they are part of something."

In an effort to identify those seniors who need help, some NORCs are copying an idea first developed in Israel. There, young and healthy retirees, known as *abbas* (Hebrew for "fathers"), are trained to do minor repairs such as fixing a faucet or a leaky toilet. However, these visitors have another agenda. They are also trained in basic social work. If they see that a resident is having trouble walking, or keeping her apartment as clean as she used to, they can identify the problem and get her some help. Using techniques such as this, or even by making an occasional phone call, NORC staffers and volunteers can help make frail seniors feel less isolated.

For a while, the federal government was supporting about forty of the eighty NORC-based projects around the country, which serve about twenty thousand seniors in twenty-five states.[13] But that grant money is drying up, and like other NORCs, the St. Louis project is scrambling to find funding. It has started to charge modest annual dues, as well as small fees for participating in some of its programs. Despite the fund-raising, though, the St. Louis NORC has had to cut its already tiny staff.

As happens too often with long-term care, slashing funding for these programs may end up costing the government more money in the long run. Not only can NORCs provide services to those who otherwise would not get them, but they can also reduce spending for social assistance or medical care.

For instance, imagine an elderly widow living alone in her small apartment. Normally, no one may know she is even there, much less that she needs help. But simply by identifying her, and connecting her with services, the NORC improves her chances of getting help before a problem turns into a crisis. And that, in turn, might keep her at home, out of the hospital, where her costly care would be paid by Medicare, or out of a nursing home, where her stay might be paid by Medicaid.

There is not yet much evidence about how well NORC services work, but it is a simple idea that makes a lot of sense.

THE VILLAGE

One warm spring afternoon, I join Norm Metzger at Murkey's, a local coffee bar on Washington's Capitol Hill. Just a half-dozen blocks from the Supreme Court, the Library of Congress, and the majestic U.S. Capitol, Murkey's sidewalk café is a window on a surprisingly diverse community that few tourists ever see.

Blocks of tree-lined streets and brick sidewalks, beautifully restored nineteenth-century row houses that are home to members of Congress, civil servants, and artists. Blue-collar neighborhoods that have been home to generations of African Americans and now are undergoing gentrification. Grim public housing complexes. Trendy apartments for young congressional staffers. It is all Capitol Hill.

Norm, who is seventy-one, was a senior executive at the prestigious National Academy of Sciences. Tall and thin, with gray hair and a bushy beard, he is dressed in tropical Washington summer regalia: a T-shirt, ratty green shorts, and Crocs. He is sipping a fancy coffee and chatting with passersby.

"When I retired, I said, 'No more meetings. No more committees.' It was a total failure."

What's ruining Norm's dreams of a lazy retirement is an experiment called Capitol Hill Village. The idea is to help people stay in their homes as they age by offering access to a wide range of basic services. The Village provides a sort of clearinghouse for a fluid mix of volunteer help and paid assistance.

This grass-roots version of the NORC is an intriguing idea. Urban neighborhoods are filled with seniors. Many need help. Others, retired and with both time and skills to give, are ready and willing to provide assistance. How can they find each other, especially when it is often so difficult in car-centric America for people to meet their neighbors?

Norm and a small group of longtime Capitol Hill residents have an answer. They are trying to create a Village, building on an idea first developed on tony Beacon Hill in Boston. It works like this: People pay an annual membership fee of $500 ($750 for couples). Those dues support a small office with a paid executive director.

With just a phone call, members get access to the kind of everyday assistance that seniors need to stay independent. It may be a ride to the grocery store or the doctor, or someone to pick up their medications at the pharmacy—all provided by volunteers. Or it may be the services of a plumber or electrician, or of a home health aide. Members pay for these professionals, although the Village has negotiated discounted rates from many. During its first year, the Village was getting about fifty calls for help each month.

"It's about staying power," says Norm. "We want to enable people to stay in their houses as long as possible by providing the services they need. We watched our parents in nursing homes and assisted-living facilities, and we don't want that for ourselves."

Volunteers have become the backbone of the Village. More than half of the members volunteer themselves, and the willingness of neighbors to help neighbors has been a key to the Village's success. But there are lots of unanswered questions.

One big challenge on Capitol Hill, at least, is architecture. Those beautiful row houses are far from friendly for those using walkers or wheelchairs. Many front doors are six steps up from the street, bedrooms are usually on the second or third floor, and putting in elevators is costly and sometimes not even possible in these narrow nineteenth-century buildings.

Can the Village be financially sustainable? Already Norm realizes that the dues probably won't be enough to make the organization self-supporting. After its first full year of operation, the Village had about 230 members, but Norm and the other founders worry that if they raise dues too much, they'll lose members.

While the Hill is very diverse, participation in the Village is not. It is almost all white and middle class and made up of people who by nature plan for their futures. Low-income people have not joined, even though the group will subsidize their dues. Neither have African Americans, although many are longtime Hill residents.

Even if the Village becomes self-sustaining in the short run, it is not clear what will happen in the long term. Now most of its members, like Norm, are relatively young seniors, mostly in their sixties and early seventies. They are healthy, financially secure, and able to give time and money to the organization. Only three members of Capitol Hill Village are frail.

By paying dues to the Village today, when they don't need its help, these relatively young and healthy members are buying a kind of insurance. When it comes time for them to collect, will a new generation of sixty-somethings be there to deliver?

"What will happen when those who volunteer now age in place and start to need services?" Norm wonders aloud. "I don't know."

"SKIN HUNGER"

NORCs and Villages are trying to take advantage of accidental communities, meeting people where they live. But there is also a small, but growing movement to create brand-new communities, where young couples with kids, seniors, and young singles all choose to live together in a housing development, with the intention of sharing time and skills. And there are seniors—perhaps a group of old friends or colleagues—who choose to create their own cooperative living arrangements: something like a new millennium version of a 1960s commune.

Scattered around the country, from rural Abingdon, Virginia, to Burbank, California, small groups of seniors are experimenting with these new living arrangements. Sometimes called co-housing or intentional communities, they are a way for people to help one another as they age.

Some are for seniors only. At Silver Sage, in Boulder, Colorado, empty-nesters live in sixteen attached homes and duplexes, all built around a community center and garden. Some units are eligible for low-income subsidies, but others are priced as high as $700,000.

In Berkeley, there is the Senior Artists Colony, a 141-unit apartment complex geared to, well, senior artists. Painters, sculptors, and retired Hollywood actors all share the urban building. No golf or assisted living here, but a film editing lab, theater, and drama classes are cornerstones of the complex.[14]

By contrast, in southwest Virginia, Dene Peterson started a very different form of adults-only living. Called ElderSpirit Community at Trailview, these twenty-nine-unit residences were initially conceived as a place where a group of former nuns, like Peterson, could grow old together. It has grown to become a home where seniors of many backgrounds share both mutual support and spirituality. About half the residents are renters and half are owners, but all are expected to help with community projects and assist one another as they need help.

Other communities have a very different philosophy. They take families of all ages. A multigenerational co-housing project sits next door to Silver Sage, for instance. The idea is to provide a trade-off. Seniors may help with, say, babysitting while young parents may drive seniors to the store. Ann Zabaldo, who lives in a family-oriented planned community in Takoma Park, Maryland, says, "These communities provide a social capital you can't buy. They change the dynamic where aging in place is another way of saying 'dying alone.'"

Janice Blanchard, former director of Aging in Denver, a hotbed of shared living arrangements, puts it another way. These close-knit communities, she says, fulfill "skin hunger"—the need for seniors to maintain friendships, help others, and escape isolation.

But there are questions about the future. For now, even seniors who live in these communities are relatively young and healthy, much like members of the Villages. And the key to their success will be similar: How will communities hold together once increasing numbers of members become frail and require significant amounts of care?

ADULT DAY CENTERS

Wherever frail seniors live, they can also take increasing advantage of adult day-care centers. In these facilities, otherwise homebound seniors can get meals and companionship, and stressed caregivers can get a break for a few hours a week. Some of these centers are taking an extra step and offering complete medical care to their participants, too.

There are about 3,500 adult day-care centers caring for 150,000 people around the country.[15] For most participants, the centers mean lunch and several hours a day spent in the company of others—and they give family members a desperately needed break from the relentless pressures of helping a frail loved one.

Adult day care provides critical respite help for May Barrett, who struggles to care for her husband, Wally. He spends three days a week at the Alzheimer's Family Day Center, which is especially set up to care for participants with dementia. It gives May a precious opportunity to take a break, but know that her husband is safe.

Not far from the Barretts, Hei Sung Lee has created the Korean Senior Center. Here, elderly immigrants enjoy a wide range of services each day. They receive traditional meals—a very important benefit for those who still struggle to eat unfamiliar American food. They learn how to talk to a doctor—not only the right words, but the way to speak to a rushed and impatient American physician. And most of all, they have the opportunity to spend time with friends, rather than sitting alone at home while their children and grandchildren are off at work or school.

Each of these efforts, in its way, tries to provide assistance to those who need it in a community-based setting rather than in a nursing home or other institution. And they have something else in common: As with so many other creative living arrangements, Medicaid and private long-term-care insurance will rarely pay for them. Although costs can be much lower than a $250-a-day nursing home bill, neither government nor private insurance has, for the most part, the flexibility to pay for care that is more comfortable and less costly or care for those who are not yet sick enough to be eligible for either government help or private insurance.

HOSPICE

Probably no service for the frail elderly is less understood, and more important, than hospice, which provides specialized care for the dying. In the words of the late humorist Art Buchwald, who was himself a hospice patient, "When the patient enters the hospice, an entire team sets to work to meet the family's needs—a doctor, a team of nurses, a case manager, a social worker, a chaplain, a nursing assistant, a bereavement coordinator, and of course, the volunteers."[16]

Although Buchwald lived for a time in a hospice facility, he was the exception. Like Gordon Fredine, half of all hospice patients are cared for at home. One quarter receive services in nursing homes. Less than 20 percent actually live in a hospice facility.[17]

It is often said that hospice helps people die. In fact, it helps them live. In many ways, the care teams that hospices use are a model for the kind of truly managed, coordinated care that so many chronically ill desperately need, but cannot get.

In part, this can happen because of the unusual way hospices are paid by Medicare. Normally, the government health program pays doctors and other medical providers through what's called fee-for-service. Under this system, the physician gets a fixed amount of money for each specific service he provides—$50 for an office visit, $40 for a blood test, $100 for X-rays. Hospice, however, is paid differently. For instance, it gets about $130 a day to take care of patients who are living at home, no matter how much care it provides. This encourages the hospice to coordinate its services carefully, which can both hold down unnecessary costs and provide better care.

Managed care has gotten a bad name because it has become so tied to the cost-cutting HMOs that were so hated in the 1980s and '90s. But carefully managing multiple symptoms, while tending to patients' spiritual and social needs, should be the aim of all health-care systems. Sadly, in the United States it is too often true that a patient needs to be dying before he can get such care.

With hospice, this coordination allows patients to live out their last days as comfortably as possible, without intensive, intrusive, and often painful medical treatment that, at most, may extend their life for only a few days or weeks.

Bill Thomas, the nursing home maverick and gerontologist, tells me about meeting with the families of nursing home residents who have suffered a major stroke: "I tell them their mom can either be given maximum treatment or maximum care, but in our country at this time, they cannot get both. If they want maximum treatment, we'll call the ambulance to take her to the hospital, she'll go to the intensive care unit, be put on a ventilator and there you go. Or we can keep her comfortable, alleviate symptoms, familiar voices and sounds can be near her. We'll see what happens, but it is very likely she is going to die."

That is the choice many Americans have as they near death, and maximum care is what hospice does.

Traditional hospices will not try to cure a patient's terminal illness, but will provide all other medical care. A new concept, called an open-enrollment hospice, will even treat that terminal disease, should a patient choose that path. Both provide all other routine medical care, and carefully manage pain.

About 1.4 million people were enrolled in hospice in 2007, three times the number a decade ago.[18] However, more than one third are enrolled for a week or less, and half participate for less than two weeks.[19]

For many patients, this means weeks or even months of needless suffering. But doctors remain reluctant to talk to patients about death, and many of those who do are not very good at it. And given the state of medicine today, they often cannot answer the single most important question potential hospice patients ask: "How long do I have?" For their part, families often say, "She is not ready yet."

Formal specialized care for the terminally ill is not new, but the modern concept of hospice was brought to the United States by an English physician, Dame Cicely Saunders, in the 1960s. In 1969, Elisabeth Kübler-Ross wrote a bestselling book, *On Death and Dying*, which dramatically raised Americans' awareness of how people die and how important it is to provide emotional as well as physical assistance in their last days.

In 1983, Medicare began financing hospice care, and today, eighty cents out of every dollar is paid for by the federal health program for seniors. However, that money comes with highly complex and controversial rules. For example, for a patient to be eligible for benefits, a doctor must certify that she has six months or less to live, assuming the disease follows its normal course.[20] But this rule far exceeds the ability of medicine to predict the life expectancy of the dying. If someone lives longer, she can be recertified. However, in an effort to hold down costs, the government caps the amount it pays for an average patient. If too many remain on the rolls for too long, and a hospice exceeds the limit, it must return some money to the federal government.[21]

Patients can also lose their benefits if their overall health improves. Because the care they get at hospice is often so much better than in other settings, it is not unusual for this to happen. For example, when patients are first admitted to hospice, their symptoms are often out of control. They are in pain, unable to eat, and may even be struggling to breathe. Well cared for, they improve. They begin to eat again and gain weight and strength. Under government rules, this can extend their life expectancy to beyond six months. The result: They lose their Medicare hospice benefit and must withdraw from the program. Although patients can reenroll if they again begin to fail, few do.

Gordon Fredine got help during his last days from a local hospice. But many of these other services were not available to him or his family. There was no NORC program where he lived, no Village, and no Schmieding-like training facility for Edith.

It is a pattern that repeats itself over and over. Creative people find ways to ease the burden for people getting care at home, and for those family members and paid aides who bear the immense responsibility of helping them. But the government, fearing these programs will be abused, imposes restrictions on their use or cuts their funding, so for most of the 7.5 million frail seniors and younger disabled people living at home, and for their families, this kind of help is little more than a dream.

EIGHT

How We Pay

John Lennon was so wrong when he told us that all we needed was love. Long-term care takes love, for sure. But it also takes money. Great gobs of it.

In 2005, America spent more than $200 billion for nursing home, home care, and other long-term-care services. About half of that, or more than $100 billion, was paid by the government, through our tax dollars. Most of the rest was financed by individual families, out of their own pockets. A small amount—less than ten cents out of every dollar—was covered by private insurance.[1]

How much is $200 billion? It is nearly $2,000 for every house-hold in the nation.

Of course, not everyone is going to need this assistance. In 2005, three researchers—Peter Kemper, Harriet Komisar, and Lisa Alecxih—used a sophisticated computer model to project the futures of Americans who had just turned sixty-five. They concluded that the average sixty-five-year-old will need three years of care before dying—about a year and a half of informal help at home and an additional eighteen months of paid assistance, either at home or in an institution such as a nursing home.[2]

But averages are deceiving. It turns out there are very big differences in the amount of care people need. The researchers found that three out of every ten seniors will never require any of this help. They will die quickly, from accidents or diseases such as aggressive cancers or heart attacks.

That still means that two out of every three will need some period of personal assistance in their old age. About 17 percent will require help for a year or less, and many of them will get by with relatively little aid from family members or friends. However, more than half will need care for at least a year, and one out of every five will need help for five years or longer.

Women are far more likely to need long-term care than men, and the odds are nearly twice as high that they'll need it for five years or more. Why? One big reason is that they simply live longer. It also may be because men are less likely to care for frail wives than wives are to aid their husbands.

The big question is: What will all this cost? The short answer is: more than most Americans have, especially for those unlucky enough to need more than a year of care. The researchers estimated that 42 percent of sixty-five-year-olds will have no long-term-care costs before they die and about 20 percent will have less than $10,000. However, about one out of every six will generate costs in excess of $100,000 and about one in twenty will incur expenses of more than $250,000.[3]

With the cost of a nursing home averaging $78,000 a year and home health agencies charging close to $20 a hour for aides, it is easy to see how quickly expenses can add up. It does not take many months before long-term care becomes a financial burden far beyond the resources of most Americans.

Long-term care rivals what some families will pay for medical care. The difference is most Americans have health insurance. While lots of attention is paid to the 45 million people without medical insurance, the fact is that nearly 250 million do have coverage.[4] Most workers get it through their employers, and nearly everyone over sixty-five has Medicare. By contrast, fewer than 7 million people have private long-term-care insurance, and except for those who are both very poor and very sick, there is no government program to pay for their care.

That means people must pay largely out of their savings. And the sad truth is that Americans seem unable—or unwilling—to build up a financial reserve for their old age. The amount of take-home pay we put in the bank or invest has been falling steadily since the early 1980s, and by 2008 we were putting away pretty close to nothing.[5] What savings Americans do have is tied up in either homes or retirement plans.

Before the real estate and stock market collapses of 2008, the median net worth of all those over sixty-five, including their home, was somewhere between $110,000 and $150,000, depending on who calculated the numbers.[6] How much long-term care can that buy? Not much.

Here is one way to think about it: If that typical senior wanted to turn his savings into regular monthly income to help pay for long-term care, he could buy an insurance product called an annuity. In 2008 a sixty-five-year-old who invested $100,000 would get monthly income of about $700. What would $700 buy? Only about three days in a nursing home each month, or forty hours of home health services. An annuity of even $150,000 would throw off only about $1,000 a month, enough to pay for just four or five days in a nursing facility.[7]

Of course, most seniors also collect Social Security, which typically pays $1,100 a month, although many widows get less.[8] That helps, but still falls far short of the cost of a nursing home. And for seniors living at home, that extra money has to pay for more than a health aide. It also must provide food, utilities, and transportation, as well as rent or a mortgage, and property taxes.

Then there are regular medical bills. In 2008 the Medicare Part B premium was nearly $100 a month, and the premium for the Part D drug benefit was at least $25. Even with this insurance, seniors face massive health bills. The government estimates that a typical Medicare beneficiary spent nearly $3,800 in out-of-pocket medical costs in 2007, or $7,600 for a couple.[9] According to one forecast, a sixty-five-year-old couple will need to put aside between $250,000 and $1.2 million to pay for health care during the remainder of their lives.[10] And remember, that projection is only for medical care. It does not include any long-term care.

These out-of-pocket health-care costs for seniors are growing rapidly. Not only are medical costs themselves rising, but the number of employers offering any health insurance for their retired workers is shrinking at an alarming speed. In 2006 only about one third of companies offered any such insurance—half the percentage that did in 1988.[11] Unless you work for the government, or for a jumbo company, there is almost no chance this insurance will be available to you after you are sixty-five. As companies continue to drop health coverage for their retirees, out-of-pocket medical costs in old age will only rise.

Those at high risk of entering a nursing home face even more severe financial stress. Among eighty-five-year-olds with no spouse and who need some help with activities of daily living, 74 percent have assets of less than $5,000, and 84 percent do not have sufficient funds to pay for even a year in a nursing home.[12]

So what do most people do if they need personal assistance over many years? For starters, they rely on free informal care from family members or friends. That's what Gordon Fredine and Walter Barrett did. It is hard to put a value on that assistance, but if families had to pay aides to do this work, the price would far exceed $100 billion a year. Add lost wages and benefits, as well as out-of-pocket costs, and the price tag explodes. The seniors' group AARP figures that in 2006 the total value of care provided by friends and relatives topped a staggering $354 billion.[13]

People rely on this informal help for as long as they can, then typically try to get by with a few hours a day of paid care. As they get sicker and frailer, the numbers stop working completely. As many as half of nursing home residents who are admitted as private-pay patients run out of funds during their stay and end up on Medicaid.[14]

LOST IN THE FINANCIAL SUPERMARKET

For those with more money, there are alternatives: long-term-care insurance, annuities, reverse mortgages, and hybrids that attempt to combine the benefits of each. But these products are costly, complex, and appropriate only for those with substantial assets. Most are out of reach for typical middle-income Americans.

The first product most people think about is long-term-care insurance. This coverage is often confused with Medicare Supplement, or Medigap, insurance. But it is very different.

Long-term-care policies won't pay for medical expenses, but they will pay for the cost of care in a nursing home and, sometimes, in an assisted-living facility or for the services of a home health aide. However, to collect, beneficiaries must be unable to care for themselves, either because they can no longer do activities such as bathing or going to the bathroom on their own or because they suffer from severe memory loss.

Long-term-care policies are expensive, especially for those who wait until they are in their sixties or older to buy. Today, a sixty-year-old can expect to pay roughly $2,000 a year for a good-quality policy.[15] Some studies show that the policies are especially costly for men, who are much less likely than women to get benefits but who pay the same premiums.[16]

They are also complicated, with lots of fine print and a complex language all their own. For instance, where other insurance policies have a deductible, long-term-care plans have what they call an elimination period, which is the number of days you must pay for care on your own before you can be reimbursed by your insurer.

Another way financial planners say you can create income in your old age is to buy just the kind of annuity that economists like to use as a benchmark when they analyze retirement savings. These investments are not easy to understand, but they are a little like buying yourself a private pension. They work like this: You give an insurance company or other financial institution a pile of money up front—say $100,000. In return, it promises to send you a check each month based on interest rates at the time you invest.

No matter what happens to the economy or the markets after that, you get the same steady monthly payment. When you die, the insurance company keeps whatever is left of the $100,000. You can arrange for those payments to continue for your surviving spouse, but the trade-off will be a smaller monthly check while you are alive.

Remember, a fixed annuity is not the same as a variable annuity, which does not guarantee a return and is often little more than a tax-sheltered mutual fund tied to extremely high fees.

By contrast, fixed annuities can make sense for some retirees, but even they can be expensive, complicated, and not very useful unless you are wealthy. If you can afford it, such an investment might be a good way to produce a steady source of income while you are relatively healthy and your needs are fairly stable.

However, these products have some big downsides for most of us. To start, they are beyond the means of many Americans, who have put aside very little in savings besides their retirement plans. Most advisers recommend that no one tie up more than one third of their financial assets in an annuity, so a prudent investor would need assets of $3 million or more to purchase a policy that would throw off enough cash to fully pay for nursing home care. And remember, this income might also have to help support the living expenses of a healthy spouse at the same time it is paying long-term-care costs.

In addition, while the security of a fixed payment seems comforting, it also creates a big problem. Because annuities generate steady income each month, they work best to help pay predictable bills such as the mortgage or utilities. When retirees are relatively young and healthy, they may occasionally splurge—maybe on a new car or a nice vacation—but they generally can estimate their costs. They can even figure, roughly, what their medical bills will be each year, since they know what their deductibles and co-payments are.

Everything becomes far less predictable, however, after a catastrophic, unanticipated health crisis, such as a stroke or the onset of Alzheimer's. Then that steady annuity income suddenly falls far short of what they need.

In fact, the spending patterns of many retirees look like a U on a graph. At first, when seniors are healthy and active, they consume a lot—on trips, golf, restaurant meals, and the like. As they get older, they go out less and spend less. Then, once they become sick or frail, their expenses rise again. And if they need long-term care, their costs explode. Getting the timing right, so that an annuity produces income when the buyer most needs it, turns out to be a big challenge.

That's especially true since, because typical annuities pay a fixed monthly amount, inflation eats away at the value of these payments as time goes on. You can buy protection against the inevitable rise in the cost of living, but once again you'll have to pay more up front. And while these newer products gradually increase monthly payments to keep up with the steadily rising cost of living, even they can't come close to financing the huge jump in expenses once someone needs nursing home care or an around-the-clock home health aide.

Now, some insurance companies and financial economists are tinkering with products that could provide a bigger burst of income just when seniors need it most—when they require costly long-term care. That's when they can easily go from spending a few thousand dollars a month to $10,000 or more.

Some new hybrids combine long-term-care coverage with other insurance. Ideas include tying long-term care to life or disability policies, or annuities, or allowing accelerated death benefits under life policies.[17] Some companies combine reverse mortgages with long-term-care insurance, so buyers can use cash from these loans to pay their insurance premiums. However, borrowing against your home to pay for insurance can be a very risky proposition.

Still other products allow people to tap into the cash value of life insurance policies. In these arrangements, investors pay you today in return for the right to collect on your life policy when you die. The advantage: you get money when you need it to help pay the costs of long-term care. The downside: Your policy pays much less upon your death, and that could leave your spouse short of funds after you're gone.

Most of these new products simply graft one already complicated product to another, which makes buying a challenge and comparison shopping impossible. They also multiply already stiff up-front fees. Financial experts advise against purchasing most of these, at least as they are currently designed.

But some ideas may have more merit. For instance, one would marry a long-term-care insurance benefit with an annuity.[18] Just as if you were buying an ordinary annuity, you would make a big lump-sum payment to an insurance company when you retire and get a steady monthly payment for as long as you live. But this policy, called a Life Care Annuity, comes with an important extra: Should you become very ill, it substantially increases your cash payments. The more severe your disability, the bigger the payment.

Of course, these extra benefits don't come for free. However, the designers believe they can keep the price down thanks to an interesting difference between those people who buy annuities and those who purchase long-term-care insurance. It turns out that annuity buyers are healthier and expect to live longer than those who prefer long-term-care insurance. With a hybrid policy, which would be sold to both kinds of people, an insurance company could internally balance those risks. That would allow it to sell the policy at a lower premium and to avoid strict underwriting.

However, the up-front price of a policy such as this is far out of reach for most sixty-five-year-olds.[19] For example, one of the designers of this plan, Mark Warshawsky, estimates that an inflation-protected policy that pays $1,000 per month in retirement income, with an additional $2,000 to $4,000 if the buyer becomes disabled, would require a sixty-five-year-old to invest more than $225,000 up front. According to one estimate, no more than 10 or 20 percent of new retirees have enough money to buy such a policy.[20]

Three Boston College economists have designed a less costly annuity that also aims to provide a source of income for old age.[21] Called an Advanced Life Deferred Annuity, it could be purchased at age sixty or sixty-five, but would not begin to pay any benefits until the buyer reached age seventy-five or older.

Because it pays nothing until the investor reaches a relatively old age, the policy is much less expensive than other annuities. For instance, with an investment of just $74,000, a sixty-year-old could buy $20,000 a year in inflation-protected income starting at age eighty-five. This is more affordable than other options, and could provide a spurt of income when it is most needed. The challenge, however, is persuading people to put money away at sixty for a benefit they might not see for twenty-five years, if ever.

TURNING HOME EQUITY INTO LONG-TERM CARE

Many seniors do have one resource, however: their house. And financial experts have been scratching their heads for years trying to figure out how people can turn their home equity into the cash they need to pay for their long-term care.

It is such an obvious source of income. While Americans are

poor savers, they are also obsessive home owners. For years they have been barraged by both government and the real estate industry with a single message: Home ownership is the American Dream. Thanks to more than $100 billion in tax benefits, and the promise of easy loans, more than two thirds of all Americans own their residences. While the bursting housing bubble in 2007 and 2008 temporarily dimmed buyers' ardor, principal residences, along with Social Security benefits and retirement plans, are by far our biggest potential source of cash in old age.

Before the mortgage bust, people nearing retirement held about $2 trillion in housing assets.[22] Even if the slumping market reduced home values by 20 percent, it still left seniors with plenty of equity to use to pay their long-term-care costs. Eighty percent have their own homes, and the average family nearing retirement owns a house worth about $200,000, with a mortgage of about $83,000.[23] That leaves them with about $120,000 to borrow for medical or long-term-care expenses—enough to pay for several years of home care.

But how can they access those assets? Houses are not like stocks: You can't sell them with a phone call or a mouse click. Home sales come with big transaction costs, including hefty fees for lenders, real estate agents, lawyers, and insurance companies. Still, one solution is to sell and move into a smaller home. That is the perfect answer for many families, but what if you don't want to move?

At first, taking out a home equity loan seems like a good answer. These loans are easy to get, relatively inexpensive, and can be used for almost anything. However, borrowers must repay principal and interest on the loan each month, which sharply reduces the cash they have left to pay for their care.

In the early 1990s, a new product became widely available that hinted at an answer. It was called a reverse mortgage. Instead of borrowers making monthly payments to the bank, they'd repay nothing until they moved or died. Interest would accrue during the life of the loan, but no payments would be required until the loan was terminated. Borrowers could take a lump sum, a steady check each month, or obtain a line of credit to use as needed. Whichever option they chose, the reverse mortgage would turn the value of their home into usable cash by converting their equity into income.

Reverse mortgages seemed like the perfect tool to finance home health care, but like annuities and insurance, these mortgages turned out to come with many strings attached. They carry high up-front fees, and their rules can be hard to understand. In addition, they work only while the borrowers still live at home. As soon as they leave their house, because they either die or move into, say, a nursing home or assisted-living facility, the lender can demand repayment. And that usually means the home must be sold. If there is anything left after repaying the loan and the accrued interest, it would go to the borrower or his family.

This can make a reverse mortgage decision very complicated. Let's say a couple takes out such a loan while both are still living at home. Should one spouse move to a nursing home or assisted-living facility, they would still be eligible to receive payments. As soon as the second spouse leaves, however, the loan must be repaid. And if it happens that both the husband and wife need institutional care at the same time, the mortgage terminates at exactly the time the couple most need cash.

Nearly all reverse mortgages are insured by the government, through a program called the Home Equity Conversion Mortgage (HECM). Only about 10 percent—mostly for higher-end houses—are issued privately. While many lenders are in the reverse-mortgage business, just three—Wells Fargo, Bank of America, and Financial Freedom—originate most of these loans.

The industry says there are millions of potential borrowers, but only a few would be able to use them to pay for long-term care. The reason is they simply don't have enough equity to use a reverse mortgage for an extended period of care. For instance, almost two thirds of home owners who need help with their daily activities have home equity of less than $100,000. Just one in ten has $200,000 or more.[24]

It is even worse for those seniors who are severely disabled. In 2002 their average household wealth totaled less than $50,000. Of that, about $36,000 was home equity—far too little to make a reverse mortgage worth the up-front fees.[25]

Use of these mortgages has increased dramatically in the past decade, but there are still only about 350,000 federally guaranteed loans outstanding[26]—only about 1 percent of all older homeowners and a tiny fraction of the 13 million who one study estimates might benefit from them.[27]

By far the biggest reason people don't take out these loans is the high fees. In a 2006 survey of reverse mortgage shoppers, nearly two thirds of non-buyers cited those costs. And it is no surprise. The AARP study found that a typical seventy-four-year-old living in a $300,000 house would have to pay as much as $30,000 in fees—half of them up front—to get a government-insured reverse mortgage. Those fees exclude interest on the loan, which steadily accrues until it is repaid when the mortgage terminates.

More troubling, while competition among lenders brought interest rates down in recent years—at least until the real estate crash—origination fees have grown four times more expensive. The maximum fees for the federal loans grew from $1,800 in 2000 to nearly $7,300 by 2006.[28] Privately insured mortgages offer lower fees but higher interest rates—sometimes three full percentage points more than the government-guaranteed mortgages.

Fees on government-insured loans are so high in part because they are based on the maximum loan borrowers can qualify for, not on the amount they actually borrow. In addition, loan fees are based on the assumption that a typical buyer—who is seventy-four—will live for another twelve years.[29] But, in reality, as people die or move out of their homes, loans are terminating after just six years for average borrowers and only four years for those who are older, and that forces them to pay these stiff fees over a shorter period of time.[30]

It also turns out that many borrowers are taking out reverse mortgages at a surprisingly young age, and for some unexpected reasons. The AARP survey found that half of borrowers took out the loans to pay for everyday expenses. A quarter said they planned to use the money to pay off existing debts. Less than one third cited health or disability as a reason for borrowing. Only 5 percent said they ended up using the loans to pay for health care or personal assistance.[31]

This could prove to be a serious problem. If people are using reverse mortgages as just another way to dip into their home equity while they are relatively young and healthy, they will have little left to borrow against when they need long-term care. And that will largely defeat the purpose of using these loans for personal assistance at home.

These premature borrowers, like so many others, will end up with far fewer financial resources than they need to care for themselves in frail old age. Most Americans, however, think that they can turn to the government for help, and that is when they will get an even nastier surprise.

Polls show that nearly 60 percent of people think that Medicare, the nearly universal health system for those over sixty-five, funds long-term care.[32] It does not. They are as wrong as John Lennon, who thought that all it took was love.

Medicare pays for some nursing and home health care, but only under very limited circumstances. For the most part, it insures only rehabilitation or care after a patient has been discharged from a hospital. And it will pay the full cost for only twenty days and a share of the cost for no more than an additional eighty. So, for example, if a woman has had a stroke, Medicare will pay for rehab in a nursing home, but only for as long as she is showing improvement, and in any case, for no more than one hundred days. As soon as she stops getting better—in other words, as soon as she begins to need long-term care—Medicare stops paying.

The government program that does help support people in

long-term care is Medicaid. But Medicaid is a welfare program, available only to those who are very poor. Created in 1965 mostly to help provide health care for poor women and their children, Medicaid has morphed into something entirely different—something its creators never imagined.

NINE

Medicaid

Natalie Fenninger and Caroline Foye have never met each other, but they have lived strikingly parallel lives. Both were born before World War I, survived the searing Depression years, and became part of the great post–World War II middle class. Natalie, who we met in Chapter 2, spent most of her years in suburban New Jersey, while Caroline lived in the suburbs of Boston. Both are artists—Natalie an accomplished poet, Caroline a talented painter. Both adopted and raised sons (Caroline adopted two).

Both women have seen their share of tragedy. Natalie's first husband was a telephone company executive who died young. Caroline's husband was a banker who fell on hard times and then suffered for years from cancer and depression. But both women persevered, buried spouses (Natalie outlived three), and, as they had planned, used their hard-earned savings for their older years. Putting aside a little something each week for your old age was almost a cliché for their Depression generation, and Natalie and Caroline both did it.

But they never imagined what their care would cost, that their money would run out, and what would happen when it did.

Natalie and Caroline—like Walter Barrett, Peggy Ingles, Granny and Pawpaw, Lisa, and millions of other Americans—are caught up in an irrational system of government health care for the elderly and disabled. It will pay tens of thousands of dollars to care for some severely ill seniors, but nothing for others who may be just as sick but who have the misfortune of suffering from the "wrong" diseases.

If your dad is over sixty-five and suffers from an acute illness such as cancer or a heart attack, Medicare will pay, often generously, to provide treatment. If he suffers from a chronic disease such as kidney failure, it will pay for the dialysis he needs to stay alive or the transplant that may allow him to resume a normal life. If he is dying, it will pay for hospice care.

But if he suffers from Alzheimer's or Parkinson's, stroke, congestive heart failure, asthma, or arthritis, Medicare will pay little or nothing for long-term care, even though it may be as critical to his well-being as surgery or prescription drugs. Neither will private Medicare Supplement insurance (often known as Medigap) or private Medicare managed-care plans (called Medicare Advantage).

Long-term-care insurance may cover this kind of care, but few Americans have it. Everyone else must pay the staggering costs of nursing home or home health care out of their own pockets. Only when they run out of money will they become eligible for Medicaid, the government's welfare-like health-care program for the poor. Then the government will pay, although not necessarily for the help people want, need, or expect.

After many comfortable years in an independent-living apartment at the Friends House retirement community, Natalie moved into assisted living back in July of 1999, just a few months after her third husband died. At eighty-five, and suffering from an unusual form of temporary memory loss called transient global amnesia, Natalie wasn't acutely ill. She just couldn't take care of herself anymore.

As the years went on and Natalie became increasingly frail, she needed more and more assistance. Her stepdaughter, Gretchen, who was her friend and caregiver, first hired private-duty aides to help out. Gradually, those care workers had to spend more hours each day with Natalie until, by 2006, she needed full-time, 24/7 help.

The cost was staggering. Some months she was burning through as much as $16,000 on assisted living, round-the-clock aides, medical equipment, and prescription drugs. After seven years, Natalie had spent nearly half a million dollars on long-term care and was going broke. So she did what millions of other once-middle-class elderly and disabled people do, she turned to Medicaid—the government's health-care program for the poor that has become the payer of last resort for long-term care.

In a perverse way, Medicaid encourages people to pay top dollar for long-term care when they first need it. After all, you can live more comfortably in an assisted-living facility knowing that once you have run out of funds, Medicaid will be there to take care of you.

To receive Medicaid assistance, however, Natalie had to move from her assisted-living apartment into a nursing home, a step she never wanted to take. And she had to do it long before she really needed such intense care.

Caroline Foye, who lives just down the road from her son Richard in a southern Vermont hamlet, also was forced to turn to Medicaid. Long before she became ill, Caroline had spent most of her money caring for her chronically ill husband, Elmer. By the time she suffered a series of strokes at age ninety-six, she had little more than her tiny house, some modest pieces of furniture, and a few strikingly beautiful watercolors she had painted years before.

Caroline was hospitalized after her strokes, and later transferred to Thompson House, a nursing facility in Brattleboro. Medicare covered most of her hospital care and, for a couple of weeks, paid $185 a day for what her son Richard describes as a "nice private room" in Thompson House. But Medicare will provide nursing care only as long as a beneficiary is showing improvement. And Caroline was not getting better, so Medicare stopped paying.

Caroline and Richard learned a hard lesson about Medicare. The near-universal health system for seniors does not cover long-term care. It pays only for short stays in nursing homes and temporary assistance at home, and even then only under very limited circumstances. But Caroline still needed extensive help getting dressed and bathed, so, like Natalie, she turned to Medicaid. And, like Natalie, she was transferred to a double room. "She was sharing a room with a demented woman," Richard remembers. "It was bad."

For Natalie and Caroline, a lifetime of careful savings didn't matter. Like millions of once-middle-class Americans, they saw all of their hard-earned money disappear into the maw of the long-term-care system. Then, once it was gone, they had only one place to turn for help.

Medicaid is not what it seems. Many think of it as a government program for poor women and children, yet in reality it has become the nation's biggest payer of long-term care for the elderly and disabled. It was supposed to provide medical care, yet much of its budget is spent on personal assistance. It is the only federal program that provides long-term care, yet most people wrongly believe that its sister program, Medicare, covers these costs. It was designed to pay for nursing home stays, and still forces many into these institutions, yet few beneficiaries want this kind of care, and many don't need it. And although Medicaid was created in the mid-1960s as a political afterthought, it has become one of the fastest-growing spending programs in the entire federal budget.

The numbers are mind-boggling. Medicaid spends $100 billion a year on long-term care and supports nearly half the total cost of all paid personal assistance. While moms and kids make up three quarters of Medicaid's 52 million enrollees, two thirds of the program's dollars go to the aged and disabled.[1]

Only about 3 million people, or about 7 percent of Medicaid beneficiaries, receive long-term care, but the costs for each are steep. In 2002, Medicaid paid $31,112 for each elderly participant and

$46,531 for every disabled beneficiary receiving long-term care.[2] By contrast, it spent only about $1,500 on a typical child.[3]

Here is another way to think about how Medicaid has come to dominate the long-term-care world: Of the nation's 1.4 million nursing home residents, more than 900,000 are on Medicaid. Only about one in five pays out of their own pocket or taps an insurance policy.[4]

How Medicaid Works

The easiest way to think about Medicaid is as a very unusual insurance program. Unlike typical insurance, in which you pay a deductible of, say, $500 or $1,000, Medicaid has a kind of open-ended deductible that is tied to your assets. You first spend nearly all of your money on medical and long-term care and other living expenses. Then, once you run out, Medicaid steps in. It is no exaggeration to say that if you have $100,000 in the bank, you must pay $98,000 out of pocket before Medicaid insurance kicks in.

To be eligible for Medicaid long-term care, people must be sixty-five or older or permanently disabled, unable to care for themselves, and have few assets and little income. An aged or disabled person is not eligible unless he meets all three tests.

While Medicaid is a joint state/federal program, states are given broad flexibility to decide who gets benefits. However, Washington places certain minimum requirements on every state.

To satisfy what Medicaid calls its functional eligibility test, a person must be unable to perform certain activities of daily living, such as eating, bathing, or going to the bathroom, without assistance. Historically, this meant he needed a nursing home level of care. Starting in 2007, however, the federal government encouraged states to use less strict medical standards, and make Medicaid more widely available to those who could be cared for at home.

However, in the real world, this home-care option often exists only on paper. In many states, it may take years before a frail senior can get one of a limited number of home-care slots. In others, financial and medical restrictions make it tough to get approved.

Financial requirements apply broadly across the states. Middle-class people often meet these limits only after they have spent down their assets on medical and long-term care. In most states, an individual is allowed to keep only $2,000 in stocks, bonds, bank accounts, and other liquid assets. A couple may have $3,000 if they are sharing a room in a nursing home. As of 2008, if one spouse is in a nursing home, the other is allowed to hold on to half of the couple's assets, up to $104,400.[5]

Couples can also keep one car, personal jewelry, other household goods, and their home. Unmarried people are not eligible for Medicaid if their house is worth more than $500,000, although states are permitted to increase that level to $750,000. If a person is in a nursing home and has no spouse or other close relative living at home, she may be forced to sell her house, often because Medicaid does not leave her with enough money to pay property taxes, utilities, or make repairs. States may also put a lien on a beneficiary's home so the government can be repaid for Medicaid nursing home payments after she dies.

To meet Medicaid's asset test, some families have used trusts and other sophisticated financial planning techniques to transfer their property to others. However, Medicaid now bars people from making such transfers for at least five years before they apply for assistance. Those who shift funds earlier are penalized by having to wait longer before they can collect benefits.

Medicaid also imposes an income test on applicants. These rules are even more complicated, and vary from state to state. They are also different for those getting care at home and those in a nursing facility.

In 2008 a person who was receiving home care was generally allowed to earn no more than $637 a month, the level at which an individual becomes eligible for Supplementary Security Income (SSI). Some states will allow Medicaid beneficiaries to earn up to 100 percent of the federal poverty level, or $867 per month. In reality, these rules bar most Social Security recipients from assistance.

Rules are somewhat more generous for people who live at home under so-called home- and community-based waiver programs. They are allowed to receive up to 300 percent of the SSI standard, or about $1,910 a month. In some states, they must contribute all of their extra income to the cost of their long-term care. In others, those who earn more than the cap are not eligible for any government assistance.

Many states impose no income test on those in nursing homes, but beneficiaries must contribute nearly all of their monthly income to the cost of their care. However, at least twenty-one states, including Ohio, Oregon, and Texas, bar individuals from enrolling in Medicaid at all if their monthly income exceeds $1,809.

While the journeys Natalie and Caroline took to Medicaid are strikingly similar, what happened to them once they got there is very different. Natalie lives in Maryland, a state that pays lip service to the idea of allowing the frail elderly to live at home, but in reality provides very little opportunity for them to do so. Thus, she spends her days sharing a small room with a stranger in a nursing home, at a cost to Medicaid of more than $4,500 a month. Caroline lives in Vermont, which actively encourages Medicaid recipients to live at home, instead of in an institution. As a result, the state pays half as much to keep her at home than it would if she were in a nursing facility.

In some ways, both women have been lucky. They are not victims of scandalous nursing homes, abuse, or neglect. They have loving and attentive families who help as best they can. Each of their stories is, in its way, ordinary. And that is what is so frightening.

Months before Natalie ran out of money, it was obvious both to her family and to Friends House what was going to happen. Like half of all nursing home residents, Natalie was going broke and was headed for Medicaid.[6]

Not surprisingly, by late 2006, her money was gone—more than half a million dollars, estimates her grandson, Rick, who manages her finances. So were the round-the-clock aides. In November, Rick began the process of applying for Medicaid. It took six months, until May of 2007, before Maryland approved his request. He stopped counting pages, but with supporting documents, he figures the application weighed six or seven pounds. "You need to prove that somebody is broke," he says. "You've got to document everything that's happened over the past five years."

Applying was only half the story. The only way Natalie's family could make sure she could stay at Friends House was to move her into the nursing wing before she became eligible for government assistance. It sounds like another tale out of Dickens, but had they waited too long, Natalie might have had to move to a distant or poor-quality facility in order to get her benefits.

Here's why: Once a resident like Natalie is in a nursing home, the facility cannot force her out when she runs out of funds and goes on Medicaid. But if she becomes impoverished while still living at home or in an assisted-living facility, it is a different story. Nursing homes often limit the number of new Medicaid patients they will take. So, while the government would still pay for her care, a family might have to hunt for a nursing home that had an empty bed for the impoverished. The facility might be fifty miles away. It might be a barely livable Medicaid mill.

Natalie was able to stay at Friends House, but like most facilities, it required Medicaid patients to live in shared rooms. So in July 2006, months before she actually needed nursing care, she was moved into the tiny double room she now shares with Helen. She is better off than many. At least she has a safe place to live.

A Sideshow in the Health-care Circus

For the past half-century, government has been struggling with what to do for seniors like Caroline and Natalie, as well as for the younger disabled such as Peggy and Lisa. The question politicians have been trying to answer is this: What obligation does society have to provide long-term care for its most vulnerable citizens—help that is both vital and mind-numbingly expensive? Where does a family's role end and the government's begin? These are the same questions we ask about health care.

This debate has been going on since the founding of the nation, but it began in earnest in the 1960s, during the heyday of the Great Society. In 1965, Congress created two landmark public health programs. The biggest was Medicare, which was supposed to provide basic medical insurance for everyone over sixty-five, regardless of income. Under Medicare, billionaire investor Warren Buffett is eligible for exactly the same benefits as a retired maintenance worker. Medicare's benefits were limited, however, since the program was designed to treat only acute episodes of those illnesses that were common in the 1960s. "They insured the fears of fifty-year-old men in suits who were afraid of dying of heart attacks," says geriatrician Joanne Lynn.

Medicare never covered long-term care. This was no accident. Even in the 1960s President Lyndon B. Johnson and his allies in Congress were aware that an open-ended nursing home benefit could bankrupt the program. So they limited Medicare's coverage to rehabilitation or convalescence after a hospital stay, as well as to basic medical care.

That meant someone recovering from surgery might get a few

days or weeks of help at home from a visiting nurse or an aide who could change surgical dressings or help them bathe. Or a patient recovering from a stroke might get some limited time for physical therapy in a nursing facility. But once a patient's condition stabilized and she was no longer improving, no longer needed skilled nursing care or help for longer than one hundred days, Medicare stopped paying. That's why Caroline Foye lost her Medicare nursing home benefit.

To make matters even more complicated, Medicare would pay for the medical care of the frail elderly, including doctor's visits, tests, and physical therapy. Gradually, over the years, preventative care and hospice were added. And in 2006, Medicare began paying for prescription drugs for both low-income seniors and those wealthier retirees who chose to purchase Part D drug insurance. But it does not cover long-term care.

If Medicare was not going to pay for what was then called "custodial care," who would, especially for the poor? The challenge was even greater because, a few years before, in 1960, Congress had created a modest nursing home benefit for the low-income elderly. The solution was a classic Washington tale.[7]

The sponsors of that 1960 bill—Congressman Wilbur Mills of Arkansas, the wily chairman of the House Ways and Means Committee, and Senator Robert Kerr, a powerful lawmaker from Oklahoma—were hardly social reformers. Kerr, a deeply conservative Democrat, was far more interested in helping the nursing home industry than in aiding the poor. Instead of trying to expand coverage, Mills was trying to torpedo a more ambitious health program for seniors that was being pushed by, among others, Senator John F. Kennedy, his own party's candidate for president that year.

Mills easily buried the Kennedy-backed plan in committee. But Mills recognized that support was growing for some form of long-term-care benefit, and felt he had to do something to relieve the political pressure. So, with Kerr, he put together a limited plan that would allow states to establish their own nursing home insurance for the poor. Many states, as Mills probably expected, never followed through.[8]

Nonetheless, Mills's effort to co-opt the broader government health insurance program succeeded only in delaying the inevitable. President Kennedy was assassinated before he could make much progress. But health care for the poor and elderly was a key element of LBJ's Great Society. By the time bills to create Medicare and Medicaid were moving through Congress in 1965, more than three hundred thousand frail elderly were already getting government nursing home benefits through the old Kerr-Mills Act. Assistance for these vulnerable seniors could not be dumped, but Johnson was unwilling to push for a comprehensive program for long-term care. So Mills simply tacked nursing home care for the poor on to the new Medicaid program, which was intended mostly to provide health care for low-income women and their children. Then, he glued Medicaid on to the far more popular Medicare bill. In the end, Medicaid long-term care was "only a sideshow in the health care circus," writes Bruce C. Vladeck, who ran the Medicare and Medicaid programs in the 1990s.[9]

This shotgun marriage has lasted for more than four decades, but it is far from a happy union. And the greatest victims of the discord are the seniors and their families the programs are intended to help.

While there have been many changes to Medicaid since 1965, its basic structure remains unchanged. Because it began as a nursing home benefit, it is still struggling to change its focus to reflect people's growing desire for care at home.

Unlike many long-in-the-tooth government programs, Medicaid has never been truly reformed. Instead, every few years, more changes are grafted on to its increasingly outmoded, forty-year-old chassis. It is a little bit like taking a 1965 Chevy and trying to update it by adding seat belts, air bags, an emissions control system, and disc brakes. Even after all that, it is still a 1965 Chevy.

The politicians were right about one thing back in the 1960s: Government assistance for long-term care would turn into a money pit for taxpayers. They largely insulated Medicare from long-term-care costs, but Medicaid's expenses have exploded. The program now spends seven times as much to care for the elderly and disabled as it did just thirty years ago.[10]

There is only one small bit of good news for Washington. Medicaid is operated as an entitlement, which means its costs automatically grow as the number of enrollees swells or prices increase. But Mills made sure that unlike other entitlements such as Social Security and Medicare, Medicaid expenses are shared by the states. On average, the feds pay a bit more than half of its costs, although that varies a lot from state to state. In 2008, for instance, the federal government paid 76 percent of Mississippi's costs but only 50 percent of Connecticut's.[11]

Through thousands of pages of complex regulations, the federal government sets the basic rules for Medicaid. However, because costs are shared, states are allowed to make some changes in the way they run the program, though usually only with the approval of Washington and only after wading through miles of red tape.

This means that decisions about who is eligible for Medicaid long-term-care benefits, and how much help they get, depends largely on where a person lives. And there are big differences. In 2004, states spent an average of $304 per resident on such services. But New York paid $833, while California spent $187, and Nevada spent just $102.[12]

In many states, seniors still have little choice but to live in a nursing home, since Medicaid mostly pays only for this type of care. This reliance on nursing home care is slowly changing, however, and in recent years the federal government has made it easier for states to help those who prefer home- and community-based care. Proponents of this initiative believe that allowing the aged and disabled to remain at home both improves their care and saves money, and in 2007, thirty-eight states had plans to expand these programs.[13] Still, only four states—Alaska, New Mexico, Oregon, and Washington—spend more than half of their Medicaid dollars on home-care programs. Twenty spend 15 percent or less.[14]

The Three-Step Program

One state that has wholeheartedly embraced the idea is Vermont. And that is where Caroline Foye lives.

Caroline, who is ninety-seven, is making her daily visit to her son, Richard, an accomplished potter who lives a half mile away, just across a creek and down a narrow country road.

You get to Richard's house by crossing two of Vermont's famous covered bridges and following a narrow, winding road through the town of Williamsville. It is little more than a wide place in the road with a general store (EST. 1828, it says over the door) and a sharp-steepled church—now for rent.

Caroline comes by most mornings to have coffee and a piece of Richard's homemade cinnamon bread. Later they will take a walk down the road—son stepping briskly along and mother gamely following, hobbling along with her aluminum walker. Before she heads home for lunch, Caroline will have a beer. Guinness usually.

Coffee and cinnamon bread, a walk, and a beer: Richard calls it his mother's three-step program. As eccentric as it seems, it may be keeping Caroline alive.

"I don't know what I'll do when she can't walk," Richard says. What he means, but can't quite bring himself to say aloud, is he doesn't know what Caroline would do, either.

Richard moved both of his parents to Vermont from their home in Topsfield, Massachusetts, in 1995, after his father was found wandering. For decades, Elmer Foye had suffered from one medical problem or another, from severe depression to cancer, and later Parkinson's and dementia. Caroline cared for him alone nearly all of that time.

For a while, Elmer and Caroline stayed with Richard, but that didn't work out. Then Elmer lived in a series of nursing homes. That was a disaster, Richard remembers. So in 1996 his parents bought their small frame house down the road. Elmer died in 2000, and for six years, Caroline lived alone.

After her strokes and her transfer to a shared Medicaid room,

Caroline wanted to come home. Richard remembered his father's days in similar facilities and figured there had to be a better way. But Caroline struggled to speak and stand, and could get around only with her walker. And she was out of money, her nest egg long since spent caring for Elmer.

Richard, who is sixty, knew his mother would need a lot of help if she was going to return home. But he is not married, has no other family to share the burden, and was already burned out from years of aiding his parents.

It is like this in rural Vermont: Richard lives in an old wood-frame house, with a breezeway that opens up to a storage area piled high with old furniture and tools. To get there, you have to climb three stone steps. It is hard not to notice the railing. Metal tubes that may be lengths of plumbing pipe do duty on the right. The handle of an old hockey stick serves as the railing on the left. It is so old that the once-bright red label has faded to near illegibility.

Here, where flatlanders visit only in summer and in high leaf-peeping season in September, practical solutions are highly prized. It is a lovely but often harsh environment: Money is usually in short supply, and the hardware store may be an hour away. So self-reliant locals use whatever is available to fix a problem. Like Richard's stair railings, the solutions surely don't need to look pretty, and sometimes can be more than a little odd. All that matters is that they work.

The problem that the Foyes needed to solve was how to care for Caroline at home. Like that broken railing, there was no off-the-shelf solution.

A nurse at Thompson House had the answer. She told Richard about a state Medicaid program that would pay for Caroline's home care, so he arranged to get her enrolled, and out of the nursing home.

Since the mid-1990s, Vermont has been actively encouraging the frail elderly and the disabled to stay at home. Instead of paying an institution to care for someone like Caroline, Vermont makes cash available for families to help their loved ones at home. With a fistful of programs with upbeat names like Flexible Choices and Choices for Care, Vermont has reduced its Medicaid nursing home population by about 20 percent.[15]

The program is similar to what Maryland is doing for Peggy Ingles. Teresa Wood, who runs the Vermont home-care project out of a nondescript office building in Waterbury, is blunt about the benefits: "We realized it is cheaper to keep people at home. We can save a lot of money, and it is what they want."

Richard used his Medicaid cash to pay Ayars Hemphill, who was his pottery student, to move in with Caroline and serve as her paid companion. Ayars is forty-eight, but with her smooth skin, red hair, and shy smile, she looks thirty. She has developed an extraordinary relationship with Caroline.

Early on a May morning that can't decide if it wants to be showery or sunny, spring is just arriving in the rural southeast corner of the state. Richard, Caroline, and Ayars are relaxing on the breezeway. It is just a covered porch, really, open in the front and back, and a fine place to watch the hummingbirds court. The hillside out back is just beginning to green up after another hard Vermont winter.

Caroline is sitting in an old chair, her face as weatherbeaten as the clapboards of Richard's faded white house. She wears sensible black shoes, tan corduroy pants, and, in the early spring chill, a white cable sweater over a purple checked shirt, all covered by a red blanket.

Ayars is quiet, at least around strangers. Caroline, who suffers from stroke-related dementia, finds it hard to speak. Yet they communicate with their body language, like old friends might.

"It's an opportunity to live with somebody and care for her," Ayars says. "I don't feel like it is all one way. What she gives me . . . it does feel like an honor to be with her."

I ask Caroline if she likes it that Ayars stays with her.

"Sure," says Caroline.

"That's it?" Ayars teases. She laughs. Caroline does, too.

The two women share their tiny wooden house. Caroline lives downstairs in a small bedroom, separated by a curtain from a smaller sitting area. Ayars lives on the second floor. The walls are mostly bare, though a few of Caroline's precise watercolors hang throughout the house. There is also a handwritten sign that says IN CASE OF EMER- GENCY. There are six names to call before 911.

The state of Vermont pays Ayars just $45 a day to care for Caroline—officially $10 an hour for 4.5 hours, although she spends a lot more time than that helping. Besides her salary, the state pays Ayars's Social Security taxes and Workers' Compensa- tion. She gets no health benefits and no vacation time. She has no 401(k).

Caroline is up at seven A.M. Ayars helps her dress, gets her breakfast, then takes her to Richard's for her daily visit. Then Ayars takes her home for lunch and, while Caroline naps, Ayars leaves to do gardening or other work to supplement her income.

Ayars is not a certified home health aide. She is a companion for Caroline, but has few of the skills she needs to provide personal as- sistance. A volunteer comes regularly to bathe Caroline—Ayars has never been trained to clean someone who is very fragile and at risk of a fall getting in and out of a tub. Caroline also gets hot dinners from Meals On Wheels.

Vermont also pays about $175 a month for Caroline's fuel and phone bill. Since Caroline owns her home, the state also helps out with her local property taxes. With fees for a care manager and other expenses, keeping Caroline at home costs Vermont about $2,000 a month—roughly half of a nursing home stay.

There is another important trade-off for Caroline. It is about risk—in some ways just as it is with the residents of the Cedar Glen small group home or at one of Bill Thomas's Green Houses. If Car- oline falls, has trouble breathing, or has another stroke, there is little Ayars will be able to do beyond calling one of the names on the emergency phone list. Given Caroline's age and health, there is a good chance that if she does have a medical emergency, she will die.

If she were living in a nursing home, she might survive such a cri-

MEDICAID   161

sis. But at ninety-seven, still able to hobble down the road with her walker and enjoy a few sips of beer every day, Caroline has made a different choice. She is willing to accept the extra risk in return for a more normal life.

And so is Richard. "I am lucky to have Ayars," he says. "I took care of [my parents] for ten years. I couldn't do it alone anymore."

Even now, even with help, Richard is exhausted. There are some things government assistance can't do. "I feel trapped," he says as we walk together down the road, his mother struggling to keep up with her walker. "I hope she dies in her sleep." He is not angry or sad. It is just the way it is after ten years. I understand.

The Woodwork Effect

As Caroline and Richard know, home care requires more than just health aides. It also requires a place to live. And for many, that is a huge—and often ignored—challenge.

Like Lisa, those who are severely disabled often can no longer be cared for at home, or have no home to return to. Many need financial assistance for more than long-term care, such as help paying their rent. They need a home they can afford, and one that can accommodate a wheelchair or walker. Unfortunately, while Medicaid does pay for room-and-board costs for nursing home residents, it does not subsidize housing for those at home or in assisted living—even under the community-care programs.

Renters such as Peggy Ingles are caught in a catch-22. If they make a decent salary, they can afford rent but will be disqualified from Medicaid. If they don't work, they might get Medicaid but must rely on dwindling government housing programs to keep a roof over their heads.

Even as the demand for such subsidized housing grows, the number of available units is shrinking. Under one program, people who are disabled, elderly, or poor pay about 30 percent of their income for rent, and the government picks up the rest. But since 2004, federal money for these projects has been drying up and the number of families helped by this initiative has plunged.[16]

Caroline is very lucky. She gets assistance only because Vermont, an especially generous state, does help out through other programs. And she can keep her home, which she might not be able to do as a widow living on Medicaid in a nursing facility.[17]

Unlike Vermont, many states remain unwilling to open up their home care programs. Some have long waiting lists. Others have different rules for different disabilities. Maryland, for instance, has separate waiting lists for those with traumatic brain injuries, developmental disabilities such as autism, and other physical limitations, as well as the aged. Peggy Ingles was able to get Medicaid home care. But there are thousands of seniors waiting to get into a similar program. By some estimates, a senior like Caroline would have to wait three years to get a home-care benefit in Maryland. Of course, most frail ninety-year-olds will die long before they make it to the top of the list.

Other states provide such paltry benefits that they are of limited use to families trying to keep their loved ones at home.[18] In Arkansas, for example, the elderly getting care at home receive no more than $400 a month. In Colorado, they can get as much as $4,000. In Vermont, beneficiaries get an average of about $2,500.[19]

Why would states limit these benefits, especially since the average cost of keeping someone at home is half of what Medicaid typically pays for nursing home care?[20] One reason is what some analysts inelegantly call the woodwork effect. The fear is that if states make it too easy for people to get Medicaid home care, more families will "come out of the woodwork" to enroll their loved ones in the government program instead of struggling to provide assistance on their own, at no cost to the state. Remember, today most care is provided by unpaid friends or relatives.

Joshua Wiener, a highly respected long-term-care economist, has reviewed twenty years of research and concluded that even though it costs less to care for a typical Medicaid beneficiary at home, states can't expect to save much money overall, mostly because more people are likely to take advantage of these home-care programs.[21] But in Vermont, officials insist this concern is wildly overblown.

"The woodwork effect is a myth. It doesn't exist," says Patrick Flood, commissioner of the state's Department of Disabilities, Aging, and Independent Living. "It's a bogeyman."

Figuring out who is right isn't easy. For one thing, it is often cheaper for Medicaid to pay for people at home simply because those beneficiaries are less sick and need less care. By contrast, a nursing facility is cheaper for someone who needs round-the-clock assistance.

Home care may also be less expensive for the state because the family is bearing the expense of food, rent, and other costs. When figuring total costs, nursing home care may be surprisingly close to home care, but Medicaid officials don't worry about overall costs. They think only about the state's share.

There is no doubt that the fear of the woodwork effect is enough to keep many states from making home care more easily available under Medicaid. As a result, in 2006, more than 60 percent of Medicaid's long-term-care money was still going to institutional care.[22]

Like everything else in the world of health care, Medicaid is all about striking a balance between care and money. How can government reduce costs by keeping people out of nursing homes while not making home care too attractive, which might increase state expenses?

As heartless as it may seem, cost is a huge issue. As long as states feel their ability to raise taxes is limited, every dollar they spend on Medicaid long-term care is a dollar not available to pay for a child's health care or for public transportation.

For states, Medicaid is the most rapidly growing service they provide, and it is busting their budgets. They spend about 18 percent of their funds on the program, more than they do for any other service except for elementary and secondary education.[23] And as program costs grow, they will continue to crowd out other popular spending, lead to substantial tax increases, or both.

For Washington, Medicaid, along with Medicare and Social Security, threatens to overwhelm the federal budget. In 2005, federal and state governments combined to spend more than $305 billion on Medicaid—ten times what they spent thirty years ago.[24] The federal share alone was $182 billion, about 1.5 percent of the nation's Gross Domestic Product (the total value of all the goods and services the United States produces each year).[25] In two decades, it is expected to rise to 2.6 percent of GDP, and by 2060 it is projected to balloon to nearly 5 percent.[26] That will make it one of the nation's biggest government programs.

As a result, governors and Washington policymakers are scrambling to slow the growth of long-term-care costs. Each solution holds the promise of controlling costs, but every possible alternative also comes with risks, and unfortunately, there is little evidence that any alternative will really save money.

Helping Medicaid recipients get long-term care at home, as Vermont has done with Caroline Foye and Maryland has done for Peggy Ingles, is one solution. But as Peggy has learned, just sending an aide or a homemaker for a few hours a day is not enough.

A PEACEFUL, HAPPY ABODE

That's why some states are trying another kind of Medicaid experiment—one that holds the promise of providing much more comprehensive care for the frail elderly who are trying to age at home. It is built on the model of adult day centers, but with some important twists.

In a blue-collar neighborhood in Baltimore, on the Bayview campus of prestigious Johns Hopkins University, about seventy people come each weekday for breakfast, activities, and lunch.

At first glance it is not so different from the kind of adult day program that Walt Barrett attends. On the day of the center's annual Christmas party, I meet Fran. She is eighty-four, short and stocky, with curly gray hair, a big smile, and no teeth.

For many years, Fran lived in a basement apartment in the grimy industrial suburb of Dundalk. Her sister Rose, a dozen years younger, lived upstairs. Then Fran started getting feisty, arguing with Rose over small things, and complaining endlessly about a job she had lost years before. Eventually she was diagnosed with dementia and placed in a nursing home.

It was a disaster. Fran quickly lost the ability to feed herself and was becoming incontinent. So Rose used a few dollars she had put away and bought a mobile home so she could bring Fran back to live with her. A couple of years ago, she found out about the Hopkins day center and got Fran enrolled. Now Fran comes every Monday, Wednesday, and Friday.

But this is not an ordinary adult day center. Instead, it is a program called PACE, created to provide a full range of services for the frail elderly. (PACE is another one of those social service acronyms. This one stands for Program of All-inclusive Care for the Elderly.) Seniors get day care, but they also have access to a full-service health center staffed by Johns Hopkins doctors and nurse practitioners.

A pharmacist manages their prescription medications, and a twenty-four-hour helpline is available to answer questions from relatives. A van picks participants up each morning and brings them home each evening, and the program will pay for home renovations, so seniors can get around more safely. Once, it even arranged to treat the fleas on a participant's dog.

"It works good," says Rose. "All I need to do is say something is going on, and they take care of it."

Since Fran has been here, she has regained the ability to feed herself and can even get to the bathroom without help. I ask her how she likes it and in reply I get a big toothless smile and a hug.

Everything PACE does is aimed at accomplishing one goal, says Karen Armacost, who directs the program that Hopkins calls

ElderPlus. "The idea is to help people stay at home. We don't provide services that are listed in page after page of government coverage manuals. We just provide the care people need."

PACE's roots go back to the Chinese community in San Francisco. In 1973 a group of local organizers began an adult day center they called On Lok (Cantonese for "peaceful, happy abode"). By 1975 they'd expanded their services to include in-home care and home-delivered meals, and in 1978 they added a medical program. In the 1980s, the federal government, with the help of three large foundations, began an experimental effort to copy the On Lok model around the country.

Not only does PACE provide a rare opportunity for one-stop shopping for both medical and social services for seniors and their families, it also enjoys an unusual source of funding. The Hopkins project is jointly supported by both the Maryland Medicaid program and by federal Medicare. Medicaid pays about $2,200 per patient per month. Medicare pays an additional $3,000.[27]

Those not eligible for Medicaid can participate in PACE, but few do, since they have to pay $3,000 a month for the program, far beyond the ability of most families. At Hopkins, only three seniors private-pay for the PACE service.[28]

Fran is a typical user. Like her, most participants are women in their eighties, more than half suffer from Alzheimer's or other memory loss, and all need a level of care equal to what they would get in a nursing home. On average, participants stay in the program for three and a half years, usually until they die.[29]

People who come to PACE are happier, healthier, and live longer than frail seniors who do not have access to the program. They also stay out of hospitals and nursing homes longer.[30]

PACE is also very important because it is a rare example of Medicare and Medicaid working together. Because the low-income frail elderly often have multiple chronic illnesses, and require both medical treatment and personal assistance, they desperately need to have all of their care coordinated. Organizing their care this way can help make sure they get the treatment they need, take their medications properly, and comply with follow-up visits and tests. Still, because Medicare pays only for health care, and because Medicaid covers long-term care, this kind of cooperation almost never happens outside of a few programs such as PACE.

Indeed, the two government programs often engage in a subtle but nasty effort to shift costs to each other. Because the line between medical care and long-term care is often blurred, it is easy for the federally funded Medicare to dump costs onto Medicaid, which is supported in part by the states. At the same time, states pay consultants millions of dollars to shift as many of their costs as possible back to the federal government. The consultants get rich. Government budgets get padded. Seniors get sick.

PACE breaks down that system and provides badly needed holistic care. Yet, of 44 million Medicare beneficiaries, barely twenty-five thousand visit forty-two PACE sites in twenty-two states.[31] Why do so few use the program?

There are lots of reasons. In part, it may be because participants must agree to give up their own physicians and use PACE doctors, a step some people may be reluctant to take. In addition, those who join must also have a home and someone to take care of them, because PACE is not set up to provide twenty-four-hour assistance. Since so many frail elderly are widows without families, they have little choice but to live in some kind of group setting, and many are unable to participate in PACE.

A bigger problem is that some states, such as Maryland, strictly limit participation. Half of the people who applied to the Hopkins program were rejected by the state because they were not considered sick enough. Recently, two dozen seniors who were already enrolled were forced to leave for the same reason.

Why? Money, as usual. Because PACE is so costly, states are trying to limit users to only the frailest. This, in turn, increases financial pressures on the nonprofits that run programs, since they must spend more to assist these sicker participants. The Hopkins program, for example, was profitable for several years, but has been losing money since the state tightened its eligibility rules. In 2008, in response to a lawsuit, Maryland said it may soon once again ease some of these restrictions.

Of course, even if kicking people out of PACE saves money in the short run, it probably costs taxpayers more in the long term. Without the help of these kinds of programs, frail seniors will get sicker and, very likely, end up in a hospital emergency room and perhaps an intensive care unit. Common but preventable illnesses such as pneumonia and urinary tract infections are a fast ticket to hospitalization, costly antibiotics, and sometimes worse. Government will easily spend ten times as much for a day of care at Johns Hopkins University Hospital than for a day at the PACE center, just a few hundred yards away.

Sadly, in the constant game of cost-shifting that drives so many health-care decisions, sick seniors may still prove to be a bargain for Maryland. Why? Because at PACE, a big chunk of the bill is paid by the state, but if a senior lands in the Hopkins intensive care unit, much of the cost is picked up by federal taxpayers through Medicare.

States are also looking to control costs through the use of privately managed long-term care. For several years, governors in states such as South Carolina and Florida have been pushing young and healthy Medicaid recipients into HMO-like managed-care programs. Now they are exploring ways to do the same thing for seniors.

In these programs, private managed-care firms are paid an annual fee for both the medical and long-term-care needs of Medicaid-eligible seniors. If they can provide care for less than that fixed payment, they can keep the difference as profit. If care turns out to be more expensive, the company loses money.

The hope is that these companies will better identify and control diseases, as well as coordinate the care of seniors who may be suffering from multiple illnesses. Like PACE and even hospice, the idea is that these programs would manage the complex care of frail seniors in a more effective way than mainstream medicine does today. As a result, they would treat patients in the least costly setting without jeopardizing quality. So, for instance, coordinated care might allow a person to stay at home rather than have to go to a nursing facility, or it would help someone already in a nursing home stay out of the hospital.

So far only a handful of states, including Arizona, Florida, Massachusetts, Minnesota, and Texas, have put managed long-term-care programs in place, and only about 2 percent of beneficiaries are in such plans.[32] One study suggests that such programs may save money by substituting more intensive, but relatively lower-cost, nursing home care for higher-priced hospitalizations.[33] However, the jury is still out on whether these programs either save money overall or improve care.

States are also looking to reduce costs in more draconian ways. Some, such as Maryland, are finding ways to limit who is eligible for Medicaid long-term care. The curbs they are putting on PACE are just one example. Another is cracking down on what some critics consider widespread efforts on the part of seniors and their families to manipulate the system. Stephen Moses, an outspoken critic of Medicaid, calls the program "inheritance insurance for Baby Boomer heirs."

In 2005, Congress responded to these allegations by putting tough new restrictions on the ability of seniors to use sophisticated financial techniques to transfer assets so they can become poor enough to qualify for Medicaid.

There is no doubt that some seniors and their attorneys do use trusts and other tools to hide assets. However, the evidence is pretty strong that widespread use of these tricks is an urban myth. The reason is simple: Most people in long-term care don't have enough money to hide. Those nursing home patients who do give their money away to relatives and others rarely become poor enough to qualify for Medicaid. Of those who do, just 5 percent transferred more than $50,000. Two thirds gave away less than $5,000, and the average gift was less than $3,000, barely enough to pay for a few weeks in a nursing home.[34]

The authors of one important study, Timothy Waidmann and

Korbin Liu, figure that with even the toughest crackdown, states are not likely to recover more than 1 percent of total Medicaid spending for long-term care.[35] The Congressional Budget Office projected that the efforts of Congress to toughen the rules in 2005 would reduce Medicaid costs by less than that.[36] In one survey, more than half of the nation's state Medicaid directors reported that the changes would make an "insignificant" impact on their costs.[37]

However, budget pressures do make seniors and those with disabilities tremendously vulnerable to other cuts in state Medicaid programs. When the economy slows, as it did in 2008, Medicaid becomes a prime target for spending cuts, and those receiving long-term-care services are often among the victims. By January 2008, these vulnerable people were seeing their Medicaid assistance slashed in nearly two dozen states. Florida, for instance, was cutting payments to nursing homes, while Rhode Island was raising the fees seniors and the disabled pay for adult day programs, according to the Center on Budget and Policy Priorities.

States understand that trimming benefits here and slicing eligibility there won't solve their Medicaid problem. So they are looking to find more dramatic ways to scale back the program and reduce the taxpayer burden of long-term care. And the easiest way to do that, states believe, is to shift the cost back to families by encouraging them to buy private long-term-care insurance. If enough middle-class people could be persuaded to purchase private coverage, the states believe, this insurance could replace Medicaid as the payer of nursing home and home health costs.

It is not likely that middle-class buyers could afford policies generous enough to pay for all of their care. But when combined with the use of their own assets, their policies might be good enough to keep many off Medicaid for a few extra months.

Is private insurance the answer to the challenges of financing long-term care? Can it provide the money people need for quality care and, at the same time, reduce the financial pressures on government? There is a lot of money riding on the answer.

TEN

Long-Term-Care Insurance

Alan Dow was a prudent man, just as you would expect from a cost accountant for General Electric. Back in the early 1990s, about the time he retired, Alan carefully organized all of the family finances into three-ring binders, including detailed instructions for his wife, Beverly, for when he died.

Alan also bought generous long-term-care insurance for himself and Beverly. Their lawyer called it a "Cadillac policy." It would pay up to $167 a day for five years of nursing home care or up to a total of $334,000—an extremely generous amount back then. The premium was steep: more than $1,900 a year for each of them, but to Alan it was worth it. Besides, the insurer was GE, his longtime employer.

Alan died just six months after his retirement and never used his policy. But Beverly lived comfortably for many years in their home in Burlington, Vermont. At least at first she was relatively healthy and, thanks to Alan's careful planning, financially secure. She spent her time volunteering with the Red Cross, just as she had been doing for forty years.

After a decade, however, Beverly began to lose her memory. She still lived on her own, but was beginning to wander. Sometimes she'd get lost even in familiar places like the grocery store.

Beverly had never managed the family finances. She'd left all of that to Alan. After his death, she tried to handle the checkbook on her own, relying on the advice in Alan's three-ring binders. For a while, it looked like she was managing okay. She was not.

Like so many frail seniors, she had become adept at fooling people, pretending all was fine whenever her kids asked. It took a long time for her adult children to realize how much trouble she'd gotten into.

As Beverly's memory faded, her son Steve and his wife, Judy, finally stepped in. What they found was a financial catastrophe. Judy remembers what it was like to work through it all: "She had twenty-five years' worth of subscriptions to all kinds of magazines. She had written three thousand dollars in twenty-five-dollar checks to all these little charities. She had taken out a life insurance policy that she owed almost nine thousand dollars on, even though the cash value was going down. She had no idea how to balance a checkbook."

Sad to say, what happened to Beverly is very common. Many seniors, especially those with dementia, can't say no to solicitations and easily fall victim to scams.

"By the time we got control of her finances, almost everything was gone," Judy remembers.

At least Beverly still had her long-term-care insurance. Somehow she had continued to pay the premiums, even though they had increased from $165.03 a month to $214. Her rates went up even though GE, like most carriers, once bragged about how it would never raise premiums once a customer bought a policy. While the fine print allowed insurers to boost costs for existing policies such as Beverly's, the companies' marketing materials hinted broadly that this would never happen.

In the end, Beverly kept her policy even longer than GE did. In 2004, disappointed in its slow growth and paltry returns, GE spun off its long-term-care operation, along with its other financial services, into a new company called Genworth. It got almost $3 billion in the transaction.[1]

At first, as Beverly's health failed, her daughter-in-law Judy struggled to care for her at home. At the same time, Judy was also trying to raise two high-school-age kids, keep a full-time teaching job, maintain a career as an artist, care for her own increasingly frail parents, and find time to be Steve's wife. Finally, exhausted, she crashed, and the Dows decided to move Beverly into The Arbors, a residential care facility in Shelburne, Vermont.

The Arbors is mostly an assisted-living facility, but it also has some nursing home beds. The minimum monthly charge for assisted care is about $5,800, but costs can be much higher, depending on how much help a resident needs.

As Beverly's dementia got worse, however, the assistance she required increased dramatically. By the summer of 2007, she was practically helpless and needed almost constant aid—far more than she could get in assisted living.

Everyone realized Beverly needed to be moved to the nursing unit, but The Arbors did not have a bed available, and Steve and Judy were not willing to move Beverly to another facility. So, for four months, while the Dows waited for a room to open up, they had to hire a private-duty aide to supplement the assisted-living care she got from the staff at The Arbors.

At least, the Dows figured, Beverly's long-term-care policy would help. They were counting on it to pick up $167, or roughly 60 percent, of each day's cost. But, instead, because she was still in assisted living, Beverly's insurance paid only half the nursing home rate, or $84 a day. Even though the Dows were spending more for assisted living and the aide combined, the insurance company was paying less than if Beverly had been in the nursing home.

For months the Dows and Genworth argued over the company's

payment. Judy and Steve even hired a lawyer to sort it out. Their anger was compounded because the insurer required that Beverly be regularly reevaluated to make sure she was still frail enough to qualify for any benefits at all.

"What the hell is this," Judy says. She is seated at her kitchen table on a warm spring day surrounded by piles of letters and other insurance documents, and twisting a flat, thin strip of wood between her fingers. "You don't get better from Alzheimer's. She cannot move. She blinks her eyes and that's it. What are they trying to do to us?"

It almost seems as if Beverly's life has been reduced to those stacks of paper, which fill two boxes, one metal and one plastic. Beverly was once a mother and wife who had her joys and times of sadness. Now so much of her has become little more than grist for lawyers, claims adjusters, and nursing home administrators. Like the raw material for some sort of industrial-age long-term-care machine, all this paper goes in one end, somehow turns into money, and eventually Beverly's care comes out the other.

Now that Beverly is in the nursing unit, the insurance is paying the full $167 a day. Soon, however, the five-year policy will come to an end. Judy and Steve don't know what they'll do then.

The cost of Beverly's care is staggering. The basic daily rate at The Arbors nursing unit is $283, or almost $8,500 per month. Then there are the extras: $1 for mouthwash. $1 for a toothbrush. $127 for adult diapers. Altogether the Dows spend almost $9,000 each month.

The insurance helps make it possible for Beverly to live in a safe and comfortable facility, but the seemingly endless battles over benefits have left a bad taste in Judy's and Steve's mouths. Says Steve, "I contract to do work. I do it. I can't understand why insurance companies won't do the same thing."

In fact, Genworth's policy did what it promised Alan and Beverly more than fifteen years ago. Steve and Judy are so frustrated because the policy is not flexible enough to adjust to Beverly's actual needs, because it is too complicated to understand, and because insurance company bureaucrats are, well, bureaucrats.

Like the government's Medicaid program, long-term-care insurance struggles to keep up with the kind of care people want and need. Most newer policies are more supple, and pay for care no matter where it is received. However, like Beverly, many of those filing claims today are stuck with older policies. Those buying updated coverage won't be getting benefits for decades. And by then, who knows, technology and medical advances may make those policies obsolete, too.

Like so much else in long-term care, it wasn't supposed to be this way. For more than twenty years, insurance company executives, governors, economists, and financial advisers saw private insurance as something of a Holy Grail. It would be, they thought, a winner for everyone.

How Does Long-Term-Care Insurance Work?

When you think about long-term-care insurance, you'll face a maze of unfamiliar words and complex and difficult choices. Comparing one policy to another is even more of a challenge, because there are no standard benefits among companies.

In general, these policies pay a share of your cost of long-term care, delivered either at home or in an institution such as a nursing home. They commonly pay for nursing and personal care, homemaker services, and respite care. Some newer policies pay family members and neighbors for providing this assistance. They do not pay for medical care—just as typical health insurance policies do not pay for long-term care or personal assistance—except in very limited circumstances.

Keep in mind that long-term-care benefits are paid only if a claimant is unable to care for himself, not if he is merely frail.

Policies also limit the amount they will pay per day, and cap the length of time for which coverage is provided. Many newer policies reduce some of this complexity somewhat by offering a "pool of money" that will pay a maximum dollar amount of, for example, $300,000 over an agreed-upon period of years.

Here are some of the things to look for if you are thinking about buying:

Do You Already Have Coverage?
Probably not. Many people who have purchased Medicare Supplement insurance (also known as Medigap) think these policies cover long-term care. They do not. Some policies may pay deductibles or other co-payments for rehabilitation or limited care at home after you have been hospitalized, but they do not pay for long-term personal assistance at home, in a nursing home, or in an assisted-living facility.

Do You Need It?
The answer to this question depends on how much money you have, your health and that of your family, the financial status of your children, and your tolerance for risk. The goal for many buyers is to provide for the long-term care of one spouse while maintaining a comfortable standard of living for a healthy spouse. In general, someone with few assets or who would have to cut back on their current housing, food, or medical care in order to pay premiums should not buy long-term-care insurance. Someone who is very wealthy may be able to self-insure. For those in the middle, which is to say most of us, the answer is: It depends.

When Should You Buy?
The typical buyer is now about age sixty, but it is a balancing act. As a general rule, the younger you are when you purchase, the lower your premiums. Of course, you will also make those pay-

ments for more years. A new purchaser at sixty-five may pay a premium that is three times as big as someone who buys at forty.

Carriers also underwrite policies for medical status, so if you have certain health conditions, they may charge you higher premiums or not cover you at all. The older you are, the more likely it is that your medical history will make it harder to buy insurance. Some insurers underwrite very carefully; others are more lax. In general, the most flexible charge the highest premiums.

For most people, the best time to buy is in their fifties.

What Benefits Should You Purchase?

Insurance is always a trade-off. The more generous the benefits, the higher the premium. What should you look for?

Elimination Period. Policies normally have an elimination period of sixty to ninety days. This operates much like a health insurance deductible, although it is expressed in days rather than dollars. During this period, you, rather than the insurance company, are responsible for paying all costs. If a nursing home in your area charges $250 a day, a thirty-day elimination period means you would pay $7,500 out of pocket before you begin to receive benefits. It is possible that Medicare might pay some of this, but only under limited circumstances. The larger the elimination period, the lower your premium will be, so the rule of thumb is to buy the longest you can manage.

Daily Benefit. How much money do you want the company to pay per day? Most people get $100 to $150 a day, but you can buy as little as $50 or as much as $200 or more. It is also important to think about inflation protection. If you buy a policy at age sixty, you may not need care for twenty-five years. During that time, costs may increase sharply. Inflation protection may help your benefit keep up with prices, although you will pay higher premiums for this feature. If you can afford it, buy it.

Length of Benefit. Eighty percent of the aged will need less than five years of long-term care, and people usually buy coverage for between two and five years. Lifetime policies to protect against truly catastrophic costs used to be relatively popular. Now their cost is well beyond the means of all but the wealthiest buyers. A typical policy provides a daily benefit of $142 for nursing home care and $135 for home care. The elimination period averages about 80 days. Coverage lasts for an average of 5.4 years for nursing homes and 5.2 years for home care. Three quarters of policies also provide inflation protection, so that benefits increase over time.[2]

Covered Services. The best policies pay for both home care and nursing home care, but many will pay a lower daily benefit for those at home. Given the increasing importance of home care and the growth of alternative-care settings, such as group homes, look for a policy that provides the most flexible benefits.

How Are Benefits Paid?
Some policies reimburse you for only those expenses you incur from an approved provider. Indemnity policies will pay up to your daily limit no matter what your actual cost, but you must still receive eligible services from an approved provider. The most flexible—and most expensive—policies simply pay you cash once you are eligible for benefits. The money is yours to use as you wish.

When Can You Collect?
First, you must show you are unable to manage the routine tasks of daily life. Most plans look at your ability to bathe, eat, go to the bathroom, dress, and get up from a bed or chair without help. Normally, once you are unable to perform two of these activities of daily living (ADLs), or if you suffer from dementia or severe memory loss, the elimination period begins. Once it ends, you can start collecting benefits.

The Lost Grail

Long-term-care policies were expected to take some of the uncertainty and financial risk out of old age and help seniors get the care they needed as they became increasingly frail. Insurance was supposed to reduce both the financial and emotional stress of adult children who were caring for their parents, and, not incidentally, help leave them a little more to inherit after their mothers or fathers died. Widespread use of private insurance could reduce budget pressures on federal and state governments. And of course the policies would be a nice profit center for the insurance business itself. What could possibly go wrong?

As it happens, almost everything. With middle-of-the-road coverage for a sixty-year-old costing close to $2,000 annually, policies are too expensive for most Americans. And, buried in jargon such as *elimination period*, *maximum benefit amount*, and *premium waiver*, they are too confusing—as the Dows discovered.

To make matters worse, many people think they already have insurance or believe that Medicare will pay for their long-term care. They are almost always wrong, but that hardly matters. No one is interested in buying coverage they are convinced they already have. Or think they won't need.

Most Americans are unaware of what even a healthy retirement, to say nothing of long-term care, will cost. Nearly two out of every three workers are confident they'll have enough money for their old age, but barely one in ten say they have even $250,000 in assets, which itself is far short of what they will need to retire at age sixty-five.[3]

Others are simply unwilling to think about old age and frailty or to discuss insurance with agents or financial advisers. After all, how many of us at fifty want to spend time imagining ourselves as frail and sickly ninety-year-olds? "It is," says one veteran salesman, "the hardest sell there is. When people are young, they won't buy it. By the time they want it, they can't afford it."

As a result, fewer than seven million Americans have coverage, in striking contrast to the two hundred million who have private health insurance. While politicians give endless speeches about how America needs to provide medical care for the uninsured, the truth is that eight of every ten non-elderly already have health coverage (nearly all seniors, of course, have Medicare).[4] By contrast, even among Americans over forty-five, barely one in two hundred has long-term-care insurance. Today private insurance pays only about 7 percent of nursing home and home health-care costs, or about $14 billion.[5] Families pay almost three times that much out of pocket, until many run out of money and go on to Medicaid. They are the real uninsured.

Without profound changes, private insurance faces an ever more difficult future. Individual sales declined each year from 2003 through 2006. While group sales grew strongly in 2002 and 2003, they fell sharply in 2004, and have grown only modestly since.[6] Overall, new sales have been falling steadily since 2002, and in 2006 dropped to fewer than five hundred thousand, their lowest level in more than a decade.[7]

In the 1980s and '90s, private companies dove into the long-term-care insurance business—and many took a financial bath. Some big-name carriers, such as GE and Travelers, eventually abandoned the business entirely. Others, after vowing they'd never raise premiums for those who'd already purchased policies, found themselves boosting prices, not once, but repeatedly. Still others imposed tougher underwriting standards, and either sharply increased premiums for new buyers who were suffering from certain diseases, or refused to sell them policies at all. These changes only drove more customers away, leaving the business in deeper trouble.

The result is that more than twenty years after it hit the market, private long-term-care insurance remains a niche product—little more than asset protection for a relatively small segment of the risk-averse wealthy. However, these policies do little for millions of middle-class Americans who make too much money to qualify for Medicaid but far too little to pay the staggering long-term-care bills many will surely face.

Do I Feel Lucky?

Private insurance is failing even though, in some ways, it should be the perfect tool for financing future long-term-care costs. To understand why, it helps to think about how all insurance works. In simplest terms, it is just a way for each of us to hedge our bets in life. In exchange for our premiums, an insurance company agrees to help pay the costs of some future event—a fire, auto accident, heart surgery, or a stay in a nursing home. We all know that someone will face these expenses. We just don't know if that someone will be us. Clint Eastwood's Dirty Harry had it exactly right: "You've got to ask yourself one question: Do I feel lucky?" That uncertainty makes insurance a convenient way for everyone to share the risk by putting a little something aside, just in case.

Some customers will suffer terrible losses, but many will have none at all. The insurance company makes money by accurately calculating the odds of these adverse events, and setting its premiums so that those with few or no claims effectively pay the expenses of those with big ones. Those monthly payments, as well as earnings on the company's investments, also pay administrative costs and leave room for some profit.

The trick is to spread that risk as widely as possible. The more people who share it, the smaller the percentage of policyholders who file claims, and the lower the premiums can be for everyone. With long-term care, many will die suddenly and never use their policies. Others will live for many years in a nursing home and receive far more in benefits than they paid in premiums.

That's why long-term-care insurance makes so much sense, at least in theory. There is a known risk: One influential research study predicts that any given sixty-five-year-old has about a 70 percent chance of needing some long-term care before dying, and the odds are fifty-fifty that a senior will need it for more than a year. To think of it in dollars, 42 percent of today's sixty-five-year-olds will have no long-term-care expenses over their lifetime, but 16 percent will generate costs in excess of $100,000 and five out of every one hundred people will suffer truly catastrophic costs, incurring expenses of more than $250,000.[8]

Of course, none of us can predict our own individual fate. Will we drop dead of a heart attack at ninety after a long and healthy old age, or linger in a nursing home for a decade? So, just as we want to buy homeowner's insurance to hedge our bets against the risk of our house burning down, we should also want to protect against the (much more likely) possibility of needing long-term care.

─────────────── **WHY PEOPLE DON'T BUY** ───────────────

So why are so few people buying it?

Money, mostly. Most insurance company executives admit policies are too expensive, and the industry's own consumer surveys find that cost is by far the biggest reason people won't buy. One study reported that 83 percent of those who talked to an agent but eventually decided not to buy said that cost was a big reason they walked away.[9]

It is no surprise. While prices vary widely among carriers, the annual premium for a sixty-year-old who buys comprehensive coverage of $150 a day for five years is roughly $2,000.[10] That is for one person. If two spouses buy, of course, each must pay.

Not only are policies expensive, but they may not be a great deal for many buyers. For a midrange policy, sixty-five-year-olds will receive about eighty cents in benefits for every dollar they pay in premiums.[11] That's a bad bargain compared to health insurance policies, which pay between ninety and ninety-four cents. Why the difference? Long-term-care insurers build in higher administrative costs, including bigger commissions for their salespeople, and they include an extra cushion to protect themselves against uncertain future costs.

It also turns out that policies may be a much better deal for women than for men. Policies are not priced by sex, so a male and female of the same age and health status pay the same premium. But women, who live longer, are far more likely to receive benefits than men. The bottom line: A sixty-five-year-old man can expect to get back only 56 cents in benefits for every $1.00 in premiums he pays, while a sixty-five-year-old woman will receive $1.04, more than she put in.[12]

That's less important if a husband and wife buy their policies together, since they usually can get a couple's discount of about 30 percent. But for many single men, long-term-care insurance can be a bad deal.

Because insurance companies have been losing money, they have become increasingly reluctant to sell to the very seniors who are most likely to need insurance. That means if you suffer from a preexisting condition, such as severe arthritis or memory loss, you may not be able to buy coverage at all, or you may have to pay an exorbitant price. As many as one in four potential buyers may be denied coverage because of their health.[13]

Insurance companies quietly slice and dice their prices to account for these preexisting conditions, so a very healthy customer may pay premiums that are 15 percent lower than those at average risk. Some companies, such as Northwestern Mutual Life, are more willing to take higher-risk clients, though they will also charge higher premiums. Other carriers, such as Mass Mutual, try to keep their premiums low by carefully screening out those with health problems.

Because insurance companies don't like to reject too many customers, many won't even accept applications from those who fail to meet their health standards. Insurance agents are usually instructed to ask potential clients what are called "never" questions, such as whether the customer has been a patient in a nursing facility over the past year. If the answer to any of these queries is yes, he will be told there is no point in even applying since he will never be covered.

That's only one reason why the active long-term-care sales force for this insurance is so small. The product can be sold by banks, stockbrokers, financial planners, and insurance salesmen. However, while tens of thousands of financial advisers are licensed to sell, just a handful account for most sales. One top insurance company executive told me, "On paper, I probably have a sales force of ten thousand. In the real world, I've got maybe four hundred or five hundred really active sellers." Many agents just don't want to deal with the many complex questions they get from potential buyers.

One way companies encourage their sales force is with generous front-end commissions. Top producers may earn half of a customer's first-year premium in commission, although their payment will fall with each annual renewal. Such a compensation structure, however, can have a big downside for buyers, who may find that once-enthusiastic agents lose interest in helping clients who are generating less and less income for them each year.

Can average people afford long-term-care insurance? That is a topic of hot debate. While it is far less costly than health insurance, long-term-care coverage may still be out of reach for many, especially once people reach their sixties.

As people age, premium prices increase rapidly. The same policy that costs $2,000 a year at age sixty costs only $1,350 at fifty, but $3,400 at seventy. By age seventy-five, it will cost nearly $5,400.[14]

State insurance commissioners have set rough guidelines for who should buy long-term-care insurance, based on a person's income and total financial assets.[15] Not surprisingly, they are more affordable for younger people. According to those standards, three quarters of those thirty-five to fifty-nine can manage to pay for coverage, but that drops to only about 40 percent of sixty- to sixty-four-year-olds, and only one quarter of sixty-five- to sixty-nine-year-olds. Only 17 percent of seventy- to seventy-four-year-olds can afford to buy.[16]

But even younger buyers may struggle to pay premiums. Researchers who have looked more carefully at who can manage these policies have found relatively few have the resources to pay the premiums. They conclude that once young people meet more urgent financial demands, such as saving enough for retirement and buying health, life, and disability insurance, only one third can afford long-term coverage.[17]

FIGHTING BACK

In an effort to hold down monthly premiums, insurance companies are aggressively marketing to younger people. The effort is succeeding. In 1995 the average age of a buyer was sixty-nine. In 2005 it was sixty-one. Almost half of buyers were fifty-five to sixty-four, compared to just one out of five a decade before.[18]

While the inclusion of more generous benefits has boosted premiums by more than 50 percent since 2000, the growth in younger buyers has partially offset this trend by driving down average premium costs by as much as one third. Still, overall premium payments have grown by 14 percent in recent years.[19]

These younger buyers have their own challenges, however. It may be thirty years before a fifty-five-year-old makes a claim. During that time, premiums are likely to increase,[20] carriers may fail, and the nature of long-term care itself may change in profound but unknowable ways.

Failing companies are a particular problem. There has already been tremendous consolidation in the business, with many companies selling out. Today, just five big firms control 71 percent of the individual market, and another five hold 97 percent of the group policies.[21] But dozens of others are still playing in small niche markets.

When a company quits long-term care, it sells its policies (called its book of business) to another carrier. The buyer may be more consumer-friendly than the original seller. Or it may be a financially strapped outfit that will battle claims every step of the way. As a consumer, you are at the mercy of the fates.

Of course, a policyholder can always drop his coverage and look to another company. But if he does, he will almost certainly pay a higher premium. Why? Because the monthly price will be based on his age when he buys the new policy. Since he'll be older, he'll pay more.

One way companies are trying to attract younger buyers is to sell to groups, such as employers or professional associations. Insurers prefer to market this way because they can attract many clients at once, much as they have done for years with health insurance. However, unlike with medical policies, employers rarely pick up any premium costs for long-term-care coverage.

Underwriting standards are sometimes easier in group policies, which may use "short-form" medical reviews. While that may make them a better deal for those with preexisting conditions, those who are healthy may be better off shopping on their own. Although the group market is growing rapidly, and represented about 40 percent of new sales in 2006,[22] it is still a tiny share of overall policies.

Because they are fighting over crumbs of a very small pie, insurance companies have been aggressive in trying to outsell one another. In recent years, carriers have tried to compete by offering ever-richer benefits. They've increased daily limits, offered more flexibility for home-based care, eased claims eligibility standards, and offered generous inflation protection. Because insurance is always a trade-off between benefits and price, the result was predictable: Premiums skyrocketed.

Now that industry-wide trend is coming to a screaming halt, and companies are headed in two dramatically different directions. Some are likely to target high-end buyers with ever-more-generous benefits coupled with high premiums. Other industry executives are looking at ways to slow the increase in monthly payments. And the only way they can do that is to trim benefits. One survey of industry professionals reported that about one third felt that the best way to increase sales is to make policies more affordable.[23]

Some are already moving in this direction. One way is to provide less protection against the likely increase in nursing home and home health costs over the coming decades.

In recent years, policies have included riders that automatically raise daily benefits by 5 percent each year to protect against cost inflation. This added coverage can easily add 60 percent to premiums for a fifty-year-old and 50 percent for a sixty-five-year-old. But, especially for younger buyers, such policies can provide important protection against inevitable increases in the cost of care.

Now some carriers, led by industry behemoth John Hancock, are offering less generous inflation protection than the standard 5 percent. In an effort to hold down premiums and maintain their own financial stability, these carriers are offering policies that tie inflation protection to the consumer price index, which has averaged just 3 percent over the past twenty years.[24] This seemingly small change can reduce premium costs by 15 percent. Trouble is, actual nursing home costs increased at nearly twice that annual rate over the past two decades.[25]

The consequences of this trade-off can be profound, especially over many years. Today's $200-a-day policy covers most of a typical nursing home stay. If prices continue to rise by 5 percent each year, that same bed will cost $560 in twenty years. However, if benefits increase by just 3 percent each year, the insurance company will pay just $375. You will have to pay the difference of $185 a day.

Some insurers are also looking to save money by cutting benefits for nursing home care. Today most policies pick up all costs of a nursing facility, up to the daily maximum of, say, $150. But some industry executives are looking at paying only for the personal assistance residents receive, not for room and board. This would allow them to reduce both the daily benefit and the premiums. But it also would require families to make up the difference.

THE COLONEL

In part because policies are so complicated, buyers don't understand when, or how, they can collect on their claims. They think they'll start getting money as soon as they become frail or move into an assisted-living facility. But in truth most people will receive benefits only after they have become severely impaired and unable to do routine daily activities, such as eating or dressing, on their own. Even worse, many policies, especially older ones, impose strict rules on where a senior can live in order to collect benefits. Some will pay only for nursing home care. Others will limit payments for those living at home. Often it is the location of care, rather than a senior's needs, that drives benefits.

As a result of this widespread confusion, longtime policyholders are often left frustrated and angry at the most vulnerable period of their lives. That's what happened to the Colonel and his family.

After a long career as an Air Force officer, Leslie Bolstridge moved back to his hometown of Corinna, Maine. He had returned to care for his own father, who died soon after Leslie arrived. But after decades of traveling the world, being back home in hardscrabble central Maine felt right. So after his dad died, Leslie and his wife just stayed.

And Leslie, who is known by family and friends simply as "The Colonel," became something of an unofficial mayor of the old mill town. He was a selectman, ran the food bank, and even created a zoning department. When he retired from his days in town government, they gave him the keys to the city.

As the Colonel has aged, things have not gone so well. Since the death of his wife in 2001, Leslie has lived alone. In recent years, he has had a series of strokes, and is now suffering from dementia. Today, at eighty-eight, he needs nearly round-the-clock care.

The Colonel doesn't have much family to help him anymore. He has a sister, but she is frail and can no longer travel up from Bangor to see him. His son, Loren, oversees his care, but Loren lives in Minneapolis and is constantly traveling for his own job. The Colonel's daughter passed away a few years ago, but her husband still looks in on Leslie and takes him to doctors' appointments when he can.

Once, the Colonel had plenty of friends in Corinna, but many have died off. Others don't come around much anymore. It happens a lot with the old and frail. Perhaps because they see too much of themselves in the sick, the healthy shun those whose health is failing.

"People feel uncomfortable," says Loren. "There is an awkwardness."

It all means that Leslie, like so many frail seniors, has to pay people to take care of him. To prepare for that possibility, he has been paying premiums for a long-term-care insurance policy for the past twenty years. Unlike a lot of older plans, his does provide a fairly generous benefit for home care. In fact, it is supposed to pay $116 a day.

But there is a catch. The help must come from an approved home health agency. For a while, the Bolstridges used a certified local firm. But it was charging $16 to $18 an hour, and as the Colonel needed more care, those costs became prohibitive. So Loren found a group of local women to take care of his dad. They cook his meals, help him get around, and keep him company—all for only about $12 an hour.

It is pretty good care. Leslie seems to like his daily helpers, and certainly enjoys the attention. But because his caregivers are not licensed and approved, insurance won't pay, so the entire cost comes out of his pocket.

Here is where the story gets stranger. If Leslie goes into a nursing home, his policy would pay double the home care rate, or $232 a day. But he doesn't want to go, and probably doesn't need to. Loren has tried to persuade the insurer to pay the $116 a day for his dad's informal caregivers, whose lower rates would make those dollars go much farther. But the company has refused.

So, like so many others in long-term care, Leslie's family is faced with a bizarre choice: They can use an approved agency and get partially reimbursed by the insurance company. But because costs are so much higher, they'd still end up spending more out of pocket. They can ship Leslie off to a nursing home, where the insurance company would pay close to all of his costs. Or they can do what they are doing—use the local women, get nothing from the insurance company, but spend less of their own money.

So, for now, they are keeping him at home, and the insurance is simply going to waste. Loren, who makes his dad's decisions now, is doing all he can to keep the Colonel out of an institution, even though the only financially sensible thing for him to do would be to send him to a nursing home. That is the perverse logic of the system.

Some newer polices attempt to avoid this problem by paying benefits in cash, so you'd get, say, $150 a day to spend any way you want. Others offer what is known as indemnity coverage, which provides more flexible benefits by reimbursing all actual costs up to a daily limit. Either kind of policy might have covered the Colonel's home care or Beverly Dow's assisted-living stay. But this flexibility comes at a stiff price. Indemnity policies, for example, cost 25 percent more than standard coverage.

COMPLEXITY

Another big reason why people don't buy long-term-care insurance is that policies and even applications are so complicated. The fine print can run a dozen pages. The National Association of Insurance Commissioners publishes a helpful consumer guide. It is sixty-two pages long.

Despite some halfhearted efforts over the years, the industry has never been willing to agree on a standard policy. Life would be much simpler for buyers if they could compare basic policies among carriers. But as things stand today, they cannot.

Take, for example, elimination periods. Some companies have ninety-day deductibles. Others are one hundred days. Similarly, policies often provide respite care, where a family can get extra help while they take a much-needed break from caring for their loved ones. Some policies offer twenty-one days. Others thirty days. Says one frustrated industry executive, "Nobody cares about whether they're getting twenty-one-day or thirty-day respite when they are buying insurance. It is just another paragraph they don't read."

But each of these seemingly minor differences affects the price and makes it hard to compare policies.

The biggest difference is inflation protection. At one 2008 industry conference, top executives of three firms argued for an hour and a half over whose inflation plan was better. One offered a 5 percent annual increase in benefits. One benefit growth tied to the government's measure of inflation. The third had an entirely different idea. It had no automatic inflation increases. However, it gave customers the chance to buy extra coverage every few years at a discounted price.

"Do customers understand these differences?" I asked one company executive after we'd listened to this debate.

"Of course they don't," he replied, "I barely understand them myself."

MEDICAID AND LONG-TERM-CARE INSURANCE

To truly understand the role of private long-term-care insurance, you need to think about how it works with Medicaid.

People who are wealthy use private insurance to preserve assets for their children or others. As long as the insurance is paying, they can spend less of their own money on care and leave more to their kids. That is why long-term-care insurance can be a good estate-planning tool.

But for low- and moderate-income people, insurance is a tougher call.

On one hand, private coverage may allow them greater choices than Medicaid in the care they get. For instance, some home health agencies and nursing homes won't accept Medicaid payments at all. Other nursing facilities limit the number of Medicaid patients they will take at any one time, but will gladly accept private insurance. In addition, despite what happened to the Colonel, it is often still easier to stay at home if you have private insurance than if you are on Medicaid.

On the other hand, many experts say private insurance is not necessarily a good buy for those with moderate incomes. Two highly respected economists, Jeffrey Brown of the University of Illinois and Amy Finkelstein of the Massachusetts Institute of Technology, argue that the very fact that Medicaid exists discourages many people from buying private insurance. Here's why: Since many middle-class people will spend so much of their money on long-term care that they will end up broke and on Medicaid anyway, all private insurance does is put off the day when government picks up the tab. Thus, for many, there is little financial incentive to buy private coverage.[26]

Very few of us understand the role Medicaid plays. But we are convinced that the government will somehow pay for our long-term care. According to one survey, nearly 60 percent of those over forty-five believe that Medicare pays for a long-term stay in a nursing home. Half think Medicare Supplement (Medigap) insurance covers such care.[27] This mistaken belief that Medicare will pay may play as much of a role in consumers' unwillingness to buy private insurance as the reality of Medicaid.

Still, this Medicaid connection explains why government is so interested in private insurance. If this coverage could reduce the number of seniors who qualify for Medicaid, or delays the time when they have to enroll, it would save both Washington and the states billions of dollars. With that kind of cash at stake, it should be no surprise that government has been aggressively encouraging people to buy private insurance, dangling tax breaks, and funding a multimillion-dollar marketing campaign. To generate interest in the product, it has even started to sell private long-term-care insurance to federal employees.

THE PUBLIC-PRIVATE PARTNERSHIP

So far, few of these ambitious ideas have encouraged more new buyers. Take the tax breaks. Both the federal government and at least twenty-four states allow credits or deductions for the purchase of long-term-care insurance. In 2007 people between the ages of sixty and seventy could also deduct from their federal income tax up to $2,950 in premiums for approved long-term-care policies.[28] However, the benefit of this deduction is limited, since it can be used only if your total medical costs exceed 7.5 percent of your adjusted gross income. As an added incentive, benefits you receive through a private policy are also generally tax free.

The trouble is that these incentives may do little more than give tax breaks to people who were already going to buy private insurance. Even with these incentives, the cost of a policy is still too steep for most potential buyers. The evidence is mixed, but it is a good bet that they won't increase sales by more than 5 to 10 percent.[29]

In another major initiative, several states are taking advantage of a program called the Partnership Act. This program, which was introduced in four states in the late 1980s and then expanded in 2006, offers long-term-care insurance buyers a trade-off. If they agree to buy a Partnership long-term-care policy, they can keep a lot more of their financial nest egg and still become eligible for Medicaid.

As many as twenty-two states are planning to participate in the enhanced program.[30] However, early evidence suggests that Partnership policies are not likely to reduce state Medicaid costs very much. In the four states that started using the program in the 1980s,[31] only 218,000 policies were purchased over nearly twenty years. And one study figures that as many as 80 percent of those purchasers would have bought long-term-care policies even without the Partnership. Because the law exempts more assets for Partnership buyers, they became eligible for Medicaid sooner than if they had purchased traditional long-term-care policies. As a result, government costs for these policy holders may actually increase.[32]

Selling Partnership policies is also a challenge for insurance salesmen. Traditional long-term-care insurance has been marketed as a way to keep potential buyers off Medicaid. Agents tell prospective buyers about the downsides to the government program: limited choices in what care they get and the poor quality of some Medicaid nursing homes. With Partnership, agents must now convince well-heeled buyers that going onto Medicaid is a good idea.

Says one financial planner, "That's not what my clients want to hear. These days we market everything around consumer choice. This doesn't fit that model at all. Sure, there are some people who think they can use this to game the system, but I'm not seeing much interest."

Before they can get buyers to consider the Partnership program, or even take advantage of the tax breaks, companies first need to make potential clients aware of the risks of long-term care. That marketing has proved to be expensive and difficult. But now the insurance industry is getting some unusual help.

In 2006 the federal Department of Health and Human Services, in cooperation with the insurance industry and several states, began an effort to encourage consumers to think about long-term care and long-term-care insurance. With $3 million in taxpayer funds, the "Own Your Future" campaign includes a government Web site (the National Clearinghouse for Long-Term Care Information) and a consumer planning kit, which governors can mail to interested seniors in an effort to encourage them to buy long-term-care insurance.[33]

In another attempt to build a market for these policies, the government has even begun selling policies to its own employees. The federal Office of Personnel Management started marketing long-term-care coverage to 20 million federal workers in 2000. Although the government does not pay any premium costs, the policies—sold by a group of private companies—are considered pretty generous. Typical premiums are 46 percent lower for singles and 19 percent lower for couples than the average price of comparable products. Still, only about 5 percent of eligible employees have enrolled in the federal plan—a rate similar to that of the market as a whole.[34]

THE DEATH SPIRAL

All of these challenges could pale in contrast to a potential problem that insurance industry executives only whisper about: genetic testing. As science allows us to know more about the genetic predicates of our future health status, it threatens to destroy the current underwriting structure of long-term-care insurance.

Today researchers are aggressively working to find genetic markers for diseases such as Alzheimer's. While they have made remarkable progress, they are not there yet. However, once a test is discovered and becomes widely used, the entire business model for long-term-care insurance will be turned on its head.

If companies learn that some potential customers have a genetic marker for diseases such as Parkinson's or Alzheimer's, they will refuse to cover them, or at least raise their premiums substantially. Those most likely to need long-term care will be underwritten out of the market.

On the other hand, some states have already moved to bar insurance companies from using such information when they sell and price insurance. At first, that will give buyers the upper hand, since those who know they are predisposed to a debilitating disease will line up to buy coverage.

It won't take long for the insurance companies to figure out what is happening, however, and begin raising premiums for all buyers— the only way they'll be able to pay increasing claims and still make a profit. As those premiums increase, only those with the greatest need will buy, which will further drive up their monthly costs. In the insurance world, this phenomenon has a name. It is known as the death spiral.

There is no way to know how long it will be before these tests become widely available. Maybe five years. Maybe ten. Perhaps, somehow, they will never be used, although that seems unlikely.

At least for now, private long-term-care insurance will remain a good deal for some wealthy buyers. Certainly no one should delay purchasing while awaiting big changes in the insurance market that no one can predict. Private insurance can generate much-needed income when a senior becomes frail or disabled, is a valuable tool to preserve assets for children and grandchildren, and provides a level of security for the risk-averse.

As currently designed, however, private long-term-care insurance is too costly, too complicated, and meshes too awkwardly with Medicaid ever to be a mass-market product. Without major structural changes and a dramatic expansion in the pool of buyers so risk can be spread more broadly, it is not likely that this product will ever play more than a niche role in financing long-term care.

So, with 77 million Baby Boomers on the cusp of retirement, what will we do? How will we balance the role of government and individuals? And where will we get the money we need to pay for a hugely expensive social need?

ELEVEN

The Boomers

In the end, it will be about the Baby Boomers. It always is.

Seventy-seven million strong, incredibly influential in defining American culture, politics, and economics from the time they were teenagers, the huge post–World War II generation will soon make one last demand on society: being cared for in its old age.

Paul Simon wrote his Boomer hit "Old Friends" in 1968. At twenty-six, he was trying to imagine life at seventy. His elegiac vision—of "old men, lost in their overcoats, waiting for the sunset"[1]—may better describe eighty-five-year-olds these days. Still, legions of Simon's aging fans can, through their laser-corrected eyes, begin to see the day when they will learn for themselves what it means to be old and frail. The first wave of the "never trust any-one over thirty" generation has passed sixty.

Today, Boomers such as Cheryl Fears, Judy Dow, and Richard Foye are caregivers who confront the daily challenges of their aging parents. But they are also beginning to think, however reluctantly, about their own old age—about that time in just a few decades when it will be their turn to be cared for.

What they face is truly frightening. As their generation grays, its needs in frail old age threaten to bring an already-rickety long-term-care system to its knees, jeopardizing not only their own retirement but the standard of living of their children and grandchildren.

The Boomers will be buffeted by a demographic storm that began blowing decades ago. Their future—and that of their children—will be defined by three immutable facts: the vast numbers of those born between 1946 and 1964, their rapidly increasing life expectancy, and profound changes in the nature of families. Their generation will begin to need assistance in a nation where half of women are unmarried, a third of children are born out of wedlock, and millions of adult children live far from their parents. In such a society, who will meet the unprecedented demand for the informal, unpaid care that has been the bedrock of our long-term-care system? And if that free assistance is not available, who will pay for the care these Boomers will inevitably require?

At the rate they are going, it won't be many of the Boomers themselves who will be struggling against both profound changes in our economy and financial headwinds of their own making. Their generation has made more money than any other in history, but has spent nearly all of it. Largely abandoned by the traditional pension system that supported their parents, yet unwilling to save for their own old age, a huge chunk of the postwar generation will simply not have the economic resources to pay for both healthy retirement and ever more costly long-term care. If nothing changes, millions will have no choice but to turn to taxpayer-funded Medicaid.

On top of all of this, not only will we have to spend more as a society on aging Boomers, we will have to do so at a time when our overall economy is growing more slowly. As Boomers retire, there will be fewer young people to replace them, so the total number of Americans working will barely increase. This is critically important for our future national wealth. While the size of the workforce is not the only driver of growth, it is the most important one, and it means that over the next thirty years, the economy is likely to expand only two thirds as fast as it has over the last thirty. That means our society will have relatively less to spend on its aging population (or anything else).[2]

Painful news? For sure. But just as each of us needs to be realistic about the health of a loved one who needs assistance, we must confront society's long-term-care challenges with our eyes open. The future is not hopeless, but it is hard.

By 2030, more than 71 million Americans will be sixty-five-plus—almost twice as many as today. By mid-century, nearly 90 million will reach that age, one of every five of us. Even more important, the old-old—those most likely to need long-term care—will be the nation's fastest-growing age group. Today, fewer than 6 million Americans are eighty-five-plus, but by mid-century, 21 million will see that once-rare age. Amazingly, as a share of the population, as many of us will be eighty-five in 2050 as were sixty-five in 1930.[3] At least statistically, it is true: Eighty-five will be the new sixty-five.

As a result, more than 20 million seniors will need some long-term care by 2050, twice as many as in 2000. Six million of them will suffer severe disabilities.[4]

WHO WILL CARE FOR ME?

Not only will millions more of us be receiving care, but family care-givers themselves will be older. Despite Simon's poignant vision, few of today's fifty-year-olds see themselves sitting on a park bench at seventy, waiting for the Big Sunset. They are more likely to envision days happily golfing and cruising. After all, one great blessing for the Boomers will be the ability of many to live healthier lives well into their old age.

But in reality, for many, life at seventy won't be about either chilly park benches or sunny nineteenth holes. They won't have the time. Many will be caring for their ninety-five-year-old parents. Or working. Or both.

Even as the Boomers need help, there will be relatively fewer people to assist them. Today, for each person over eighty-five, there are more than thirty adults between the prime caregiving ages of twenty and sixty-four. By mid-century, there will be just eleven.[5]

This shortage of potential caregivers will be profoundly affected by other shifts in our society. Today most informal assistance is provided by spouses and daughters. But families are changing in ways that will make that help much harder to come by.

More than 14 percent of the postwar generation is divorced, and almost that many never married at all. As a result, more than one out of four are heading into their sixties with no spouse to assist them in old age. The problem is gravest for women: Nearly one third are unmarried.[6]

As adult children, millions of Boomers have taken on the responsibility of caring for their parents. But it is much less likely that their kids will be there for them. In part, that's simply because we have had fewer children. One in five women now in their forties has never had kids. The typical Boomer mother averaged fewer than two, compared with nearly three for her mom.[7] And perhaps most troubling, nearly four in ten children born in 2007 were delivered to unwed mothers. What are the chances that, as adults, they will care for fathers or grandfathers they barely know?

Even if they are inclined to help, it may be much more challenging for the daughters of Baby Boomers to find the time to care for their parents. A big reason is that they are more likely to be working than their mothers. As recently as the 1980s, fewer than half of married women between the ages of forty-five and sixty-four—the period when they are most likely to be asked to care for aging parents—were employed. Today, nearly two-thirds have jobs outside their homes, and experts expect the numbers of working women to continue to grow. For them, taking time to care for parents will be an even greater financial burden than it is today.

All of these changes will mean more families will have to turn to paid caregivers, such as nurses' assistants and personal care aides, to help their parents. By mid-century, the elderly and disabled will need at least twice as many direct-care workers as they have today.[8]

Demand for these aides will explode because Boomers will be aging, of course. But that isn't the only reason. Since more people are demanding care at home, their need for paid assistance will grow even faster. After all, it takes many more aides to travel from home to home, visiting one client at a time, than it takes to help dozens of patients who all live in the same nursing facility. For all of their problems, nursing homes are very efficient places to deliver personal care. Single-family homes are not.

The problem will become even more severe if the United States continues to restrict immigration. It is becoming increasingly difficult to persuade U.S.-born workers to do these jobs. Nationwide, about 20 percent of aides are foreign-born,[9] although in many cities far more care workers have immigrated from Africa, the Caribbean, the Philippines, and Central America. Continuing efforts to bar those workers from entering America will only squeeze the number of available helpers even harder and push up wages for those willing to do this difficult work.

Indeed, unless these aides are paid more and treated better, this huge workforce simply won't be there for the Boomers' old age, which will further drive up costs. Even if wages grow at the same rate they have in recent years, today's $200-a-day nursing home bed will cost $417 in just fifteen years. For a year's stay, that adds up to an almost-unimaginable $152,000.[10] But if we give these workers better pay and benefits, prices will rise even more.

The Boomers won't need just more aides. They will need tens of thousands more physicians and nurses specially trained to care for the frail elderly. As they live longer, Boomers are more likely to suffer from multiple chronic conditions such as arthritis, high blood pressure, and congestive heart failure, as well as from falls, memory loss, and malnutrition. Their need for specialized care will be compounded by the high number of medications they'll be taking. A typical eighty-five-year-old today fills more than eighteen different prescriptions each year,[11] and given advances in pharmaceuticals, the Boomers are likely to use even more. The interaction of these drugs can cause severe health issues that often go unrecognized by doctors, nurses, and pharmacists who are not well trained in geriatric medicine.

Yet even today there are far too few medical professionals who specialize in caring for the elderly. As the Boomers age, a chasm will open between their needs and those who are trained to meet them.

Today there are barely seven thousand doctors certified in geriatric medicine—for thirty-eight million seniors. As the population of sixty-five-year-olds balloons, the need for these physicians will increase four-fold or more. Yet the pipeline of newly trained specialists is nearly bone-dry. According to the prestigious Institute of Medicine, in the entire United States, only 253 doctors took one year of advanced geriatric training in 2006–2007, filling just half of the available fellowship slots. Only sixty-eight specialized in geriatric psychiatry.[12] According to one estimate, by 2030 the nation will face a shortage of twenty-eight thousand geriatric physicians.[13] One reason: They are paid roughly half of colleagues such as dermatologists.

It is much the same with nurses, who are aging faster than they can be replaced. Today two thirds of all nurses are themselves between the ages of forty-one and sixty, and by 2030, at the height of the coming age wave, many will be receiving care, not giving it.[14] Yet just three hundred newly trained nurses are being certified each year as advanced-practice geriatric RNs. Overall, the nation will face a shortage of more than eight hundred thousand RNs over the next two decades.[15]

Even if aging Boomers can find expert care, they will need somewhere to live. Staying home will be a growing challenge for them, especially for those with no family to help. There will be plenty of senior living options, of course, from group homes to new-style senior communities—for those who can afford them. But housing assistance for low- or moderate-income seniors is rapidly disappearing, yet another victim of government budget cuts. And despite the widespread distaste for nursing homes, the exploding population of the old-old will mean that as many as five million will still require care in these facilities.[16] Yet nursing home operators are dumping long-term-care beds in favor of more lucrative rehab and assisted-living facilities—a trend that will create even more challenges for the postwar generation.

TECHNOLOGY FOR THE STAR TREK GENERATION

In a future without enough health aides or family support, how will the frail Boomers get care? Not surprisingly, a cadre of engineers and entrepreneurs is looking to technology for the answer.

Technology has already had a major impact on the quality of life for seniors. Much of it is now so universal that we take it for granted. For instance, drug therapies, combined with exercise regimes, allow those who suffer from arthritis to remain independent for years. Laser surgery for eye cataracts gives people full lifetimes of sight instead of an old age of blindness.

Similarly, some simple devices make daily life infinitely easier as we age. Walkers, grab bars in showers, and those ubiquitous plastic pill dispensers have made it possible for many seniors to stay home with little or no extra help.

Because aging Boomers are such a huge potential market, major technology companies such as Intel, General Electric, and Motorola, as well as research universities from Virginia to California, are working full-speed to develop new assistive devices. Those Boomer consumers who bought Mustang convertibles in the sixties, lava lamps in the seventies, and Volvos and infant car seats in the eighties will soon be in the market for some very different products, for example:

- Remote sensors that allow one nurse to monitor the blood pressure, weight, heart rate, blood sugar, and other vital signs for dozens of patients from a single console located miles away.

- Computer- or phone-based systems that actively remind a memory-impaired senior it is time to take a pill, and that automatically dispense the correct tablet from a preloaded container.

- Devices that help people get up from a bed or chair, or measure the gait of someone unsteady on her feet.

- Robots that roll down the halls of nursing homes to deliver food and even conduct rudimentary physical exams.[17]

All these gizmos are on the market today or well along in the design stage. And they all seem somehow appropriate for the *Star Trek* generation.

Promoters hope this new technology will allow people to stay home longer or reduce costs of caring for residents in assisted-living or nursing facilities. In some cases, it may very well improve the health and safety of the frail elderly. However, it is worth remembering that rather than reducing expenses, medical technology often increases overall costs. The reason: Many more people come to rely on this costly gear.

Think about what happened when heart bypass surgery was largely replaced by angioplasty, in which clogged arteries are opened with a balloon catheter and kept clear with a tiny mesh tube. The cost of each newer procedure is half the price of the old method. But so many more people get angioplasties, which are safer and much easier to recover from, that total spending on cardiac care has increased by more than 50 percent over the past two decades.[18] It is not hard to imagine the same thing happening with those digitized pill dispensers.

Whether new technology saves money or not, caring for elderly Boomers will require massive, unprecedented dollars. By mid-century long-term care is expected to cost nearly $600 billion a year, an amount that will approach 10 percent of our total national income.[19]

CAN BOOMERS PAY FOR THEIR OWN CARE?

Who will pay for it all? Some have argued that the Boomers will be richer in old age than their parents. Many will, of course, but for most, this may be little more than wishful thinking. The demise of both traditional pensions and health insurance coverage for retirees, the likelihood that Social Security benefits will grow more slowly, higher costs for both out-of-pocket health care and Medicare premiums, and steep household debt will leave many Boomers much worse off in retirement than their parents.

The wealthiest 10 percent of Boomers hold more than 40 percent of all their generation's wealth,[20] and most of them will be fine in retirement. The same can't be said for the other 90 percent. By one measure, more than six out of every ten Boomers may find themselves unable to maintain their standard of living in retirement.[21] Even before they have to pay for long-term care.

This would be a profound turnaround in the financial well-being of retirees. Today's seniors—the Greatest Generation and the Silent Generation—are far better off than their parents. Today's elderly own homes and have steady incomes and medical insurance in retirement.

That once-stable ground is trembling under the Boomers. In large part it's because a growing share of retirement risk is shifting from employers to workers. Once, companies provided a safety net of both pension income and health insurance for their retired workers (and, often, for their spouses). Not anymore. In the high-risk, high-reward world of today's "ownership society," these burdens are falling squarely on retirees themselves. And since they are likely to be living longer, the Boomers' chances of outliving their retirement funds are growing every day.

Think, for instance, about what is happening to pensions, where steady, reliable, old-style retirement plans have given way to 401(k)s. On one hand, this trend has benefited the high-income, better-educated, and financially savvy. For example, the wealthiest 10 percent of retired couples can expect to have more than $1.2 million in 401(k) assets by the time they retire in 2040.[22]

At the same time, this trend is eroding the value of total retirement assets for many middle-class families. According to one study, the pension wealth of a typical household was 10 percent lower in 2004 than it was in 1992.[23] After the stock market collapse of 2007–2008, it is lower still.

Thirty years ago, 30 million workers participated in traditional plans, where a company invested money on behalf of its workers, who then got a regular monthly retirement check for life.[24] In the 1970s and early 1980s, more than 90 percent of all retirement contributions were made to these "defined benefit" plans.[25]

That world has been completely turned on its head. Now 90 percent of all retirement contributions are made to 401(k)-type plans.[26] Fewer than 20 million active employees participate in traditional pensions, while more than 50 million have 401(k)s, which were almost unknown three decades ago.[27] In these plans, the worker is responsible for putting money aside from each paycheck, and deciding where to invest it.

For workers who take full advantage of them, 401(k) plans can be excellent retirement savings tools. Unfortunately, too many Boomers either didn't save at all, started too late, put aside too little over the years, or invested poorly. Many withdrew cash from their accounts to pay for children's college, emergencies, or even boats or trips.[28] At the end of 2006, before the financial markets crumbled, the average worker in his fifties had a 401(k) balance of just under $150,000.[29] And even that amount can be misleading. One of every seven of these fifty-somethings had a 401(k) balance of less than $10,000, and 60 percent had less than $100,000.[30] The stock market collapse of 2008 shrunk these assets, even more.

According to the Urban Institute, by October 2008, 401(k) balances for typical fifty-somethings had plunged to below $100,000. Worse, in many parts of the country, home values plunged by nearly 20 percent in 2008, further savaging those assets that many Boomers were counting on to support their old age. For younger Boomers—those in their forties and fifties—there is still time to recover those losses. For older Boomers, as well as for many current retirees, it may be too late. All they can do to provide a somewhat more secure old age is to work longer. That way, they will not only spend less in retirement, but also have the chance to put aside some extra cash.

Sadly, however, many will face financial disaster in the last years of their working lives. They'll lose their job or suffer a major illness. Such catastrophes are surprisingly common—as many as 70 percent of us may suffer such a shock in our fifties or sixties. And the impact on savings is disastrous. If you are laid off in middle age, you will lose an average of 23 percent of your wealth, as you have to dip into savings to pay living expenses and lose your chance to put aside any additional money for retirement. If you become disabled and have to stop working, your wealth can be slashed by more than 40 percent.[31]

Then there are women such as Cheryl Fears, who sold her small business and quit working completely to help her parents, Granny and Pawpaw. As she scrambles every day with a new crisis, the last concern on Cheryl's mind is saving for her own retirement.

Even men, once largely immune from caregiving obligations, are working—and saving—less. Steve Dow, a self-employed contractor, says he's probably given up $80,000 in business over the past few years because of the time he's had to spend caring for his mom. I ask if he's been able to put anything away for retirement in recent years, and he just laughs. "You can't even think about that. When our time comes, the only thing we'll be able to do is pile in a bus and drive it over a cliff."

Not only is the Boomers' wealth—and potential income—in retirement falling short, but they are very likely to see big increases in their out-of-pocket medical costs. With health expenses growing much faster than the economy, this will be a problem for everyone. But for the Boomers, as with so much else, it will be especially acute.

Overall, a couple retiring in 2021 (that is, a husband and wife born in 1955) will have to put aside more than $280,000 just to pay out-of-pocket medical costs for the rest of their lives. A typical couple retiring a decade later (the youngest Boomers) will have to save almost $380,000.[32] A long-lived couple with very high medical costs might have to put away $1 million to pay for their health care.[33] And that's before they pay any long-term-care costs.

Several trends, nearly all bad, are conspiring to make this happen. To start, retiree health insurance, once a staple, is going the way of the gold watch and the retirement party. Except for those working for government or for a few big unionized companies, this medical coverage is rarely offered to new hires and is even being slashed for longtime workers.[34] Those retirees fortunate enough to get health insurance will pay higher premiums and out-of-pocket costs.

Medicare will still be there. However, because health-care costs are rising so fast, pressures on this program will be even more severe than on Medicaid. Indeed, Medicare's own hospital insurance trust fund already takes in less money than it spends each year.[35] Premium costs for both the Part D drug benefit and Part B hospital insurance are rising fast, and unless something unexpected happens to bring overall medical expenses under control, those monthly premiums will explode. Today drug insurance costs about $25 a month, and Part B is about $100. The Boomers will be paying lots more.

Most retirees have their Medicare premiums deducted from their monthly Social Security checks, so it is easy to see the problem: Even if Social Security benefits continue to rise with inflation, medical costs will increase significantly faster. Every year, Medicare premiums will be absorbing a greater and greater share of our Social Security checks.

By 2040, if Social Security benefits are not scaled back, a typical retiree can expect to receive about $1,335 a month in today's dollars. But they'll be paying almost $300 a month in premiums for Medicare Parts B and D—more than 22 percent of their total retirement benefit. This will put a growing financial burden on all retirees, but especially for the one in five who has no pension, 401(k), or other source of income, and who relies on Social Security for all of their income in old age.[36] For them, it means they will have to live on a bit more than $1,000 a month. Imagine $1,000 to pay for food, transportation, housing, utilities, and, of course, those out-of-pocket health costs that are not covered by Medicare.[37] And it will leave nothing at all for long-term care.

Remember, that's if promised Social Security benefits are not cut for future retirees. But they almost surely will be.

While some worry that Social Security will disappear, there is no chance that will happen. Nor will current retirees get their benefits slashed. The program has far too much political support for either step. However, for decades, Washington has been spending the money it was supposed to be putting aside to pay benefits. As a result, the government will have only enough resources to pay about two thirds of what it has promised the next generations of retirees.

Given these financial pressures, there is an excellent chance that at the very least, benefits will grow much more slowly than they have in the past. The retirement age, which is already being gradually increased to sixty-seven, may be pushed back again, and annual cost-of-living increases in benefits may be scaled back.

Economists measure the value of Social Security benefits through what they call the replacement rate, which is a fancy way of asking how much of a typical worker's current income will be picked up by the government retirement plan. In the mid-1980s, Social Security covered about half of average earnings. In recent years, it covered just 40 percent,[38] and in coming decades, it will provide barely one third, even without reductions in future benefits.

STEIN'S LAW

Now, here is the paradox. Even as the Boomers risk bankrupting themselves in retirement, they will still be getting a staggering amount of financial assistance from government. So much help, in fact, that the government risks bankrupting itself.

The amount of financial support Washington has promised the postwar generation in retirement is mind-boggling. A couple who will turn sixty-five in 2030—the last of the Boomers—can expect to get an unimaginable $1.2 million in government benefits, even if they never need Medicaid's help to pay for long-term care. After adjusting for inflation, that's nearly twice what a couple who retired at the beginning of the twenty-first century received and five times what 1960s-era retirees got.[39]

Despite popular belief, most of this growth in government assistance will come from Medicare's health benefits. Boomers will get more from Social Security, of course, in part simply because they will live longer. But Medicare is another story. For decades, overall medical costs have been growing far faster than the economy. Unless these skyrocketing expenses can somehow be brought under control, families and government will find themselves marching, arm in arm, off a financial cliff. As rapidly as the price of premiums and out-of-pocket costs rise, the government's bill will grow even faster.

The consequences for Medicare alone are enormous. In 2000 the government health program for those sixty-five and older paid a typical couple about $350,000 in benefits over their lifetimes. In 2030, even after adjusting for inflation, the program will provide that couple more than $600,000 worth of medical care.[40]

Medicaid, as we have seen, will have its own challenges. The number of frail elderly will grow as the Boomers head for very old age, and their need for government assistance will increase as they run out of money in their eighties. Unless something changes in a very big way, a massive additional burden is about to fall on taxpayers through an explosion in Medicaid costs. Today we spend about $400 billion, or 2.6 percent of our national income, on this state/federal program. By 2025 we may be spending more than 4 percent, nearly as much as Social Security, and by 2045, Medicaid will absorb 6.5 percent.[41] That is more than the nation spends today on national defense. It will be the same problem for the states, whose long-term-care costs will rise far faster than state taxes can pay for them.

In just two decades, just as the first Boomers hit their eighties, government will be spending an extraordinary one quarter of our total national income, or GDP, on those sixty-five and older. That is, 25 percent of the value of everything the nation produces each year will be spent on Social Security, Medicare, and Medicaid benefits. In modern American history, we have spent that kind of money for only one other venture: the four intense years of World War II.[42] However, when it comes to caring for our aged, we will be paying out these dollars year after year, with no end in sight.

To understand what this means, keep in mind that today we spend about 20 percent of our national income to run the entire federal government. It is what we pay for every single thing Washington does. It is also roughly what we collect in taxes each year.

If we are going to be spending 25 percent of our total economy on just three government programs, we must find some way to pay for it. Unless we make some big changes, government will face three impossible choices: It can either slash everything else it does—no more parks, roads, health care for kids, or national defense. We can saddle our children and grandchildren with massive, unsustainable debt. Or we can impose crushing taxes on them.

As terrifying as they are, these official forecasts may actually be optimistic. That's because we don't know the answer to one key, but unanswerable, question: How long will the Boomers need care in their old age? We know there is a good chance they are going to live longer than their parents. But will they also need help for more years?

Think of it this way: A woman who turns sixty-five today can expect to live to be nearly eighty-four[43] and need some care for the last three and half years of her life. A woman turning sixty-five in two decades is likely to live a year longer, to eighty-five.[44] What will that extra year be like? Will she need more assistance, or the same amount, but beginning a year later? How long will she live, in the words of Joanne Lynn, on the precipice?

The answer depends on unknowable advances in medical science, changes in the kinds of diseases that afflict us in old age, and development of those high-tech devices to help us cope with the physical challenges those illnesses create.

In recent years, the amount of disability in old age has been steadily falling, mostly because seniors have been able to better manage illnesses such as heart disease and high blood pressure.[45] All the official projections of both long-term-care and medical costs assume that decline will continue, but what if ruined knees from years of jogging cause more cases of severe arthritis, or if our current epidemic of obesity results in more heart disease and diabetes? What will happen if the very old suffer from higher rates of dementia? It turns out that even if the official predictions of disability in old age are just a bit optimistic, annual long-term-care costs could rise by another $50 billion.[46]

For most of us, the most frightening unanswerable is the future of Alzheimer's and other dementias. Sadly, as people live longer with cancers and heart disease, they are more likely to develop dementia. That's because as more of us reach our eighties, the chances of getting one of these brain-related diseases (there are more than one hundred kinds) rise rapidly. The Alzheimer's Association predicts that as many as fourteen million Boomers will eventually suffer from some form of dementia, and ten million will develop Alzheimer's, twice as many as today. By 2050 the group expects as many as one million new cases will be diagnosed each year.[47]

John Rother, the head of public policy at AARP, says the potential impact of dementia on Boomers' old age is so great that the key to our future long-term-care policy won't be better insurance or Medicaid reforms. It will be, he says, a pill to prevent or reverse Alzheimer's disease. He is not joking.

Researchers are working hard to find such a drug, but they've got a long way to go. While today's medications sometimes improve memory or speaking ability for a few months, they do nothing to slow the actual progression of the disease.

But let's say the optimists are right, and the Boomers are more active and less disabled in very old age than their parents. Even then, they and their families will still face long-term-care expenses far beyond their means.

Judy and Steve Dow's two children, Adam and Jessica, have both recently married. In a few decades, they will confront the prospect of helping Judy and Steve at a time when long-term-care costs will be far more than they can possibly afford. Richard Foye, unmarried at sixty, will have no family to care for him when, like his mother, an uncertain walk down the road and a Guinness will be the highlight of his day. If Richard, Judy, and Steve run out of money, Vermont will still have to find a way to pay the burgeoning cost of caring for them.

And Washington, scrambling to pay for long-term care even as it wrestles with Social Security and out-of-control medical costs, will still be faced with the same three grim choices: raising taxes, running up trillions of dollars more in ruinous debt, or slashing spending for everything else it does.

It is all the classic example of an economic aphorism known as Stein's Law. This rule was coined in the 1980s by Herb Stein, a top adviser to Richard Nixon, father of comedian Ben Stein, and the most trenchant economist I have ever known. Herb used to put it two ways: "If present trends can't continue, they won't," or, for variety, "If something cannot go on forever, it will stop."

The ability of the Baby Boomers and the following generations to live longer, healthier, and more productive lives than their parents and grandparents is, on the whole, a wonderful thing. But despite their fervent wishes, Boomers are not immortal. The time will come when they will confront their last months or years. And they will need help. When they do, how will our society find the financial resources necessary to get them the care that they, in their turn, will need and deserve?

It won't happen the way it does today. As Herb Stein told us, that is simply not possible. If our society is going to be ready for the old age of Judy, Steve, Richard, and seventy-seven million others like them, something very big must change.

Fortunately, the United States is not the only country struggling to answer the question of how to finance and deliver long-term care. There are lessons we can learn from other nations, some of which are far ahead of us in finding a way to pay for this assistance.

TWELVE

How the Rest of the World Does It

Imagine if Walt Barrett, Natalie Fenninger, or Granny and Pawpaw lived in Germany, instead of the United States. In many ways, of course, their lives would be the same. They'd still face physical struggles. Walt would be suffering from Parkinson's. Granny would be afflicted with dementia, and Natalie would probably still be living in a nursing home. At the same time, they would have the same loving relatives caring for them. None of that would change.

But in other ways, their lives, and those of their families, would be very different. Natalie would not have impoverished herself and ended up on the welfare-like Medicaid program. Walt's wife, May, would have a nurse helping her develop a plan to care for him, and insurance benefits to pay for home health aides or other assistance. Granny and Pawpaw's daughter Cheryl would have gotten money to help with the addition she built for them, and Granny would very likely still have an adult day program to attend.

That support—not readily available to ordinary, middle-class fam-

ilies in the United States—would come from a long-term-care insurance program, but one quite different from what we have in
America. That's because in Germany, everyone is required to buy
long-term-care insurance from either the government or a private
company. Since Germans start paying as soon as they begin working,
monthly premiums are relatively cheap. Because no one can be rejected for health or other reasons, everyone is covered. The basic insurance pays about half of a typical family's cost of long-term care.

This kind of coverage operates much like Social Security and
Medicare (but not Medicaid) in the United States. The idea is that
nearly everyone contributes to a government program that, in turn,
provides benefits to all. Over the past decade, most of Europe and
the developed countries of Asia have adopted some version of this
system for long-term care. As a result, much of the industrialized
world is years ahead of the United States in confronting the key
question of how to pay for personal assistance.

The good news, says long-term-care expert Joshua Wiener, is
that, in contrast to health care, we don't have the worst system in
the developed world. The bad news: We are no better than average
in the way we care for our disabled and aged. We are, Wiener says,
"in the middle of the pack."

While we continue to patch together a desperately out-of-date
system with the policy equivalent of bubble gum and bailing wire,
most major nations have moved on. Many long ago abandoned
welfare-like systems where only the impoverished receive financial
assistance for long-term care. And while private insurance maintains a small niche in Germany as it does here, the bedrock of financial support for the care of the elderly is built on government-run
social insurance.

In many industrialized countries, benefits are based on disability,
rather than income. So, for instance, Gordon Fredine, the former
government biologist who had steady income from a good pension,
might get the same benefits under the German system as Caroline
Foye, the impoverished widow who lives in rural Vermont.

Other countries structure payments so that the poorest get more assistance than those who are better off. In France, for instance, Caroline would get much more financial help than Gordon. But even though the Germans and other countries pay roughly the same share of their national income on long-term care as we do, public benefits are much more widely available than in the United States.[1] All families can get help with long-term care when they need it.

Still, these public systems are far from perfect. They are supported by tax dollars, often higher Social Security–type payroll taxes that are deducted from workers' paychecks. The downside to these heavier taxes is that they increase labor costs and make it tougher for workers to compete with lower-paid labor in countries such as China. Where employers pay a share of these higher taxes, they make up for it by paying lower wages, which leaves workers with less cash to spend.

Reforms have also turned out to be much more expensive than first thought, and several countries have had to scale back benefits in order to save money.

Germany, France, Japan, and others began fundamentally restructuring their long-term-care financing systems back in the 1990s. Still, not every country has been able to pull off these reforms. For instance, England, like the United States, has struggled to solve its financing problems. After years of high-level commissions and studies, it continues to rely on a welfare-based system that looks a lot like ours.

In some ways, reform has been easier for Europe and Japan than for us. That's because these nations have designed long-term care that fits with their well-established public health insurance systems. That match is by no means perfect, but it can make the marriage between health care and long-term care much smoother than in the United States. Here we struggle with a Rube Goldberg–like health system where a senior may be getting medical benefits from traditional Medicare, private Medicare Supplement Insurance (Medigap), Medicare managed care, employer-sponsored retiree health insurance, or Medicaid. Matching a long-term-care benefit to such a tangle of private and public insurance is much harder than linking it to a single, public program.

But the real reason Europe and Japan have acted more quickly is that they have had no choice. Their populations are aging faster, and they have fewer young people to provide care for the disabled and elderly.[2] Increasingly they, like us, must rely on immigrant workers to provide assistance to their parents. And finding high-quality care among poorly paid aides is a struggle almost everywhere.

What's often called the age wave in the United States will be more like a tsunami in Europe and parts of Asia. For example, in 2000 about 12.4 percent of the U.S. population was sixty-five or older. In England, it was nearly 16 percent, and in Japan it was more than 17 percent. By 2040 these age differences will become even more dramatic. About one in five Americans will be sixty-five or older. But in Japan and Europe, a stunning one out of every three people will have reached that age.[3]

In some ways, this massive demographic time bomb has already forced these countries to act. In Japan, everyone over forty participates in a government insurance plan run by local municipalities and funded by Social Security–like payroll taxes. The frail elderly get benefits in the form of direct services such as a home health aide or care in a nursing home. In France, assistance is available to everyone over sixty through cash payments that families may spend in any way they choose. There, everyone is eligible for some benefits, although they are lower for people with higher incomes.

The most interesting experiment of all may be in Germany. While their model is far from perfect, it is one that many Americans are looking to copy.

GERMANY

In 1994, Germany created a mandatory, universal long-term-care insurance system in which everyone participates. It was initially funded with a payroll tax of a bit less than 2 percent, half paid by workers and half by employers.[4] A solidly middle-class man such as Walt Barrett, who now struggles with Parkinson's and dementia at his home in Virginia, might have paid an annual premium of about $1,000 or $1,200 (or between $85 and $100 a month) during his working life.[5] To many in the United States, those contributions look a lot like a tax. To Germans, they feel more like an insurance premium.

It probably shouldn't be a surprise that Germany took the lead in long-term-care financing reform. After all, modern social insurance was invented by German chancellor Otto von Bismarck in 1881 to provide benefits for those "disabled from work by age and invalidity."[6] Although it took more than one hundred years for the Germans to include long-term care, the idea was hardly foreign to them.

Their government insurance covers about seventy million Germans. Another nine million higher-income individuals choose to buy private insurance, rather than participating in the public program. All workers, however, must have some long-term-care coverage.[7]

If they want to, Germans can buy an additional private policy that supplements the benefits they get under the basic plan. However, people with preexisting health problems can be denied such insurance or charged higher premiums, and only about 1 percent of Germans have bought extra coverage.[8]

Basic government insurance covers both home and institutional care, which is usually provided according to a plan designed by a nurse. Families may take benefits in one of three ways: they can get cash, use government-approved services, or rely on a combination of the two. The cash payments are smaller than the value of the approved services, but provide lots more flexibility.

That's why most people take the cash. Those who choose to stay at home, rather than move into a nursing facility, receive a monthly stipend that funds about half their costs. So, for example, if Walt and May Barrett lived in Germany, they could use the money to hire family members, neighbors, or professional aides to help out or pay for Walt's three days a week at the adult day center and for transportation to get there or to a doctor.

If families don't want the responsibility of managing cash payments, they may opt for an in-kind service benefit, where care is provided directly by an approved agency under contract to the insurance program. So, for instance, Natalie might still be living at a nursing home like Friends House, and insurance would be paying for part of her care.

Germans can also choose a combination of cash and services. That way, the insurance might bring in an aide for a few hours a day, but also provide money to help support a daughter who keeps an eye on her mom when the paid helper is not there.

How much money would recipients get? In Germany, someone like Walt, who needs around-the-clock care at home, would get a cash benefit of about $1,030 a month, plus an extra $725 because he has severe dementia. If the Barretts chose to hire an approved aide instead, they'd get about $2,200 worth of benefits. Natalie would get the same amount to help her pay for her nursing home care.[9]

There is one huge difference in the way Germany pays for nursing home benefits. In Germany, the payment is based only on the cost of care in a nursing home, but does not include room and board. That means that Natalie, or her family, would have to find a way to pay for those extra housing expenses each month, which may add up to one third of the regular bill. The idea is Natalie would have to pay for rent and food whether she was sick or not, so this cost is not covered by insurance.

However, the social insurance program does pay for many other benefits, including medical equipment such as wheelchairs and walkers. Walt would finally get that combination commode/wheelchair May and Michelle have been trying for months to get from Medicare.

It also pays for caregiver training and respite care, so, for instance, Cheryl Fears could hire their aide, Allen, for some extra hours while she takes an occasional break from helping Granny and Pawpaw. Benefits are available for both the aged and the disabled.

However, before receiving assistance, applicants must show a considerable need for care, similar to the level of frailty they require to get private long-term-care insurance benefits in the United States.[10]

Germany still maintains a small welfare-like program for the very poor, but has sharply reduced the number of long-term-care patients on public assistance, especially for those getting help at home.[11]

Today about 2 million Germans receive benefits under the insurance program, and about two thirds of them choose home care.[12] However, more have been going into nursing homes since the program was created—a surprise to many experts. In 1997, the first full year that institutional care was funded under the new program, about a quarter of beneficiaries chose nursing homes. By 2005, use of these facilities had grown by about 10 percent and spending was up by nearly 15 percent. Now nursing homes account for almost half the cost of the entire program.[13]

German long-term care is operated as a parallel but separate system to its public health insurance. It is governed and financed through states (called *länder* in Germany). And although it was financially stable when it started, the program is beginning to have some money problems.

Because it never linked benefits to increases in the cost of care, the insurance is paying a smaller and smaller share of a frail senior's actual expenses each year. When it began in 1995, the program was designed to pay about three quarters of costs, but by 2008 it was funding only about half. Families must pick up the rest, by either paying for services out of pocket or providing the additional care themselves.

At the same time, because premiums were frozen at 1995 prices, the insurance pool has been paying out slightly more each year in benefits than it collects in contributions.[14] Some Germans are troubled by this trend, especially as they look ahead to the rapidly growing number of elderly and to the shrinking percentage of workers who will be paying premiums.[15]

As a result, Germans have had to raise both benefits and payroll taxes. When the program began in 1995, the tax was 1.7 percent of wages, with half paid by workers and half by employers. Starting in 2005 those with no children were required to pay an additional premium of 0.25 percent, since they probably will not have a relative to take care of them and will require more paid care. In 2008 the basic premium was raised to 1.95 percent of wages. Still, according to one estimate, the contribution rate will have to nearly double by 2040 to maintain even current benefits.[16] This could be a real problem, since it would drive up the cost of labor and mean higher unemployment in a nation already plagued by joblessness.

Still, despite its problems, Germany has found a way to provide universal coverage for long-term care without huge increases in costs—at least so far. It has reduced the number of people getting public assistance, and the system remains financially viable, despite these warning signs.

Consumers seem very happy with the new system. Surveys show that 90 percent of families are satisfied, whether their loved ones are getting care at home or in a nursing facility. Like us, the Germans still struggle to maintain the quality of both institutional care and home health agencies.[17] While they have a way to go before they can deliver top-quality care, they seem to have designed a financing system that works.

JAPAN

Not every reform looks like Germany's, however. In 2000, Japan created its own social insurance system for long-term care, but instead of providing assistance for all regardless of age, Japan limits most benefits to those sixty-five and older. Those who are forty to sixty-four are covered only if they suffer from age-related diseases, such as dementia. Someone like Peggy Ingles, who suffered her serious spinal injury in her forties, would get no long-term-care benefit until she turned sixty-five.

The Japanese reformed their system in an effort to fix several problems at once. First, they wanted to reduce the burden of home care on families of the elderly. At the same time, they were looking to provide more comprehensive care by more closely linking medical treatment and personal assistance. And they were trying to control costs by tying benefits to premiums and cutting the number of hospitalized elderly.[18]

Japan faces one of the toughest population challenges of any developed nation in the world—far more difficult than the United States or even Germany. Because Japanese live many years but also have few children and allow almost no immigration, they are already battling the problem of a rapidly growing population of seniors with relatively few people to care for them. If the fuse on our demographic time bomb is lit, theirs is already blazing.

Making matters even more difficult, as more women began taking jobs outside of their homes, they started resisting their centuries-old role of caring for their mothers and mothers-in-law.[19]

Finally, Japan was struggling with a huge problem in the way it provided and paid for long-term care. For years, Japan offered free hospitalizations to the frail elderly through its national health system, but provided no long-term-care benefits outside of these institutions. Thus—no surprise—for many elderly Japanese, hospitals became the care setting of choice. They were no longer going to hospitals just to be treated for some acute injury or illness and then being discharged. Instead, they were living permanently in these facilities at great cost. It was as if someone like Caroline Foye had been admitted to the hospital after her stroke, and never left.

Before the reforms were adopted, a third of elderly Japanese patients were spending a year or more in the hospital.[20] By contrast, the average hospital stay for an American age sixty-five or older is shorter than five days.[21]

The system Japan created at the dawn of the new century is financed with a combination of both individual contributions and general tax revenues. The taxes are divided among the central government, prefectures (like U.S. states), and municipalities. The social insurance piece is financed by a combination of payroll taxes and modest monthly premiums.

Unlike Social Security in the United States, the Japanese system is designed to pay the same amount in benefits that it takes in each year. This pay-as-you-go arrangement is very different from, say, a pension plan, which accumulates income while its participants are young, builds up a big balance, and then pays it out slowly as they age over many years.

All workers aged forty to sixty-four pay a contribution of just under 1 percent of their wages, divided equally between employers and employees. In the United States, that would add up to $500 or $600 a year for someone who is comfortably middle class. This tax is in addition to their health insurance payroll tax. Those sixty-five and older also pay a monthly premium based on their income, much like Medicare Part B beneficiaries do in the United States. In Japan, the long-term-care premium averages about $30 a month and covers about 17 percent of the program's cost. Altogether, the premium and payroll tax pay for about half the program. Beneficiaries also must make a 10 percent co-payment for all services.[22]

Like the German plan, the Japanese cover both nursing facilities and home care. But unlike Germany, Japan provides only approved services, not cash benefits, so in Japan Walt would have to hire a government-certified home health agency to take care of him. He could not use cash to pay his wife, May, or a friend from church to help out.

As in Germany—and most other countries—insurance in Japan pays only for the personal care in nursing homes, not room and board. So Beverly Dow would be covered for only part of her nursing home bill and she and her family would have to make up the rest. However, they would not have had a squabble over where she was being cared for, as they did with her private policy.

The Japanese program is managed through a very complicated

system. The insurance is provided by each of Japan's 3,200 municipalities, which are allowed to set their own eligibility rules and premiums. So Walt Barrett might be paying a very different premium if he lived in Tokyo than if he were in Osaka. However, the cost of care and the amount of patient co-payments are fixed by the central government.[23]

Once someone applies for benefits, she is given a medical assessment and approved for one of six levels of care. Benefits range from around $600 to $3,500 a month. Someone like Beverly Dow, who is totally bedridden, might get the maximum $3,500, while Granny would get a lot less.[24] Patients are also assigned a case manager, who helps them build an appropriate care plan.[25] In 2003 about 3.7 million Japanese were certified as needing long-term care, and 2.7 million were actually getting benefits.[26]

As in Germany, costs have been higher than the government first expected. So in 2005 it raised fees and cut benefits. Among the changes: Families were required to pay an extra $300 a month for nursing home care, and benefits for those requiring the lowest levels of care were limited to preventative services only.[27]

Still, the system continues to face financial strains. In 2004, long-term-care insurance costs were the equivalent of $50 billion, but by 2025 they could reach $250 billion.[28] And they may be showing some symptoms of the woodwork effect that so worries U.S. economists: Instead of continuing to provide informal care, Japanese are demanding more paid help, both in homes and in nursing facilities, especially for the least seriously ill. Since the social insurance system was established, the waiting list for nursing home beds has grown dramatically.[29]

FRANCE

While Germany and Japan built their long-term-care benefits around a classic system of universal social insurance, France decided to combine public insurance with benefits based on financial need. Everyone who is frail enough gets some assistance, but it is reduced for high-income seniors. It is a bit like a mix of our Medicare and Medicaid. Instead of funding their program with contributions and payroll taxes, the French pay for theirs entirely with general tax revenues. Thus, it feels more like government assistance than insurance.

France adopted its new system, called the Allocation personalisée d'autonomie (APA)—the Personalized Independence Allowance— in 2002. It offers a monthly cash benefit that individuals may use for a wide variety of long-term-care purposes, from hiring caregivers to installing wheelchair ramps. The money may also be used to hire most family members as caregivers, although not spouses.

The APA is based on four levels of need. However, it is much tougher to get benefits than to collect on private insurance in the United States. In France, you get no payment unless you need help with at least three activities of daily living—compared with the two required by private long-term-care insurance in the United States.[30] Furthermore, benefits are available only for those age sixty and over. Peggy Ingles would be eligible under the medical standard, but she'd be too young to get any assistance.

Everyone in France who meets the minimum disability test is eligible for some benefits. However, the amount of assistance they can get declines sharply for those with higher income. For instance, someone who earns just $1,440 (€915) per month or less is eligible for monthly benefits of up to $1,680 (€1,067). By contrast, a person with the same level of medical need but a monthly income of $4,800 (€3,049) would get only $335 (€213).[31] Under this system, Granny would get a lot less assistance than, say, Caroline Foye, even though they are about equally frail.

The program is managed by regional governments. However, the central government redistributes funds to compensate for differences in resources across regions, in much the same way that Washington contributes more Medicaid funds to Mississippi than to Connecticut.[32]

When the APA was designed, the French did not know how many people would participate. Two previous attempts at reform had failed, in part because so few elderly signed up. The latest effort, however, has been a huge success. Unfortunately, as a result, government expenses have been far higher than anticipated. The expected first-year cost was $3.4 billion (€2.5 billion), but actual expenses were a shocking 50 percent higher, or $5 billion (€3.7 billion).

The French responded just like the Japanese. In 2003 the government began trimming benefits. Among the changes: Families had to wait longer before they could obtain assistance, new restrictions were placed on how the benefits may be spent, and the maximum income at which families can receive full benefits was slashed.[33]

UNITED KINGDOM

The British long-term-care system is in many ways remarkably like Medicaid in the United States. Personal long-term-care services, known as social care, are provided only to those who are relatively poor, and are coordinated by local governments (in the United States, of course, they are managed by the states). As in the United States, the British system is funded with a mix of central government grants, local taxes, and out-of-pocket co-payments by beneficiaries.[34] Overall, the UK spends $27 billion (£15.5 billion), or about 1.5 percent of its GDP, on long-term care, roughly the same as the United States. In England, about one third of paid long-term-care costs are financed privately, while the government pays the rest[35]—a split also roughly comparable to the United States.

However, England is in many ways far more generous with its public support than the United States. In 2006 someone with assets of up to $41,600 (£21,000) was eligible for government aid. In the United States you can't have more than $2,000.

In England, people who have no spouse or partner are expected to contribute all of their income, minus a small personal care allowance, to the cost of long-term care in a nursing facility. Those who are married must contribute their state pension, along with half of any personal pension.[36]

The other huge difference is that in Britain, skilled nursing care both at home and in facilities is provided at no cost to everyone through the National Health Service. Only personal care, which is excluded from the NHS, is financed separately through the long-term-care system.[37]

Still, while there is broad consensus that the system for financing long-term care in the United Kingdom does not work very well, there has been no agreement on what to do about it. So over the past ten years, Britain has produced one prestigious study after another calling for reform, but very little has been done.

In 1999 a royal commission proposed that both nursing and personal care be paid through general tax revenues, and that everyone be eligible, regardless of wealth.[38] Scotland adopted all of the recommendations, but England accepted the reform only for nursing care.

Then, in 2006, the prestigious Joseph Rowntree Foundation released a scathing report on long-term care in England. Among its blunt conclusions: "The public finds the present system incomprehensible and considers its outcomes unjust."[39] A 1999 report by the same group had reached similar conclusions and was roundly ignored. The same fate largely befell its 2006 study.

In the same year, another high-powered group, called the King's Fund, issued its own report on long-term care. This study was authored by Derek Wanless, a former chairman of the bank NatWest and an influential adviser to the government of then–Prime Minister Tony Blair. The Wanless Report, as it was known, proposed giving the frail elderly a minimum guaranteed level of care at no cost. It estimated the plan would cover about two thirds of their needs—much like the initial design of the German model. However, the proposal would have substantially increased both overall costs and government spending for long-term care. It, too, has gone nowhere.[40]

Despite calls for reform, the British have made only modest changes. Starting in 2003, local governments began providing a cash alternative to traditional in-kind service benefits. However, so far at least, less than 1 percent of those over sixty-four have taken the cash.[41] Unlike the Germans, most still prefer direct services in approved nursing homes or through certified home health agencies. To control costs, the fees charged by these providers are set by contracts with local governments, although they vary widely throughout the country.

The United Kingdom also provides an additional carer's allowance—an extra cash benefit to low-income families who provide an especially intensive level of care to loved ones.[42] Overall, the idea of expanding government support for long-term care has been the subject of heated policy debate in the United Kingdom for a decade, but there has been little action.

Despite the UK's inability to fix its long-term-care system, the rest of Europe and Japan have shown that reform is possible. True, the changes they have made have not been perfect. Costs have gone up, and the quality of care in many places still leaves much to be desired. Still, there are lessons we can learn from their experiences as we seek our own solution to the long-term-care financing mess.

THIRTEEN

Solutions

So here is the challenge: Find a way to deliver and finance the long-term care that future generations of aged and disabled need and deserve, but do it in a way that does not break the nation's fiscal bank.

To write this book, I spent more than two years studying long-term care, learning from experts in the United States, England, Germany, and Japan. I talked to academics; government officials; and owners and managers of nursing homes, assisted-living facilities, and home health agencies; as well as doctors, nurses, and aides. And I spent countless hours with the families who are living the long-term-care story. This is what I discovered: There is no easy or perfect solution. Each reform has its problems. But nearly everyone I spoke with agrees on one principle: The current system is failing. We can find better ways to deliver and pay for this critical assistance. But we must do so quickly—before the Baby Boom generation begins to reach frail old age.

It will be easier to change the way we deliver this help than to fix the way we finance it. The problem is, unless we get the money right, we'll never really do a better job of providing assistance to those with disabilities and the frail elderly. We run the risk that long-term care will become even more like our medical system, where an impenetrable tangle of inside-out financial incentives encourages poor but expensive treatment instead of good care.

How Will We Live?

How can we do a better job of providing personal assistance for the frail aged and disabled? Start with the idea of aging in place, which has become the latest mantra for both advocates of the elderly and those businesses that see billions of dollars in new opportunities dancing in their heads.

More than 80 percent of the aged and those with disabilities live at home already, so the idea is really nothing new. And for many, this choice makes both financial and emotional sense. They are most comfortable in their own house, can avoid a painfully disruptive move, and remain close to their family and friends. Especially for those who need minimal help with, say, bathing or cooking, it is far less expensive than moving to an assisted-living facility or even to an independent-living senior community. It is also what people want. And insurance, whether provided by government or private companies, needs to be flexible enough to help pay for it.

But the life of Peggy Ingles should be a lesson for all who embrace the idea of aging in place. If you are disabled or frail, living at home is hard. It requires a large and complicated support system. Daily chores that the rest of us take for granted can become overwhelming.

Peggy, who was a business owner before her horse-riding injury, is a natural problem-solver, and her mind is sharp. Yet she struggles every day with aides who don't show up on time, mail that does not get delivered, medical equipment that breaks, and van services that arrive late. Even with her dad—her ever-ready "napalm man"—and the help of the advocates at the Coordinating Center, each day for Peggy is a challenge.

The typical senior in long-term care has little of this support. She is likely to be an eighty-five-year-old widow with some dementia who will never be able to advocate for herself as Peggy does. And instead of relying on a retired father with the time and energy to battle on her behalf, this elderly widow may have only a daughter who lives a hundred miles away and is struggling to balance caring for her mom with a job and two kids.

Even with a spouse at home, it is a struggle. Just ask Edith Fredine.

Putting together a home care system—hiring aides and arranging for transportation, repairs, deliveries, medical care, and all the rest—is like running a small business. Did you remember to pick up the pills at the pharmacy? Did you pay "nanny" taxes for the home health aide? Did you call the taxi service for the ride to the adult day center? It is not easy, even if you are not eighty-five, alone, and suffering from memory loss.

Staying at home takes more than management skills, however. Even if families can afford paid aides for part of a day, there will be many hours when a spouse or adult child will be home alone with someone who may need assistance getting out of bed, eating, or going to the bathroom.

And helping takes special skills. With the frail elderly, even the simplest activities are a challenge. Moving from a bed to a chair can be the prelude to a catastrophic fall. A damp or ill-fitting bit of clothing can lead to painful, or even deadly, bedsores. Bathing a disabled senior is not like bathing an infant. And just ask May Barrett what it is like to help a husband suffering from Parkinson's and dementia get out of bed.

If Medicaid and long-term-care insurance are going to encourage the frail elderly to stay at home, we need to be sure a support system is in place to make it all work. That includes high-quality training for both paid aides and family members.

Today this is almost impossible to come by. The Schmieding

Center in Arkansas, which taught Cheryl Fears and aide Allen Wood, is a model. But Schmieding exists only because one wealthy bene-factor was willing to write a check for $20 million. If we want more facilities like it, we are going to have to find better ways to pay for them.

As obvious as it seems, home care also requires a place to live. For many disabled and frail elderly, finding appropriate, affordable hous-ing is a major struggle. Housing is the single largest expense for many seniors, and despite the recent bust, costs have exploded over the past decades even as government subsidies are drying up. In 2005 the av-erage rent payment in the United States was greater than the amount of a government disability check—which is supposed to be sufficient to cover food, transportation, and utilities as well as rent.[1] Just a small fraction of houses or apartments are wheelchair-accessible. And find-ing a place to live that is close to public transportation, a necessity for a senior who can no longer drive, is a huge challenge. Today, in most states, housing aid and Medicaid are run as entirely separate pro-grams, which rarely speak to each other. States should find ways to combine this assistance for the poor, disabled, and frail elderly.

For many, however, even a safe and secure place to live won't be enough. They are alone and no longer able to walk or drive. For them, home can be terribly lonely. Peggy has her daughter and a large circle of friends. Wally Barrett has May, Michelle, and his other children, as well as members of his church. But Edith and Gordon had only their kids, who lived many miles away. Colonel Bolstridge has only his aides and a son, who is half a continent away. For them, an oc-casional phone call or friendly visit, or especially a hug, can be as precious as gold. But so can an adult day program and transporta-tion services to get them there.

Grassroots experiments in both practical and emotional com-munity support are cropping up across the country, including government-funded NORCs; the Village experiments such as those on Beacon Hill in Boston and Capitol Hill in Washington; the intentional communities from rural Virginia to Berkeley, California; and countless informal-assistance programs run through churches, synagogues, and mosques.

Some of these ideas will work, while others will fail, but in some form the help of neighbors and friends will be essential if more of us are going to live at home, especially as families change. Three hundred years ago American communities pulled together to help their frail and disabled neighbors. It is time they do it again.

Even with all this help, many seniors will still not be able to stay at home. They will be too frail and won't have that support system. Where will they go?

For those who can afford it, assisted-living facilities or continuing-care complexes that combine independent and assisted living with nursing care on the same campus will be alternatives. But the operators of these facilities will have to change the way they think. For a long time, hotel companies and others in what is often called the hospitality industry were running senior-living facilities. Whether "active adult" communities or assisted living, the idea was to make these places as much like resorts as possible. Maybe, though, it makes more sense to make them more like homes.

Operators of small group homes such as Cedar Glen in Potomac, Maryland, have already figured this out. There, ten residents, all with dementia, live comfortably in a house in a suburban neighborhood, assisted by two nurse's aides. In many states, however, regulations discourage these homes. If they are going to expand, as they should, states will need to open the door to professionally run homes that care for eight to ten seniors who have their own rooms, but share communal dining and living areas.

And what of nursing homes—which remain the very image of long-term care in America? In one way it is easy to see the future of this care in skilled nursing facilities: Despite the coming wave of frail elderly, the percentage of the aged living in them will continue to shrink. In an environment where seniors say they'd rather die than live in one, and where operators don't think they can make money running them, we are facing something of a social and financial race to the bottom.

Saddled with outdated facilities, massive employee turnover, poor regulation, and an irrational government payment system, nursing homes for long-term care are a dying business. Mom-and-pop facilities are folding, and big chains are selling out to private investors, who are looking to cut costs and restructure these businesses to become more profitable.

With 20 percent of their beds empty at any one time, many nursing facilities survive only because of Medicaid, which is trying to cut their payments. That leaves nursing homes scrambling to fill beds with money-losing patients. Like airlines, another deeply troubled business, they are slashing costs and trimming services—but many are still running in the red. There is an old joke about a pushcart salesman who loses money on every tomato he sells, but thinks he can make it up on volume. He can't, and in the long run, neither can nursing homes.

That's why operators are converting long-term-care beds to assisted living, which are less regulated and cheaper to manage, or to more lucrative rehabilitation facilities, which are paid for mostly by Medicare and private health insurance. Some owners are even trying to get into the home health business, effectively competing with themselves for patients. The mantra among nursing home owners these days is "the continuum of care," which is another way to say they want to diversify out of their traditional long-term-care business.

In this gloomy environment the few remaining optimists include Bill Thomas and his fellow revolutionaries in the "culture change" movement. Thomas believes that no matter what we do, many frail elderly will still need intense personal and nursing care in a group facility. That's why he and others see a future for long-term care in nursing homes built around a model of smaller facilities with more personalized care. Like Thomas's Green Houses, they will be more homelike, encourage closer relationships between aides and residents, who will have as much freedom as possible to live in the way they choose.

Thomas's Green Houses and similar facilities may fill the niche for those who both need a high level of care and have the money to pay hundreds of dollars a day. But how many low-income residents can these facilities support?

Wherever people live, they are going to need the help of committed, hardworking aides who are willing to do some of the most physically and emotionally demanding work imaginable. With the increase in the number of old-old and the growing demand for home care, our need for front-line workers will skyrocket in the coming decades. It is absurd to expect someone to clean feces from a dementia patient every day for nine dollars an hour and no benefits. Like all the rest of us, good aides will work harder and better with improved training, more responsibility, and better pay. Building this huge new caregiving workforce will also require us to reopen our borders to immigrants willing to work hard in jobs that few Americans are willing to do.

We will also need more doctors, nurses, and pharmacists who are specially trained to care for the frail elderly, and this, too, will take more money and a new level of respect for the work they do.

These changes are all necessary, but alone, none of them is enough. Geriatrician Joanne Lynn argues that we need to stop thinking about care as something that comes from disconnected institutions, such as hospitals, nursing facilities, or home health agencies. Instead, she says, we should design a seamless system of both medical care and personal assistance that will follow each of us through our lives.

Her idea is that a team of medical professionals, social workers, chaplains, and others should work together to create an appropriate care plan that will evolve as our health changes. If you break a leg, you move seamlessly from the orthopedic surgeon to rehab to occupational therapy. She calls the model "bridges to health."[2] Such a structure could be especially important in our final years or months, no matter where we happen to be living.

With her rimless glasses and comforting smile, Lynn looks for all the world like everyone's favorite third-grade schoolteacher. But talking with her over pizza in a neighborhood bistro, I can't help but sense how absolutely outraged she is about the way we treat those who are ill, old, and frail.

"Why," she asks, "are we doing this so badly?"

Joanne Lynn is one of the world's most creative thinkers when it comes to a subject no one wants to think about—end-of-life care. Like Bill Thomas, she is an agitator who wants to force American society to come to grips with the needs of its chronically ill and dying.

A longtime hospice doctor who has cared for more than two thousand patients in their last days and hours of life, Lynn is a teacher, author, and passionate advocate for the proposition that those who are approaching death deserve the same high level of care as everyone else. It is not the same care, for sure, just as dying is not the same process as it once was. Not long ago, she writes, "People 'got sick and died'—all in one sentence and all in a few days or weeks." Now, she says, "Most Americans will grow old and accumulate diseases for a long time before dying. It is possible to live for years in the valley of the shadow of death."[3]

For instance, imagine a woman with cancer. Typically, she can expect to live relatively well for a long time until she begins to fail rapidly and dies. Lynn would give her top-quality medical treatment while she is stable, then transition to hospice care as she declines.

By contrast, an aging patient who is gradually becoming frail and perhaps suffering from dementia would get very different care. His family might be trained to provide personal assistance, or he might receive the help of paid aides or even nursing home care, all geared to helping him live his remaining days as comfortably as possible. When a fall or pneumonia eventually pushes him off what Lynn calls the precipice, he'd be cared for according to a prearranged end-of-life plan.

Lynn believes that a standard set of medical and social services can be designed for each of these people, in what she calls mass customization. Some tailoring would be needed for specific patients, of course, but for the most part, the road map for everyone with dementia will be similar. Team members, whether they are doctors, pharmacists, or social workers, would step in and out as needed, but care would be consistent and reliable. Standardization would allow professionals to develop best practices to ensure the highest-quality care.

Doing all this would require profound changes in the way we think about the last years of life. But Lynn's idea of fully coordinated health care for the chronically ill, integrated with social work, personal assistance, and spiritual care, isn't exactly new. In fact, it follows, in many ways, the hospice model Lynn knows so well.

But here is the difference: Lynn insists you shouldn't have to be actively dying to get high-quality coordinated care. It ought to be available to everyone throughout their lives.

There are, in truth, other models out there—modest programs aimed at Lynn's big goal. One small step in that direction is the idea of a medical home where all of the complexities of a patient's treatment are coordinated by a family practice doctor (who, not incidentally, is paid a little extra for the work). Another is the PACE program, where home care needs are linked with adult day programs, other social services, and medical care. These should be expanded and copied. Government should encourage participation and stop throwing up roadblocks.

Hospice can both save money and make for happier patients and their families, especially for those who participate for months, rather than days. Done right, there is at least some evidence that these smaller programs might achieve some of the same results. But Lynn is correct. It may be time we try this on a much bigger stage.

How Will We Pay?

Whether we adopt Lynn's vision or attack the challenges of delivering long-term care piecemeal, we still need a steady source of revenue to pay for our growing demand for this assistance. And over the long run, our existing system of Medicaid for most and private insurance for a few is not sustainable. So how will we pay?

First, remember how we finance long-term care today: Roughly half is provided for "free," informally by family and friends. Half of paid care is funded by Medicaid, the government health care program for the poor, while the medical costs for the frail elderly and some disabled are paid by Medicare. Less than 10 percent of paid long-term care is funded by private insurance. Most of the rest comes straight out of the pockets of the aged and disabled and their families. Altogether, we pay more than $200 billion annually for long-term care.

You remember the sad state of Medicaid. It is busting the budgets of states, governed by an unintelligible hodgepodge of rules and regulations, and leaves impoverished seniors at the mercy of arbitrary program cuts. Because its funding is divided between the states and the feds, governors spend millions of dollars a year on consultants who shift as many costs as possible to Medicare, which is all Washington's responsibility. Worst of all, since many frail elderly get their long-term care from Medicaid but their health care, including drugs and medical equipment such as wheelchairs, from Medicare, it is almost impossible to coordinate their care. It is even harder to imagine two separate payment systems supporting the sort of holistic system Joanne Lynn embraces.

Then there is private long-term-care insurance. Too expensive, too complicated, unavailable to those who are already ill, and a poor value for many potential buyers (even though it makes sense for some), this insurance is on financial life support. Fewer policies were sold in 2006 than a decade earlier, and companies are raising premiums for older policies as well as new ones. A handful of federal initiatives, from marketing campaigns to tax breaks, have done little to build a market. The only way this product can ever become attractive and affordable is for tens of millions more people to buy it, thus spreading the risk more broadly and reducing premiums.

SOLUTIONS   241

Most troublesome of all, if genetic testing makes it possible for
either insurers or their customers to know who is at higher risk of
developing diseases such as Alzheimer's, the business model for
private voluntary insurance will collapse.

In theory, Americans could pay out of their pockets for care,
without the need for either insurance or government help, except
that they are notoriously poor savers. Millions have no hope of having
enough money to support themselves in healthy old age, much less
handling the staggering costs of long-term care. Besides, needing
such care is the sort of risk that ought to be covered by insurance.

So what to do? A good place to start is to get Medicaid out of
the long-term-care business. The next step is to fundamentally
change the nature of long-term-care insurance. One way to do both
is to make insurance mandatory. In effect, we would force people to
save for the care they need in old age by requiring them to buy insurance when they are young.

Mandatory insurance may sound positively un-American, but we
require people to buy it for many other purposes. You can't drive without auto insurance. You can't have a mortgage without homeowner's
insurance. You pay taxes all your working life to help fund Social Security and Medicare, a transaction akin to mandatory insurance.

What would this coverage look like? There are two basic versions. One, which is pure social insurance, would mimic the way the
Germans finance long-term care. Every worker would pay a premium that would look a lot like the Social Security and Medicare
payroll tax. In return, they would get government-sponsored long-
term-care insurance for life.

Two plans already follow this model. One, proposed by the American Association of Homes and Services for the Aging (AAHSA), a
trade group representing nonprofit long-term-care providers, would
cover about $75 a day (the benefit would rise each year with infla-
tion.)[4] A similar proposal by Senator Edward M. Kennedy (D-Mass.),
called the Class Act, would cover $50 or $100 a day for life, depending on how much care you need.[5]

In one version of these proposals, people would be encouraged to enroll as soon as they join the workforce, but could choose to go without. An alternative would require coverage, or penalize those who wait by making them pay higher premiums when they finally enroll. With optional insurance, twenty-somethings, who often don't even buy health policies, are unlikely to purchase long-term-care coverage. After all, they probably won't need care for sixty years, and they'd rather spend their money on iPods or designer coffee. Unfortunately, when fewer people participate, especially those least likely to need insurance, premiums for everyone else are bound to go up.

Because the Kennedy and AAHSA plans offer fairly modest benefits ($75 a day would cover about four hours of home care, but barely one third of the daily nursing home rate), you could buy additional insurance from private companies to cover extra costs. Alternatively, you might be able to use home equity to fill in any gaps. More about that in a bit.

There are a few problems with public insurance. To start, it would generate hundreds of billions of dollars in annual premiums that would not be paid out for decades. But what would happen to the money in the meantime? With private insurance, premium payments are invested until they are eventually paid in claims. But the government has a long track record of spending money on bridges to nowhere, wars, or tax cuts rather than saving for future needs. That's why it runs chronic deficits. Sadly, there is little reason to believe the same thing would not happen to those billions of dollars in long-term-care insurance premiums the government would collect each year.

The Germans solved this problem with a quasi-private agency that acts much like an insurance company. It collects the premiums, invests the money, and pays out benefits years later. Unfortunately, since we have nothing like that in the United States, we'd have to invent such an entity.

The other problem is political. While the Germans consider

their regular payments to be a contribution or a premium, to Americans they would look a lot like a tax. What else would most of us call a mandatory payment to the government? And Americans, of course, hate taxes.

So there is another option. Instead of buying insurance directly from the government, you could purchase from private, authorized companies. The government would be sure these carriers are financially secure and that their policies provide standard, minimum benefits, so it would be easy to compare one insurance plan with another.

This model also exists already. Medicare Supplement Insurance (also called Medigap) works this way. So does the Medicare Part D drug benefit. They are not mandatory, but most people buy these standardized, government-approved private policies. This is also the way federal employees purchase their own medical insurance.

Now, these plans are not perfect, either. Administrative costs for private plans would probably be much higher than they are for government coverage. It is true for health insurance, in which the costs for private plans are nearly 20 percent greater than they are for regular Medicare. That's not a surprise, since private companies have to build in marketing costs, executive salaries, other overhead, and some margin of profit. On the other hand, Americans might feel better about paying mandatory premiums to a private company than paying a tax to the government.

In truth, it doesn't make a lot of difference. Either way we all would have coverage, and because everyone would buy at an early age, premiums would be relatively low. Neither the government plan nor the private policies would be allowed to reject anyone based on health, so no one would be left out. In either system, low-income people would get subsidies to help them buy coverage.

Another benefit: Since all would have insurance, relatively few would require government assistance. In addition, because middle-class and wealthy participants would be paying market rates for their premiums, overall government costs for long-term care should decline—an important advantage at a time of severe fiscal stress on both the states and Washington. Even with a premium subsidy for low-income people, providing long-term care should cost the government far less than the $100 billion annually it pays today. An analysis done for AAHSA estimates that its plan would cut Medicaid long-term costs in half.[6]

The welfare-based Medicaid system we have today would largely disappear. Most important, everyone who could afford it would pay their share of long-term-care costs, and we'd all be far better prepared for old age than we are now.

This new structure would permit some other big changes. Families could receive benefits in cash, an option now available only on a limited basis through Medicaid and private insurance. Cash benefits are expensive; they add at least 30 percent to the cost of private insurance today. But cash would give the frail elderly and their caregivers plenty of flexibility in how they structure assistance. They could use the money to build a wheelchair ramp or hire their niece to help them. Remember how the Barretts could not get a combination wheelchair/commode for Walt because Medicare would not pay? That would no longer be a problem.

There is still one big hole in these plans. To keep overall costs down, the Kennedy and AAHSA plans provide relatively skinny lifetime benefits. But $75 a day won't go very far when a nursing home costs more than $200. It certainly would not pay for the kind of coordinated care that Joanne Lynn has in mind. To help with those extra costs, people could always buy additional private insurance. However, if they did, they would also have to pay extra monthly premiums.

But there is another approach. Imagine you were responsible for paying the first part of your long-term care, but knew the government was there to pick up catastrophic costs—either really large daily bills or care that lasts for many years. There are several possible versions of this: You might have to pay out of pocket for all expenses for the first three years, and pick up room and board costs in a nursing home after that (remember, in Europe, families are expected to pay these costs).[7] You might be required to pay the first, say,

$100,000 out of pocket, with Medicare picking up the rest.[8] Or you might be required to buy a private long-term-care policy that paid up to, say, $150 a day for five years. In that plan—one version has been proposed by William Galston of the Brookings Institution—anyone who needed care for longer (about one in five of those sixty-five or older) would get full government catastrophic coverage.[9]

What would all this cost?

Premiums for the Kennedy plan would be less than $100 a month, with enrollment starting at age eighteen.

The AAHSA plan would also cost about $100 a month, if enrollment were mandatory starting at age twenty-one. If younger workers were allowed to opt out, the cost for those who did participate would go up. Both benefits and premiums would rise with inflation each year.

Premium costs would not be much different for $75-a-day coverage for five years—about $90 a month. However, buying a $150-a-day cash benefit for five years starting at age forty would be extremely expensive, with a monthly premium of $230.[10]

When thinking about long-term care, it is hard to ignore the biggest asset many Americans have: their home. While many frail elderly have no house, millions of seniors have substantial equity locked up in their residences despite the housing market collapse of 2007–2008.

Today there are only two ways they can tap into that money. They can sell their home or take out a reverse mortgage. As we've seen, these loans are very expensive and loaded with high fees.

But what if the government worked out a deal with seniors? What if it agreed to pick up an extra share of their long-term-care costs, without requiring them to buy a supplemental insurance policy? In return, once both spouses died, the government would be paid back with the proceeds from the sale of their home. In this system, seniors might not be able to leave their home to their kids, but they'd get the care they needed without having to pay additional insurance premiums or the big up-front fees that go with private reverse mortgages.[11] For many, this home equity trade might be an affordable supplement to a modest mandatory insurance policy, such as Senator Kennedy has proposed.

There is one more downside to all of these ideas. Once long-term-care providers knew they'd have a steady stream of revenue from mandatory insurance, they might raise prices—a lot. That's what happened when Medicare first provided near-universal health care for the aged, and it could happen again.[12] Today, Medicaid negotiates prices with nursing homes and home health agencies, but it would be largely out of the long-term-care business in the future. The new government plan, or the private carriers, might also try to negotiate prices, perhaps by creating the same kinds of networks health insurers use today for doctors and hospitals. But for now, at least, such low-cost networks are extremely rare for long-term care.

Still, while none of these plans is perfect, and making all the pieces fit will be a challenge, each of them is better than what we are doing today. The upcoming debate on health-care reform is a perfect opportunity for lawmakers to confront long-term care as well. But they will need a push.

THE PERFECT AND THE GOOD

The eighteenth-century French philosopher Voltaire warned that "the perfect is the enemy of the good."[13] He was not thinking about long-term care. But his warning fits, nonetheless. In their zeal to find the perfect solution, long-term-care experts have been unable to come together on ways to improve the unsustainable mess we have today. Neither have long-term-care industry lobbyists, who are often driven by a self-serving search for the most profitable solution for their individual companies. Even advocates for the elderly and disabled have failed to agree among themselves on what to do. And politicians, terrified by the potential costs, baffled by the complexities, and unwilling to wade into these internecine wars, simply ignore the issue.

Individual families are terrible advocates for the long-term-care cause, in large part because they are so overwhelmed by their roles as caregivers that they have little time to lobby their representatives. And once their loved one dies, the last thing most want to do is re-live their ordeal for some politician. All they want to do is get back to their lives.

But the Baby Boomers won't sit quietly for much longer. They are used to getting what they want, and soon they will begin to tell their elected officials that what they want is a way to care for their parents and themselves without facing financial ruin. And the politi-cians better be ready with an answer. To learn why, let me tell you one last story.

FOURTEEN

Dorothy

Dorothy Stevenson's life got so much worse after she died.

Dorothy was eighty-three. Only ten months before, she buried Herbert, her husband of six decades. She laid him to rest in the old Lakeview Cemetery, just up the maple-covered hill from their beloved house on the shore of New Hampshire's Lake Winnipesaukee. You can see the lake from up there, especially when the leaves are gone.

After spending three years caring for Herbert, whose mind and body were gradually ravaged by dementia, the always-practical, no-nonsense Dorothy ordered the lawyers to write her up a living will. That document said no extreme measures should be taken to keep her alive should she suffer a life-threatening illness or injury.

It was very like her. Dorothy had always been in control. She ran the house. In the antiques business she and Herbert shared for four decades, Dorothy was boss. "Mother was the closer," remembers Stephanie, their only child.

Very much her mother's daughter, Stephanie pulls out a black-and-white photo from a family album. Dorothy and Herbert are standing in front of the Taj Mahal, each perhaps in their sixties. "What is he holding?" Stephanie asks. It isn't hard to miss. In his right hand, Herbert is clutching Dorothy's large, dark handbag. He is not self-conscious at all. It wasn't the first time. "That's the way it was," Stephanie recalls. Dorothy was in charge.

So it was no surprise that Dorothy was going to do everything she could to make sure she would not die the way Herbert had, slowly fading away, month after month, year after year. No heroic measures for her. She'd be in charge.

Dorothy didn't mind being cared for, mind you. She liked it, really. Herbert, after all, had always brought her breakfast in bed, even when he was sick. But she would not be helpless. That was different. Of all things, Dorothy was not going to spend her last days dependent, incontinent, and suffering.

Except she did. Not the first time, of course. The first time Dorothy died was on a lovely midsummer afternoon, just a few days after the plumber found her unconscious in the house by the lake.

He called the emergency rescue people, who took her to the hospital just down the road. Dorothy was suffering from an unusual heart ailment with the oddly benign name of sick sinus syndrome. But this disease isn't about the occasional runny nose. It causes an irregular heart rhythm that interrupts the flow of blood to the brain, which sometimes causes brain damage.

For a couple of days after her collapse, Dorothy seemed to be doing better. But then, in the afternoon, in a hospital bed, with her doctor sitting right there by her side, Dorothy Stevenson's heart stopped. She was quietly slipping away, just as she wanted.

But with modern American medicine being what it is, Dorothy did not die for long. Despite her living will and her request not to be revived if her heart stopped, she was brought back to life. Then her heart stopped again. And she was revived again. And her heart stopped for a third time. And for a third time, the doctors and nurses brought out the high-voltage paddles, attached them to her chest, and shocked her heart back into its proper rhythm. Then, for good measure, they wheeled her into an operating room and installed a pacemaker.

You could say that the hardworking medical team restored Dorothy to life.

But maybe it is better to just say they got her heart working again—because the new life they gave her was nothing like the one she'd had just days before. Maybe it was the heart disease. Maybe it was the effect of those repeated cardiac arrests on an eighty-three-year-old. But, Stephanie remembers, "It was like her hard drive had been wiped clean. She never regained her short-term memory. Her long-term memory came and went."

Like ten million elderly and disabled Americans, Dorothy Stevenson would never again live independently. For nearly a decade, she was moved from hospitals to assisted living facilities to nursing homes. Sometimes she got good care. And sometimes she was treated like an abused animal. Stephanie remembers the day she walked into one of Dorothy's nursing homes to see a nurse struggling to move her from a wheelchair to her bed: "She is screaming at my mother, 'You get into that bed or I'm going to drop you on the floor.'"

In the end, Dorothy lived out her final three years in a nursing facility in Frederick, Maryland, not far from Stephanie, her husband, Tom, and their teenage son, Eric. It was a nice enough place. They seemed to care about this woman who could barely move, could not speak or feed herself, and who, as the days dragged on, recognized no one.

It all took a terrible toll on Stephanie, an only child, who managed her mother's care mostly by herself. After a time, Tom could not bring himself to visit Dorothy. At first, Eric came to visit on school breaks, but not during those final three years.

Stephanie came every week. Truth be told, she did it for a woman she'd never gotten along with very well. "We were never close," Stephanie remembers. "She was very controlling."

Still, even in those last years, when Dorothy's mind slowly emptied of everything familiar, Stephanie came. There wasn't much to say. There was nothing to say, really. But Stephanie came. And sat or, on nice days, wheeled Dorothy outside. And met regularly with the nursing home staff to be sure her mother was getting the best possible care.

And she wrote checks. A typical month cost $6,500, but that was just to start. There were the extras, such as medications and diapers, and transportation if Dorothy needed to see a specialist. A few times a year she'd even go to a dentist. All told, those added costs often ran another $1,000 each month. "Mother was running through money like you wouldn't believe," Stephanie remembers.

By the time Dorothy died the last time—unaware of her surroundings, no longer able to recognize her own daughter—she had run through her lifetime of savings, and more. The cost of all that care: $800,000.

Over the years, Dorothy and Herbert had made a nice living buying and selling antiques. At first they had a shop on Rivington Street, in New York City's Lower Manhattan. That neighborhood has gone trendy now, but in the years after World War II, it was a busy working-class section of town. Later they moved the shop to Scotch Plains, New Jersey. Herbert was the buyer. "He was good with the little old ladies," Stephanie remembers. Dorothy sold. Business was pretty good. "We were not rich," remembers Stephanie, "but we were not poor, either."

Dorothy and Herbert loved to travel, first on buying trips and later, after they retired, just for the enjoyment of it. They lived in the old colonial town of Westfield, New Jersey, but their hearts were elsewhere. For many summers they vacationed at the lovely lake in central New Hampshire, and dreamed of the day they could build their own home and retire there.

Finally, in 1972, they built the beautiful shingle house that sat on the edge of a quiet cove. They filled it with favorite antiques collected over a half-century.

But after her mother's savings were gone, Stephanie sold that beloved house on the shore of Lake Winnipesaukee and all its contents to help pay for the nursing homes. They asked $1.2 million for the house, but in the end got half that much. "We had to get rid of it," Stephanie remembers. "There was one offer. We took it. We needed the money. I didn't have any choice."

She got another $50,000 for her mother's jewelry and the furniture. But soon that was gone too. Then, her husband, Tom, took $130,000 out of his own retirement savings.

Even after all that, before it was all over, Dorothy—proud, self-reliant Dorothy—ended up on Medicaid. For the last eighteen months or so, the government paid for her nursing care.

Like Dorothy, Americans like to think of themselves as strong and self-reliant. Government assistance is for the lazy. It is not for us. Except that when it comes to long-term care, it is for us.

Sitting with Stephanie, listening to this story, you get a sense of just how great her family's pain was. It was losing her parents, of course. Becoming an orphan, even in middle age, is a hard thing. But there was something else. There was the house on that beautiful little cove.

With the balm of time, Stephanie tells her brutal story in a measured, detached way.

It is October. The roads are quiet. The trees are still full of the red and gold that are the primary colors of a northern New England autumn. But on this day, the colors are muted. The maples—and the mobs of leaf-peeping tourists who come to gawk—are perhaps a week past. And it is a gray day, more November than mid-October.

The weather is changing. There is a rumor of the year's first snow in the White Mountains, just a few miles to the north. It is cloudy and still, and fog is lying over the lake. A white-hulled sailboat rides silently at anchor, and a small, pine-covered island sits perhaps one hundred yards beyond. It is perfect, except for a house, just barely in view.

In the New England quiet, Stephanie, a solid, no-nonsense

woman of middle age, talks about her mother and father and how their collapsing health and ultimate deaths consumed her life for thirteen years. She talks about how old age took their minds, then their bodies. She talks about how it took their bank accounts, their stocks, and finally that house and its lifetime of furnishings.

We are sitting in Stephanie's and Tom's own comfortable summer house, just a few hundred feet from her parents' old home. But Stephanie can't get her mind off the gray shingled house beyond the trees, just off to the right, along a narrow curving sand beach. Standing in her kitchen, you can just see glimpses of it through the last October leaves.

She doesn't get along well with the couple who bought it. And there is something in her voice. Not anger, exactly. Not bitterness, either. It is a hint of how unfair it all was.

Stephanie says she usually cries at the drop of a hat, but there are no tears as she tells this story about how so many years of her life, and so much else, were lost. "It was part of my life. It was just something, you know, that I did."

In the coming decades, it is something that millions of us are going to have to do, this taking care of our parents. And we are not ready.

The United States is quietly heading for a financial, medical, and social meltdown. Unless you are like Stephanie, who has already lived this story, it is hard to imagine what is about to happen, not just to millions of individual families, but to our nation. It will profoundly change tens of millions of lives, ruin carefully planned retirements, and profoundly alter the way we think of our government.

When I think about Dorothy and all the others, there is a biblical passage I cannot get out of my mind.

The book of Deuteronomy nears its end with a succession of curses aimed at those who do not heed the word of God. They are what translator Robert Alter calls "a catalogue of bloodcurdling catastrophes." And there, among the madness and blindness, and burning rashes and rotting carcasses, is this:˙ Your society will be destroyed by a "fierce-faced nation that will show no favorable face to an old man."[1]

If we, in fact, turn our backs on the old men and women among us, that nation will be ours. That curse we suffer will be one of our own making.

Afterword

After my dad's death, my mother stayed alone in their Florida apartment for nearly two years. But as more of her friends died or became increasingly frail, Marilyn decided to move to a retirement community about ten minutes from Ann and me. She enjoyed her time there immensely, and we cherished our opportunity to be with her. But just after Thanksgiving 2000—only a year after she came to Maryland—Marilyn developed shortness of breath.

Undetected ovarian cancer had spread to her lungs. She was hospitalized in early December and, on the morning of December 29, 2000, just as we were arranging to bring her home, my mother died.

Walter Barrett is still living at home, and his wife, May, remains his primary caregiver. In June 2008, just a month after his ninetieth birthday, May enrolled Walt in hospice. She also decided to hire a private-duty aide who helps Walt get up each morning and get to bed in the evenings.

For about nine months after Gordon Fredine died, his wife, Edith, remained in the house they had shared for so many years. But she was growing noticeably more frail and said she was having trouble remembering things. So, in the spring of 2007, Edith moved to a senior housing community in Austin, Texas, where she could be close to her son, Jack. The year 2008 was tough, however. First, an untreated abrasion on her shin developed into a painful open sore. Then, in September, Edith fell and fractured her pelvis. She is still living in her apartment, but needs a round-the-clock aide. Jack is thankful that Edith moved to Texas before these incidents. If she had remained in Bethesda, he figures, "it would have been a nightmare."

Beverly Dow can no longer speak or move. Steve Dow serves on a resident family council that advises The Arbors on patient concerns. Steve and Judy worry about what will happen when Beverly's long-term-care insurance runs out. Meanwhile, Judy struggles to care for her own parents, who remain in their own home.

Colonel Bolstridge continues to live in Corinna, Maine, with the help of his local aides. He is still not being reimbursed by his long-term-care insurance policy.

Granny and Pawpaw are living with their daughter Cheryl Fears and her family. While Allen Wood continues to help out as their weekend aide, Cheryl is scrambling to find additional assistance. No new adult day program has yet opened in Springdale, so, for now, Granny and Pawpaw are home nearly all the time.

In the spring of 2008, Cheryl thought she'd found a solution. She discovered a program run by the Veterans Administration that provided an additional twenty hours of home care for her mom and dad, who is an Army vet. But after a few months, the aide suddenly stopped coming. Cheryl would like to use Allen for the extra twenty hours, but she would have to hire him through a designated agency that pays only $9 an hour. So for now, Cheryl, who fell and broke her own kneecap in the summer of 2008, is trying to handle it all herself. "Some days," she says, "I'm at a loss."

Caroline Foye broke her leg in August of 2007. Soon after, the state agreed to increase her companion Ayars Hemphill's hours to six each day, but it was not nearly enough. Caroline was growing increasingly anxious and lonely living at home, especially since Ayars had to spend so much time out of the house working other jobs. So Caroline moved into the Vernon Green nursing home, where she seems comfortable. She celebrated her ninety-ninth birthday there in October 2008.

Lisa has suffered a series of health crises in recent months, including a severe infection probably caused by the improper insertion of a urinary catheter. As she feared, she has run out of money, and is now awaiting the state's approval of her application to enroll in Medicaid.

With her walker and the help of an aide, Peggy Ingles can walk down a hallway. She continues to do her physical therapy at home and helps raise funds for other injured equestrians. In the summer of 2007, she achieved her goal of once again riding her champion horses, Sohn and Post Exchange.

Sadly, just a few months after Peggy got back on her beloved Sohn, he died. On that last ride, she remembers, "He was great with me. It was special to be able to ride him again."

Natalie Fenninger died quietly at Friends House on October 16, 2007. Gretchen and two of Natalie's closest friends from the Quaker community were with her, singing her favorite hymns as she quietly passed away.

"She stropped breathing, but we sang for another ten minutes," remembers Ruth Stern, who was with Natalie at the end. "They say your soul is still in you for a time after you die. It felt like hers was."

Natalie's grandson Richard, who joked that he'd help take care of her as long as he didn't have to come to her funeral, did come, of course.

"I didn't think she'd mind," Richard says.

Natalie's stepdaughter Gretchen still leads Sunday hymns at Friends House.

At Natalie's memorial, they read her last poem, which she wrote just two weeks before she died.

MY ROSE UMBRELLA

White splashes fleck
The dark gray pond
The days begun to wane
My rose umbrella, like a drum, reverberates with rain

A cluster of umbrellas
Drips down the window pane
My rose umbrella, like a drum, reverberates with rain

The thirsty land is grateful for light flooding on its plain
My rose umbrella, like a drum, reverberates with rain

Acknowledgments

Long-term care has been on my mind for more than a decade. For many years, I told the story in bits and pieces through short magazine articles. But the more I learned about how we get and pay for the assistance, the more I realized that it would take more than a few thousand words to tell this story. Turning it into a book, however, was a special challenge. Like most authors, I could not have done it without a huge amount of support.

The book would never have been possible without the cooperation of the many families who so generously shared their stories: the Barretts, the Bolstridges, the Dows, the Fearses, the extended Fenninger family, the Fredines, the Foyes, the Ingelses, the Stevenson/Curtis family, the Weils, "Lisa" and her family, and so many others. Thanks also to the aides who make their lives so much easier, including Ayars Hemphill, Marybelle Kamara, Mimi Noamassi, and Allen Wood. Naressa Moore, who was so important to my own family, will always have a special place in my heart.

Special thanks as well to those who showed me what it is like to work on the front lines of long-term care, including Beth Vaughn-Wrobel, Dr. Larry Wright and the dedicated staff at the Schmieding Center, Terry Sitz and Karin Lakin at Cedar Creek Associates, Ellen Greenberg and her staff at the Senior Helpline of the Jewish Council for the Aging of Greater Washington, Norm Metzger and Gail Kohn at Capitol Hill Village, Dr. David Greer, Karen Love, Bill Thomas, Margi Helsel-Arnold, Robert Bullock, and Nancy Fiedelman.

I was fortunate that so many policy experts spent countless hours helping me understand these issues. There are too many to name here, but a few deserve special recognition, including Lisa

Alecxih; John Cutler; Judy Feder; Harriet Komisar; Josh Wiener; Molly O'Malley and Tricia Neuman at the Kaiser Family Foundation; John Rother, Don Redfoot, Susan Reinhard, Enid Kassner, and Mary Jo Gibson at AARP; Larry Minnix, Barbara Manard, Robyn Stone, and the staff at the American Association of Homes and Services for the Aging; Richard Johnson and Brenda Spillman at the Urban Institute; and Eileen Tell at the Long Term Care Group.

Gregory Watson of the Moran Company, who patiently crunched numbers for me, deserves special recognition.

I was extremely fortunate to get invaluable comments on my first drafts from a cadre of willing readers, including Gloria Eldridge, Melissa Favreault, Bill Galston, Steve Goldberg, Gail Hunt, Rich Johnson, Morris Klein, Nora Jean Levin, Dr. Joanne Lynn, Nancy Ellen Roth, Julie Salamon, Gene Steuerle, Anne Tumlinson, and Tom West. Each made the book both more accurate and readable. The usual disclaimer applies: Any mistakes are mine alone.

My gratitude as well to those who helped fund this project: the Kaiser Family Foundation, whose media fellowship program got me started; the Center for Retirement Research at Boston College, where I've had the great pleasure of being a visiting fellow for the past two years; The Brookings Institution; and the Tax Policy Center, which gave me a professional home for the past year. Thanks especially to Penny Duckham, Deidre Graham, and my fellow fellows at Kaiser; Alicia Munnell at B.C.; Bill Gale at Brookings; and Len Burman at TPC.

Thanks as well to *Kiplinger's Retirement Report*, which published several articles based in part on my reporting for this book.

This project came together with the help of my agent, Gail Ross, and my editor at St. Martin's, Phil Revzin, two pros who believed that a first-time book writer could produce. Thank you both.

A quick note on sources: There are hundreds of how-to books on long-term care. One of the first and best is *How to Care for Your Parents*, by my friend Jean Levin. More recent volumes are *The Idiot's Guide to Long-Term Care*, by Marilee Driscoll, and *How to Care for Your Parents' Money While Caring for Your Parents,* by Sharon Burns and Raymond Forgue.

By contrast, surprisingly few books look at the structure of our long-term-care system. Josh Wiener has written two of the best—*Sharing the Burden*, with Laurel Hixon Illston and Raymond J. Hanley (1994), and *Caring for the Disabled Elderly: Who Will Pay?* with Alice M. Rivlin (1988). Both remain invaluable for anyone exploring this issue.

To learn about the history of nursing homes, there is still no better book than *Unloving Care: The Nursing Home Tragedy*, by Bruce C. Vladeck. The classic study on the sociology of these institutions is *Asylums*, by Erving Goffman. *Nobody's Home: Candid Reflections of a Nursing Home Aide*, is Thomas Edward Gass's horrifying first-person account of life in a nursing facility. For a very different first-person account, read *It Shouldn't Be This Way: The Failure of Long-Term Care*, by Robert L. Kane and Joan C. West. It tells what happened when Kane, a doctor and highly respected long-term-care researcher, and West, an educator, had to care for their mother after she suffered a stroke. If they couldn't do it . . . Bob and Rosalie Kane have written hundreds of articles on long-term care. *The Heart of Long-Term Care* is a good overview of what they have learned.

The body of literature on "culture change" in nursing homes is small but growing. *Old Age in a New Age*, by Beth Baker, is an excellent survey of what is happening. The prolific Bill Thomas has published a fistful of books, including *The Eden Alternative* and *Life Worth Living: How Someone You Love Can Still Enjoy Life in a Nursing Home.*

There have been even fewer books on home care and the life of caregivers. *The Cultures of Caregiving* is a valuable set of essays edited by Carol Levine and Thomas Murray. *A Family Caregiver Speaks Up* is a personal look from in the trenches by Suzanne Geffen Mintz, who is both a caregiver and founder of the National Family Caregivers Association.

Most of the other research in long-term care appears in monographs and academic research papers, many of which were invaluable to my own work. Much of it comes from the Urban Institute, the Kaiser Family Foundation, the Commonwealth Fund, and the National Alliance for Caregiving.

Finally, thanks to my best editor, my wife, Ann Kline—novelist, hospice and nursing home chaplain, and helpmate—and to Malka, whose enthusiastic demands for walks got me up and away from the computer when I most needed breaks.

Notes

ONE

The Phone Call

1. Peter Kemper, Harriet L. Komisar, and Lisa Alecxih, "Long-Term Care Over an Uncertain Future: What Can Current Retirees Expect?," *Inquiry* 42, no. 4 (2005): 335–50.

2. "Family Caregivers—What They Spend, What They Sacrifice," Evercare/ National Alliance for Caregiving, 2007. The estimates of family caregivers vary widely, from thirty million to as many as forty-four million.

3. Richard Johnson and Joshua M. Wiener, "A Profile of Frail Older Americans and Their Caregivers," The Urban Institute, 2006. These very poor seniors are often the most ill, unable to manage at least "three activities of daily living" such as bathing, eating, dressing, or going to the bathroom without assistance. About 57 percent live alone. Two thirds are women. More than one quarter living outside of a nursing home suffer from dementia, and nearly half suffer from depression.

4. "Caregiving in America," International Longevity Center–USA, 2006.

5. Harriet L. Komisar and Lee Shirey Thompson, "National Spending for Long-Term Care," Georgetown University, Long-Term Care Financing Project, 2007.

6. Ibid.

7. "Metlife Market Survey of Nursing Home and Assisted Living Costs," Metlife Mature Market Institute, 2007.

8. Mary Jo Gibson and Ari Houser, "Valuing the Invaluable: A New Look at the Economic Value of Family Caregiving," AARP Public Policy Institute, 2007.

TWO

Natalie

1. Digest of Education Statistics, U.S. Department of Education, 2006.

2. From *The Principles and Practice of Medicine*, by William Osler, 1897, cited in Joanne Lynn, "Living Long in Fragile Health: The New Demographics Shape End-of-Life Care," *Improving End of Life Care*, The Hastings Center, 2005.

3. "Older Americans 2008," Federal Interagency Forum on Aging Related Statistics, 2008. Someone who turns 65 today is expected to live an additional 18.7 years. The life expectancy of an 85-year-old woman is an additional 7.2 years, for an 85-year-old man, it is 6.1 years. At younger ages, life expectancy varies widely by race, but after 85, there is no difference between whites and blacks.

4. United States Department of Commerce, Bureau of the Census, National Center for Health Statistics, 2008. Many experts think this forecast is very conservative, and that children born in the near future will live far longer than this projection. Demographers Jim Oeppen and James W. Vaupel, for instance, argue that by mid-century, the life expectancy for women in the United States and other industrialized nations could reach one hundred. See "The Future of Human Life Expectancy: Have We Reached the Ceiling or Is the Sky the Limit?" *Research Highlights in the Demography and Economics of Aging,* March 2006.

5. Atul Gawande, "The Way We Age Now," *The New Yorker,* April 30, 2007.

6. U.S. Bureau of the Census, "65 + in the United States," 1996.

7. Lisa Alecxih, "Long-Term Care in the United States," The Lewin Group, 2006.

8. Brenda Plassman, Kenneth Langa, David Weir, and Robert B. Wallace, "Prevalence of Dementia in the United States: The Aging, Demographics, and Memory Study," *Neuroepidemiology* 29 (2007): 125–32.

9. Kemper, Komisar, and Alecxih, "Long-Term Care Over an Uncertain Future."

10. Joanne Lynn and David Adamson, "Living Well at the End of Life," RAND, 2003.

11. Ibid.

12. Elizabeth Bragg, "The Status of Geriatrics Workforce Study," University of Cincinnati, 2007.

13. Testimony of Todd Semla, president, American Geriatrics Society, before the United States Senate Special Committee on Aging, April 16, 2008.

14. "Retooling for an Aging America: Building the Health Care Workforce," Institute of Medicine, 2008.

15. Testimony of John W. Rowe, MD, chair, Committee on the Future Health Care Workforce for Older Americans, Institute of Medicine, before the U.S. Senate Special Committee on Aging, April 16, 2008.

16. Interview with author, October 22, 2007.

17. National Long-Term Care Survey, "2002 Medicare Current Beneficiary Survey," Centers for Medicaid and Medicare Services Minimum Data Set, U.S. Department of Health and Human Services, 2005.

18. The MetLife Market Survey of Adult Day Services and Home Health Aides, MetLife Mature Market Institute, 2007; author's estimates.

19. The MetLife Market Survey of Nursing Home and Assisted Living Costs, MetLife Mature Market Institute, 2007.

20. Ibid.

21. Uniglobe Travel Designers average per-person cost on Carnival Cruise Lines.

22. Enid Kassner, Susan Reinhard, Wendy Fox-Grage, et al., "A Balancing Act: State Long-Term Care Reform, AARP Public Policy Institute, 2008.

23. Centers for Disease Control, "United States Fire/Burn Deaths and Rates Per 100,000," 2004.

24. "Elder Abuse Prevalence and Incidence," National Center on Elder Abuse, 2005.

25. Barbara Lyons, A. Schneider, and K. Desmond, "The Distribution of Assets in the Elderly Population Living in the Community," Kaiser Commission on Medicaid and the Uninsured, 2005.

26. Jack VanDerhei, Sarah Holden, and Craig Copeland, "401(k) Plan Asset Allocation, Account Balances and Loan Activity in 2006," Employee Benefit Research Institute, 2007.

27. Richard W. Johnson, Gordon Mermin, and Cori Uccello, "How Secure Are Retirement Nest Eggs?," Center for Retirement Research at Boston College, 2006.

28. Paul Fronstin, Dallas Salisbury, and Jack VanDerhei, "Savings Needed to Fund Health Insurance and Health Care Expenses in Retirement: Findings from a Simulation Model," Employee Benefit Research Institute, 2008.

29. "A Report on Shortfalls in Medicaid Funding for Nursing Home Care," The American Health Care Association, 2007.

30. Book of Ruth, *The Bible: New Revised Standard Version*, Peabody, Mass.: Hendrickson Publishers, 1989: 187.

THREE

"This Is What I Do, 24/7"

1. "Caregiving in the United States," AARP, 2007.

2. Ibid.

3. Jennifer L. Wolff and Judith D. Kasper, "Caregivers of Frail Elders: Updating a National Profile," *The Gerontologist* 46 (2006): 344–56.

4. Richard Schultz, et al., "Health Effects of Caregiving: The Caregiver Health Effects Study," *Annals of Behavioral Medicine* 19, no. 2 (June 1997). An excellent review of all of this literature is in Richard Johnson, "The Burden of Caring for Frail Parents," testimony to the Joint Economic Committee, United States Congress, May 16, 2007.

5. Author's not-for-attribution interview with an official at the Department of Health and Human Services, March 27, 2007.

6. "Valuing the Invaluable: A New Look at the Economic Value of Family Caregiving," AARP Public Policy Institute, 2007.

7. Johnson and Wiener, "Profile of Frail Older Americans."

8. "Family Caregivers—What They Spend, What They Sacrifice."

9. "Caregiving in the United States," National Alliance for Caregiving and AARP, 2004.

10. Richard W. Johnson and Anthony LoSasso, "The Impact of Elder Care on Women's Labor Supply at Midlife," *Inquiry* 43, no. 3 (2006): 195–210.

11. "Family Caregivers—What They Spend, What They Sacrifice."

12. Johnson and Wiener, "Profile of Frail Older Americans." The authors estimate that when one spouse is caring for another, she is the sole caregiver nearly 75 percent of the time.

13. Alzheimer's Association and National Alliance for Caregiving, "Families Care: Alzheimer's Caregiving in the United States," Alzheimer's Association, 2004.

14. Brenda C. Spillman and Sharon Long, "Does High Caregiver Stress Lead to Nursing Home Entry?" U.S. Department of Health and Human Services, 2007.

15. Johnson and Wiener, "Profile of Frail Older Americans."

16. Robert N. Butler, "Who Will Care for You?," *AARP Bulletin*, 2007.

17. Bureau of Labor Statistics, National Compensation Survey, August 2006.

18. "Caregiving in America," International Longevity Center, 2006.

19. "Depression Among Adults Employed Full Time," Substance Abuse and Mental Health Services Administration, 2007.

20. "Elder Abuse Prevalence and Incidence," National Center on Elder Abuse, 2005.

21. Toshio Tatara and Lisa Kuzmeskus, "Trends in Elder Abuse in Domestic Settings," National Center on Elder Abuse, 2006.

22. Linda M. Woolf, "Elder Abuse and Neglect," Webster University, 1998.

23. Butler, "Who Will Care for You?"

FOUR

The Champion

1. 1996 Medical Expenditure Panel Survey, U.S. Department of Health and Human Services, 1996.

2. National Spinal Cord Injury Association at www.spinalcord.org, July 14, 2008.

3. "Who Gets MS," National MS Society, August 25, 2008.

4. U.S. Centers for Disease Control and Prevention, "Birth Defects: Frequently Asked Questions," available on the Web at http://www.cdc.gov/ncbddd/bd/facts.htm#CommonBD. Accessed December 23, 2007.

5. "Americans with Disabilities: 2002," U.S. Bureau of the Census, 2006.

6. Ibid.

7. Ibid.

8. "Nursing Home: Fact Sheet," AARP Public Policy Institute, 2007.

9. *Olmstead v. L.C. 527 U.S. 581* (1999).

FIVE

The Claws of the Dragon

1. Erving Goffman, *Asylums*, New York: Anchor Books, 1961: 6.

2. This section relies heavily on three books that describe the history of long-term care in the United States. *The Discovery of the Asylum*, by David J. Rothman, is a classic history from postcolonial days through the late nineteenth century. It was first published in 1971, but I relied on the revised 1990 edition. "The Evolution of Long-Term Care in America," by Martha Holstein and Thomas R. Cole, is an excellent brief history of the topic. It was published as a chapter in *The Future of Long-Term Care*, edited by Robert H. Binstock, Leighton E. Cluff, and Otto Von Mering, Baltimore, Md.: Johns Hopkins University Press, 1996. Finally, Bruce Vladeck's *Unloving Care: The Nursing Home Tragedy*, New York: Basic Books, 1980, brings the perspective of both an academic and a public policy expert to the long-term-care story.

3. Rothman, *Discovery of the Asylum*, 5.

4. Vladeck, *Unloving Care*, 31.

5. Rothman, *Discovery of the Asylum*, 39.

6. Ibid., 183.

7. Ibid.

8. Charles Dickens, *Oliver Twist*, New York: Random House, 2005: 12.

9. Ibid., 188.

10. Binstock, Cluff, and Von Mering, *Future of Long-Term Care*, 28.

11. Ibid., 33.

12. Nancy J. Altman, *The Battle for Social Security*, New York: Wiley, 2005: 18.

13. Binstock, Cluff, and Von Mering, *Future of Long-Term Care*, 34.

14. Ibid.

15. Charlene Harrington, Helen Carrillo, and Courtney LaCava, "Nursing Facilities, Staffing, Residents and Facility Deficiencies 1999–2005," University of California at San Francisco, 2006.

16. National Health Expenditures, U.S. Dept. of Health and Human Services, 2007.

17. Jennifer L. Wolffe, "Long-Term Care Preferences Among Older Adults: A Moving Target," Johns Hopkins Bloomberg School of Public Health, 2007. This survey did find that about 7 percent of those with more serious care needs would choose a nursing home and nearly half of those with dementia prefer such a setting.

18. National Nursing Home Survey, National Center for Health Statistics, 2004.

19. Harrington, Carrillo, and LaCava, "Nursing Facilities, Staffing, Residents and Facility Deficiencies."

20. The MetLife Market Survey of Nursing Homes and Assisted Living Costs, MetLife Mature Market Institute, 2007.

21. Bureau of Labor Statistics. The average hourly wage of certified nurse's aides in 2006 was $9.60.

22. Ibid.

23. Thomas Edward Gass, Nobody's Home: Candid Reflections of a Nursing Home Aide, Ithaca, NY: ILR Press, 13.

24. Robert Kane and Joan C. West, It Shouldn't Be This Way: The Failure of Long-Term Care, Nashville, Tenn.: Vanderbilt University Press, 109.

25. Christian Palmer, "Ahwatukee Nursing Home Fails Inspection, Loses Medicare Funding," Arizona Capitol Times, January 25, 2008; Christian Palmer, "State Advises Evergreen Nursing Home Residents to Move," Arizona Capitol Times, February 1, 2008.

26. Harrington, Carrillo, and LaCava, "Nursing Facilities, Staffing, Residents and Faculty Deficiencies."

27. Lucette Lagnado, "Prescription Abuse Seen in U.S. Nursing Homes," Wall Street Journal, December 4, 2007: 1.

28. U.S. Department of Health and Human Services, HospitalCompare Web site at www.hospitalcompare.hhs.gov. Payment varies based on many factors, including geographical location and the number of low-income patients.

29. Kindred Healthcare Annual Report, 2007.

30. The MetLife Market Survey of Nursing Homes and Assisted Living Costs, MetLife Mature Market Institute, 2007.

31. In a study funded by the for-profit nursing home industry, the consulting firm BDO Seidman estimates that Medicaid pays an average of $13.15 less per day than it costs the facility to care for the resident. "A Report on Shortfalls in Medicaid Funding for Nursing Homes Care," BDO Seidman, 2007.

32. PowerPoint presentation, Patricia Brady, senior consultant, Sellers Feinberg, April 22, 2008.

33. Ibid.

34. U.S. Census Bureau, "65 Plus in the United States," 2005.

35. Robert D. Mollica, Kristin Sims-Kastelein, and Janet O'Keeffe, "Residential Care and Assisted Living Compendium, 2007," U.S. Dept of Health and Human Services, 2007.

36. National Center for Assisted Living, "Assisted Living Profile." Available on the Web at www.ncal.org/about/facility/cfn. Accessed November 18, 2007.

37. The MetLife Market Survey of Nursing Homes and Assisted Living Costs, MetLife Mature Market Institute, 2007.

38. The National Center for Assisted Living, "Top 40 Assisted Living Chains," 2007.

39. Robert D. Mollica, "Residential Care and Assisted Living: State Oversight Practices and State Information Available to Consumers," U.S. Agency for Healthcare Research and Quality, 2006.

40. The National Center for Assisted Living, "Top 40 Assisted Living Chains," 2007.

SIX

Changing the Culture

1. The Green House Project at The Village of Redford, Operations and Finance, PowerPoint presentation, 2007. Author interviews with Redford staff, December 12–13, 2007.

2. Ibid.

3. Rosalie Kane, "Resident Outcomes in Small-House Nursing Homes: A Longitudinal Evaluation of the Initial Green House Program," *Journal of the American Geriatrics Society* 55, no. 6 (2007).

SEVEN

Everyone Wants to Stay at Home

1. Wolff, "Long-Term-Care Preferences."

2. Richard W. Johnson, "In-Home Care for Frail Childless Adults: Getting By with a Little Help from Their Friends?" The Retirement Project Discussion Paper Series, The Urban Institute, 2006.

3. Brian Burwell, K. Stredl, and S. Riken, "Medicaid Long-Term Care Expenditures, FY 2006," Thomson Healthcare, 2007.

4. Ibid.

5. Enid Kassner, Susan Reinhard, Wendy Fox-George, et al. "A Balancing Act: State Long-Term Care Reform," AARP Public Policy Institute, 2008.

6. National Association of Insurance Commissioners, Long-Term Care Insurance Experience Reports, 2006.

7. Harriet L. Komisar and Lee Shirey Thompson, "National Spending for Long-Term Care," Fact Sheet, Georgetown University Long-Term Care Financing Project, 2007.

8. For a typical example, see California's regulations at "Background Paper: Proposal for the Regulation of Geriatric Health Care Assistants," California State Senate, 2005.

9. National Commission on Nursing Workforce for Long-Term Care, Final Report, 2005.

10. Institute for the Future of Aging Services, "The Long-Term Care Workforce: Can the Crisis Be Fixed?," 2007.

11. David Gould, "Family Caregivers and the Healthcare System: Findings from a National Survey," *The Cultures of Caregiving,* edited by Carol Levine and Thomas H. Murray, Baltimore, Md.: Johns Hopkins University Press, 2004.

12. Sandra Potthoff, Robert L. Kane, and Sheila J. Franco, "Improving Hospital Discharge Planning for Elderly Patients—Patient-Centered Care," *Health Care Financing Review* 19, no. 2 (1998): 157–63.

13. Kerry Hannon, "Aging at Home with Government Help," *U.S. News & World Report*, November 5, 2007.

14. Patricia Leigh Brown, "At New Rentals, the Aim Is to Age with Creativity," *The New York Times*, September 10, 2006.

15. "Adult Day Services: The Facts," National Adult Day Services Association, 2007.

16. Art Buchwald, *Too Soon to Say Goodbye*, New York: Random House, 2006.

17. National Hospice and Palliative Care Organization, NHPCO Facts and Figures: Hospice Care in America, 2007.

18. Ibid.

19. National Hospice and Palliative Care Organization, NHPCO Facts and Figures: Hospice Care in America, 2008. 792–99.

20. Hospice Payment System Fact Sheet, U.S. Department of Health and Human Services, 2007.

21. Kevin Sack, "In Hospice Care, Longer Lives Mean Money Lost," *The New York Times*, November 27, 2007.

EIGHT

How We Pay

1. Komisar and Thompson, "National Spending for Long-Term Care."

2. Kemper, Komisar, and Alecxih, "Long-Term Care Over an Uncertain Future."

3. Ibid. These estimates represent discounted value. The costs may be paid out of pocket or, in part, by Medicaid.

4. Of those under 65, 174 million have private insurance and 28 million have Medicaid. Another 44 million—mostly over 65—have Medicare. Data on total non-elderly with insurance from John Hollohan and Allison Cook, "The U.S. Economy and Changes in Health Insurance Coverage, 2000–2006," *Health Affairs*, 2007, Web exclusive. Total Medicare participation is from the Kaiser Family Foundation, www.statehealthfacts.org, available at http://www.statehealthfacts .org/comparemaptable.jsp?ind=290&cat=6.

5. Massimo Guidolin and Elizabeth A. La Jeunesse, "The Decline in the U.S. Personal Savings Rate: Is It Real and Is It a Puzzle?," 2007, *Federal Reserve Bank of St. Louis Review* 89, no. 6 (2007): 491–514.

6. There are many different estimates of seniors' net worth. The Federal Reserve Board's 2004 Survey of Consumer Finances estimated median family net worth at about $190,000, when the head of household was aged sixty-five to seventy-four. But many of those households included couples. Lisa Alecxih of The Lewin Group estimated that the median net worth of the elderly was $110,000, including their home. Excluding their residence, it was only $25,000. Lisa Alecxih, "Long-Term Care in the United States," The Lewin Group, 2006. Others estimate individual net worth after sixty-five at about $150,000.

7. Annuity estimates based on U.S. Government Thrift Savings Plan, annuity calculator.

8. Social Security Administration, Monthly Statistical Snapshot, December 2007. Available at http://www.ssa.gov/policy/docs/quickfacts/stat_snapshot/.

9. Centers for Medicare and Medicaid Services, "Annual Report of the Boards of Trustees of the Federal Hospital Insurance and Federal Supplementary Medical Insurance Trust Funds," Washington, D.C.: U.S. Department of Health and Human Services, 2007.

10. Paul Fronstin, Dallas Salisbury, and Jack VanDerhei, "Savings Needed to Fund Health Insurance and Health Care Expenses in Retirement: Findings from a Simulation Model," Employee Benefit Research Institute, 2008.

11. "Retiree Health Benefits Examined: Findings from the 2006 Kaiser/Hewitt Survey on Retirement Health Benefits," Kaiser Family Foundation, 2006.

12. Barbara Lyons, Andy Schneider, and Katherine A. Desmond, "The Distribution of Assets in the Elderly Population Living in the Community," Kaiser Commission on Medicaid and the Uninsured, 2005.

13. "Valuing the Invaluable: A New Look at the Economic Value of Family Caregiving," AARP Public Policy Institute, 2007.

14. Joshua M. Weiner, Catherine Sullivan, and Jason Skaggs, "Spending Down to Medicaid: New Data on the Role of Medicaid in Paying for Nursing Home Care," AARP Public Policy Institute, 1996.

15. Price estimate is from the Office of Personnel Management, Federal Long-Term Care Insurance Program.

16. Jeffrey R. Brown and Amy Finkelstein, "Supply or Demand: Why Is the Market for Long-Term Care Insurance So Small?" National Bureau of Economic Research, Cambridge, Mass., *Journal of Public Economics* 91, no. 10 (2007).

17. Marc Freiman, "Can 1+1=3? A Look at Hybrid Insurance Products with Long-Term Care Insurance," No. 2007-11, AARP Public Policy Institute, 2007.

18. Mark Warshawsky, "The Life Care Annuity," Georgetown University Long-Term Care Financing Project, 2007. Christopher Murtaugh, Brenda Spillman, and Mark Warshawsky, "In Sickness and Health: An Annuity Approach to Financing Long-Term Care are and Retirement Income," *Journal of Risk and Insurance* 68, no. 2 (2001).

19. Warshawsky, "Life Care Annuity."

20. Judy Feder, Harriet Komisar, and Robert B. Friedland, "Long-Term Care Financing: Policy Options for the Future," Washington, D.C., Georgetown University Long-Term Care Financing Project, 2007.

21. Anthony Web, Guan Gong, and Wei Sun, "An Annuity People Might Actually Buy," Center for Retirement Research at Boston College, 2007.

22. Barbara Stucki, "Use Your Home to Stay at Home: Expanding the Use of Reverse Mortgages for Long-Term Care: A Blueprint for Action," The National Council on Aging, 2005.

23. Alicia Munnell, Maurico Soto, and Jean-Pierre Aubry, "Do People Plan to Tap Their Home Equity in Retirement?" Center for Retirement Research at Boston College, 2007.

24. Stucki, "Use Your Home to Stay at Home."

25. Johnson and Weiner, "Profile of Frail Older Americans."

26. Donald L. Redfoot, "Reverse Mortgages: Niche Product or Mainstream Solution?" AARP Public Policy Institute, 2007.

27. Stucki, "Use Your Home to Stay at Home."

28. Redfoot, "Reverse Mortgages." In 2008, Congress passed a law that limits origination fees for federally insured reverse mortgages to 2 percent for up to $200,000 of a home's value, plus 1 percent for the amount that exceeds $200,000, up to a maximum of $6,000. The law does not limit other fees, however.

29. Ibid.

30. Edward J. Szymanoski, James C. Enriquez, and Teresa R. DiVenti, "Home Equity Conversion Mortgage Terminations: Information to Enhance the Developing Secondary Market," U.S. Department of Housing and Urban Development, 2007.

31. Redfoot, "Reverse Mortgages." Buyers could cite multiple reasons for taking the loans.

32. AARP, "The Costs of Long-Term Care: Public Perceptions Versus Reality," 2006.

NINE

Medicaid

1. Georgetown University Long-Term Care Financing Project, "Medicaid and Long-Term Care," Fact Sheet, Washington, D.C., 2007.

2. Kaiser Commission on Medicaid and the Uninsured, 2006. "Medicaid's Long-Term Care Beneficiaries: An Analysis of Spending Patterns."

3. Congressional Budget Office. "Medicaid Spending Growth and Options for Controlling Costs," Testimony of Donald B. Marron before the Special Committee on Aging, U.S. Senate, July 13, 2006. In 2002, Medicaid spent an average of $2,100 on adults under sixty-five. By contrast, the cost per elderly beneficiary was $13,358, while payments per disabled enrollee were $12,475.

4. American Health Care Association, "Nursing Facility Patients by Payor," 2006.

5. Department of Health and Human Services, National Clearinghouse for Long-term Care Information at http://www.longtermcare.gov/LTC/Main_Site/Paying_LTC/Public_Programs/Public_Programs.aspx. For 2007 updated benefit levels and income eligibility, see AARP at www.aarp.org/nltp.

6. Timothy Waidmann and Korbin Liu, "Asset Transfer and Nursing Home Use: Empirical Evidence and Policy Significance," Kaiser Commission on Medicaid and the Uninsured, 2006.

7. This account is taken largely from Vladeck, *Unloving Care.*

8. Richard Harris, *A Sacred Trust*, New York: New American Library, 1966: 99–109.

9. Vladeck, *Unloving Care*, 51.

10. Donald Marron, "Medicaid Spending Growth and Options for Controlling Costs," Testimony before the U.S. Senate Special Committee on Aging, July 13, 2006.

11. Kaiser Family Foundation, www.Statehealthfacts.org. The average federal share of the program is about 50 percent; http://www.statehealthfacts.org/comparetable.jsp?ind=184&cat=4.

12. Ellen O'Brien, "Long-Term Care: Understanding Medicaid's Role for the Elderly and the Disabled," Kaiser Commission on Medicaid and the Uninsured, 2005.

13. Kaiser Commission on Medicaid and the Uninsured, 2006.

14. Enid Kassner, et al., "A Balancing Act: State Long-Term Care Reform," AARP Public Policy Institute, 2008.

15. Vermont Department of Disabilities, Aging, and Independent Living, "Shifting the Balance: Act 160," PowerPoint presentation, 2007.

16. AARP, "Home and Community-Based Long-Term Services and Supports for Older People," 2006. In 2004, only about 270,000 low-income rental units were available for all seniors in the United States through the primary government subsidy program, called Section 202.

17. Medicaid's home ownership rules for unmarried people living in a nursing home are complicated. Officially, the rules say a recipient may keep her home only if she intends to return there. Otherwise, she must sell her house within six months of moving out. However, states have very different interpretations about what that means.

18. "Across the States: Profiles of Long-Term Care and Independent Living," AARP Public Policy Institute, 2006.

19. Brenda C. Spillman, Kirsten Black, and Barbara J. Ormond, "Beyond Cash and Counseling: The Second Generation of Individual Budget-Based Community Long-Term Care Programs for the Elderly," Kaiser Commission on Medicaid and the Uninsured, 2007.

20. Anna Sommers, Mindy Cohen, and Molly O'Malley, "Medicaid's Long-Term Care Beneficiaries: An Analysis of Spending Patterns," Kaiser Commission on Medicaid and the Uninsured, 2006.

21. Joshua Wiener and David Brown, "Home and Community Based Services: A Synthesis of the Literature," Washington, D.C., Administration on Aging, 2004. Weiner concluded: "Expanding home and community-based services does not reduce aggregate long-term-care expenditures, although average per consumer costs are less than nursing home care in many studies."

22. Brian Burwell, Kate Sredl, and Steve Eiken, "Medicaid Long-Term Care Expenditures, 2006," Thomson Healthcare, 2007.

23. National Association of State Budget Officers, 2006.

24. Congressional Budget Office, 2006.

25. Congressional Budget Office, Monthly Budget Review, 2006.

26. Government Accountability Office, 2006.

27. Interview with Karen Armacost, December 17, 2007.

28. Ibid.

29. Ibid.

30. David Grabowski, "The Cost-Effectiveness of Noninstitutional Long-Term Care Services: Review and Synthesis of the Most Recent Evidence," *Medical Care Research and Review* 63, no.1 (2006).

31. National PACE Association.

32. Paul Saucier, Brian Burwell, and Kerstin Gerst, "The Past, Present and Future of Managed Long-Term Care," Washington, D.C., Office of the Assistant Secretary for Planning and Evaluation, U.S. Dept of Health and Human Services, 2005.

33. Robert Kane, Gail Keckhafer, Shannon Flood, Boris Bershadsky, and Mir Said Siadaty, "The Effect of Evercare on Hospital Use," American Geriatrics Society, 2003.

34. Waidmann and Liu, Kaiser Commission on Medicaid and the Uninsured, 2006.

35. Ibid.

36. "The Cost and Financing of Long-Term Care Services," Testimony of Douglas Holtz-Eakin before the Subcommittee on Health, Committee on Energy and Commerce, U.S. House of Representatives, April 27, 2005. The CBO projected that asset-protection changes would generate $2.4 billion over five years, about 0.2 percent of the program's projected costs.

37. Kaiser Commission on Medicaid and the Uninsured, 2006.

TEN

Long-Term-Care Insurance

1. Steve Gelsi, "Genworth's IPO Fights Back to Flatline: GE Spinoff Raises $2.83 Billion as Biggest So Far in 2004," CBS Marketwatch, May 25, 2004; http://www.marketwatch.com/News/Story/Story.aspx?guid={A74ED04F-264F-4C76-83C3-BAC9C27EB9CF}.

2. America's Health Insurance Plans, "Who Buys Long-Term Care Insurance," Washington, D.C., 2007. These averages are for plans purchased in 2005. Many earlier plans, which remain in force, are less generous.

3. Employee Benefit Research Institute, 2008 Retirement Confidence Survey.

4. U.S. Census Bureau, "Health Insurance Coverage, 2006. Available at http://www.census.gov/hhes/www/hlthins/hlthin06/hlth06asc.html.

5. Komisar and Thompson, "National Spending for Long-Term Care." This estimate includes costs paid by both long-term-care insurance and post-acute home and nursing home care paid by health insurance. It is not possible, using current government data, to know what share is paid by long-term-care insurance alone.

The long-term-care insurance industry estimates that it paid between $3.5 billion and $5.8 billion in claims in 2005. Those estimates, however, may be incomplete, since they are based on voluntary self-reporting by carriers.

6. LIMRA International, 2007.

7. Congressional Budget Office, "The Outlook for Spending on Health Care and Long-Term Care," presentation to the National Governors Association's Health and Human Services Committee, 2008.

8. Kemper, Komisar, and Alecxih, "Long-Term Care Over an Uncertain Future." For a closer look at the odds, about two thirds of those over sixty-five will need some long-term care in their lives, and they will require assistance for an average of three years. However, 31 percent will require no long-term care at all, 29 percent will require care for two years or less, 20 percent for two to five years, and 20 percent for more than five years. The cost estimates represent present discounted value. The costs may be paid out of pocket or, in part, by Medicaid.

9. American's Health Insurance Plans, 2007. These non-buyers were individuals who had some contact with an insurance agent. AHIP did not survey the public at large.

10. Price quote is from the U.S. Office of Personnel Management (OPM), which sells insurance to government employees. Private market premiums can be somewhat higher; http://www.opm.gov/insure/ltc/.

11. Brown and Finkelstein, "Supply or Demand." Life annuities pay 85 to 87 percent. Joel Gold, David Vanderlinden, and John S. Herald, "The Financial Desirability of Long-Term Care Insurance Versus Self-Insurance," *Journal of Financial Planning* (November 2006), reached similar conclusions.

12. This return may be even lower when correcting for policies that are allowed to lapse before they go to claim. Brown and Finkelstein estimate that a sixty-five-year-old man has a 27 percent chance of ever entering a nursing home, while a sixty-five-year-old woman has a 44 percent chance. Men who are admitted to a nursing home spend an average of 1.3 years, and have only a 5 percent chance of staying more than 5 years. Women spend an average of two years and have a 12 percent likelihood of staying more than five years. See also Gold, Vanderlinden, and Herald, "Financial Desirability."

13. Christopher Murtaugh, Peter Kemper, and Brenda Spillman, "Risky Business: Long-Term Care Insurance Underwriting," *Inquiry* 32, no. 3 (1995): 271–84. *Inquiry* projected that between 12 and 23 percent of sixty-five-year-olds do not meet underwriting standards. In a forthcoming work, Spillman, Murtaugh, and Warshawsky estimate that as many as 28 percent would not qualify for coverage. Brown and Finkelstein ("Supply or Demand") estimate that 15 percent of those aged sixty to seventy suffer from medical conditions that might disqualify them from coverage. There appear to be no credible widespread industry experience data publicly available to test these estimates.

14. U.S. Office of Personnel Management. Available on the web at https://www
.ltcfeds.com/ltcWeb/do/assessing_your_needs/ratecalcOut.

15. The National Association of Insurance Commissioners advises that
people over sixty should not buy if premiums exceed 7 percent of their income
or they have less than $35,000 in financial assets (excluding a house, for
instance).

16. Kaiser Family Foundation, 2003. Premiums increase rapidly with age and as
seniors begin to suffer from preexisting health issues.

17. Mark Merlis, "Private Long-Term Care Insurance: Who Should Buy It and
What Should They Buy," Washington, D.C., Kaiser Family Foundation, 2003.
Also Feder, Komisar, and Friedland, "Long-Term Care Financing."

18. AHIP, 2007.

19. Ibid.

20. Although carriers have promoted the promise that they will not raise premiums once a policy has been purchased, many have. According to the California
Department of Insurance, more than thirty carriers nationwide have increased
rates since 1990, including eight carriers still writing policies. Data available at
http://www.insurance.ca.gov/0100-consumers/0060-information-guides/0050-
health/ltc-rate-history-guide/rate-history-active-long-term-care.cfm.

21. Ibid. There is very little overlap in carriers in these two markets. Only John
Hancock is in the top five for both group and individual sales.

22. LIMRA International, 2007.

23. LIMRA International, 2006.

24. U.S. Bureau of Labor Statistics, 2007.

25. Cost of a private-pay nursing home bed, Center for Disease Control, National
Center for Health Statistics, author's calculations.

26. Jeffrey R. Brown and Amy Finkelstein, "The Interaction of Public and Private
Insurance: Medicaid and the Long-Term Care Insurance Market," Cambridge,
Mass., National Bureau of Economic Research, 2006; American Economic Review, forthcoming. Individuals are not eligible for Medicaid until they have exhausted their wealth. In addition, Medicaid is a secondary payer for
long-term-care services after any private insurance. As a result, many individuals
will pay premiums for private insurance that provide benefits that Medicaid
would otherwise have paid. Brown and Finkelstein estimate that 60 percent of
the private insurance benefits due a male with median wealth (about $222,000)
would be paid by Medicaid if that person had no insurance. For a woman, the
amount of such redundant coverage is 75 percent.
        Here is a very simple example. Let's say you have $150,000 in cash and mutual
funds and move to a nursing home that charges $75,000 a year. If you have no

insurance, you will spend down your assets in two years and then go on Medicaid, which will pay all of your remaining nursing home costs for the rest of your life. A private policy that pays $100 a day for three years will finance $36,500 of your first year, while you will pay the difference, or $38,500. After three years, when your insurance coverage ends, you will have spent $115,500 of your $150,000 nest egg. Then you will have to pay all nursing home costs until you deplete your remaining $34,500 (in about five months) and you become eligible for Medicaid, which will cover your costs until you die. Thus, without private insurance, you end up on Medicaid after two years. With coverage, you will be eligible after three and a half years. Over twenty years, you will have paid perhaps $30,000 in premiums and saved the government a year and a half of nursing home payments.

It won't always end up like this, of course. If you have a spouse living at home while you are in a nursing home, you can keep your house and some other assets even while you go on Medicaid. If you die sooner—in, say, a year—your heirs would come out ahead if you had insurance. Similarly, they'd do better if you had a more generous policy. On the other hand, with a private policy that pays $50 a day, you'd run out of money even faster.

27. AARP, "The Costs of Long-Term Care: Public Perceptions Versus Reality," Washington, D.C., 2006. This same survey also reports that nearly one third of all respondents think they have private long-term-care insurance. This is three times the percentage of those who actually have purchased such coverage.

28. Tax-qualified policies must meet certain basic consumer protection standards. More than 95 percent of all policies sold in 2006 were tax-qualified.

29. Anne Theisen Cramer and Gail A. Jensen, "Why Don't People Buy Long-Term Care Insurance?" Washington, D.C., *Journal of Gerontology: Social Sciences* 61 (2006): 185–93. While the authors did not specifically look at the impact of tax subsidies, their analysis of Health and Retirement Survey data found that the demand for coverage is relatively price inelastic. They concluded that even a 25 percent price discount—far more than is available through tax incentives—would increase demand by only 11.2 percent.

30. Urban Institute and Kaiser Commission on Medicaid and the Uninsured, 2006.

31. California, Connecticut, Indiana, and New York.

32. Government Accountability Office, "Long-Term Care Insurance: Partnership Programs Include Benefits That Protect Policyholders and Are Unlikely to Result in Medicaid Savings," GAO-07-231, Washington, D.C., 2007.

33. For details on the program, see http://www.longtermcare.gov/LTC/Main_Site/index.aspx.

34. Government Accountability Office, "Long Term Care Insurance; Federal Program Compared Favorably with Other Products and Analysis of Claims Trend Could Inform Future Decisions," GAO-06-401, Washington, D.C., 2006.

ELEVEN
The Boomers

1. "Old Friends," 1968, words and music by Paul Simon. Simon, by the way, is not a Boomer himself, since he was born in 1941.

2. McKinsey and Co., "Talkin' 'bout My Generation: The Economic Impact of Aging US Baby Boomers," 2008.

3. Data: U.S. Census Bureau, cited in "Older Americans 2008," Federal Interagency Forum on Aging-Related Statistics, 2008.

4. Richard W. Johnson, Desmond Toohey, and Joshua M. Wiener, "Meeting the Long-Term Care Needs of the Baby Boomers," Urban Institute, 2007.

5. Joshua Wiener, Projecting the Future of Long-Term Care: The NIC Compendium Project, PowerPoint presentation by Joshua Wiener, Lewin Group Analysis of U.S. Census Bureau Data, 2008.

6. Data from U.S. Census Bureau, 2006 American Community Survey.

7. Johnson, Toohey, and Wiener, "Meeting the Long-Term Care Needs of the Baby Boomers."

8. Robert B. Friedland, "Caregivers and Long-Term Care Needs in the Twenty-first Century: Will Public Policy Meet the Challenge?" Georgetown University Long-Term Care Financing Project, 2004.

9. Institute of Medicine, "Retooling for an Aging America: Building the Health-care Workforce," 2008.

10. Assuming a 5 percent annual increase in prices.

11. American Society of Consultant Pharmacists.

12. Institute of Medicine, 2008.

13. Alliance for Aging Research, "Medical Never-Never Land: Ten Reasons Why America Is Not Ready for the Coming Age Boom," 2002.

14. U.S. Department of Health and Human Services and U.S. Department of Labor, "The Future Supply of Long-Term Care Workers in Relation to the Aging Baby Boom Generation: Report to Congress," 2003.

15. Institute of Medicine, 2008.

16. American Council of Life Insurance, "Long-Term Care Insurance or Medicaid: Who Will Pay for the Baby Boomers' Long-Term Care?" 2005.

17. Updated information on uses of technology for long-term care is available at www.agetech.org, the Web site of the Center for Aging Services Technologies.

18. Howard Gleckman, "Welcome to the Health Care Economy," *Business Week*, August 26, 2002: 144–48.

19. American Association of Homes and Services for the Aging, "Financing Long-Term Care: A Framework for America," 2006.

20. McKinsey and Co., "Talkin' 'Bout My Generation."

21. Alicia Munnell, Mauricio Soto, Anthony Webb, Francesca Golub-Sass, and Dan Muldoon, "Health Care Costs Drive Up the National Retirement Risk Index," Center for Retirement Research at Boston College, 2008.

22. James Poterba, Steven Venti, and David Wise, "New Estimates of the Future Path of 401(k) Assets," National Bureau of Economic Research, 2007.

23. Olga Sorokina, Anthony Webb, and Dan Muldoon, "Pension Wealth and Income: 1992, 1998 and 2004," Center for Retirement Research at Boston College, 2008. The authors conclude that after adjusting for inflation, the mean pension wealth of a middle-income household fell from $127,000 in 1992 to a little less than $114,000 in 2004.

24. Employee Benefit Research Institute (EBRI), "Retirement Trends Over the Past Quarter Century," 2007.

25. Poterba, Venti, and Wise, "New Estimates."

26. Ibid.

27. Employee Benefit Research Institute, 2007.

28. By some measures, well over half of plans are cashed out. See Poterba, Venti, and Wise, "New Estimates."

29. Jack VanDerhei, Sarah Holden, Craig Copeland, and Louis Alonso, "401(k) Plan Asset Allocation, Account Balances, and Loan Activity in 2006," Employee Benefit Research Institute, 2007.

30. Ibid.

31. Richard Johnson, Gordon Mermin, and Cori Uccello, "How Secure Are Retirement Nest Eggs?" Center for Retirement Research at Boston College, 2006.

32. Munnell, Soto, Webb, Golub-Sass, and Muldoon, "Health Care Costs." This is something of a mid-range estimate. According to another study, a couple that turns sixty-five in 2018 will need to put aside between $250,000 and $1.2 million to pay for medical care over their remaining lifetimes. The amount depends on how long they will live, what retiree health benefits they have, and their tolerance for risk. Fronstin, Salisbury, and VanDerhei, "Savings Needed."

33. Fronstin, Salisbury, and VanDerhei, "Savings Needed."

34. Henry J. Kaiser Family Foundation, "Kaiser/Hewitt 2006 Survey on Retiree Health Benefits," 2006. The percentage of employers offering health insurance to retirees fell from 66 percent in 1988 to 35 percent in 2006. Most of the companies providing coverage are large. Even those that still offer coverage are sharply scaling it back by raising premiums, cutting benefits, eliminating coverage for spouses, and limiting coverage to longtime employees. Even among the largest employers, who are the most generous, three quarters reported raising premiums for retirees from 2005 to 2006.

35. Board of Trustees of the Federal Hospital Insurance and Federal Supplementary Medical Insurance Trust Funds, 2006 Annual Report.

36. Social Security Administration, "Income of the Aged Chartbook, 2002." Available at http://www.socialsecurity.gov/policy/docs/chartbooks/income_aged/2002/iac02.pdf.

37. Howard Gleckman, "The Real Retirement Time Bomb," *Business Week*, January 31, 2005. Based on an unpublished analysis by Richard Johnson and Melissa Favreault of the Urban Institute. As soon as 2010, a typical retiree will be spending nearly 40 percent of his Social Security benefit on Medicare premiums and out-of-pocket health costs combined, according to a study by the Employee Benefit Research Institute (Fronstin, Salisbury, and VanDerhei, "Savings Needed").

38. Social Security Administration, 2007 Annual Report of the Board of Trustees.

39. C. Eugene Steuerle, "Defining Our Long-Term Fiscal Challenges," Testimony before the U.S. Senate Budget Committee, January 30, 2007.

40. Ibid.

41. Richard Kronick and David Rousseau, "Is Medicaid Sustainable? Spending Projections for the Program's Second Forty Years," *Health Affairs* 26, no. 2 (2007): 271–87. (Published online February 23, 2007.)

42. Budget of the United States Fiscal Year 2008, Historical Tables, Office of Management and Budget. Spending for World War II peaked at 37 percent of GDP in 1943 and 1944. By contrast, defense spending during the peak of the Vietnam War was less than 10 percent of GDP, and spending for the wars in Iraq and Afghanistan absorbs less than 5 percent.

43. Centers for Disease Control, National Center for Health Statistics at http://www.cdc.gov/nchs/fastats/lifexpec.htm.

44. 2004 Annual Report of the Board of Trustees of Federal Old-Age and Survivors Insurance and Disability Insurance Trust Funds.

45. Robert Schoeni, Vicki A. Freedman, and Linda G. Martin, "Why Is Late-Life Disability Declining?" *The Milbank Quarterly* 86, no. 1 (2008): 47–89.

46. Joshua Wiener, Laurel Hixon Illston, and Raymond J. Hanley, *Sharing the Burden: Strategies for Public and Private Long-Term Care Insurance*, The Brookings Institution, 2004: 45.

47. Alzheimer's Association, 2008 Alzheimer's Disease Facts and Figures.

TWELVE

How the Rest of the World Does It

1. OECD, "Long-Term Care for Older People," 2005. In 2000, the United States spent about 1.37 percent of its gross domestic product on long-term care; Germany

spent 1.35 percent. The average among major industrialized countries was 1.25 percent.

2. Ibid.

3. Ibid. Another way to look at the aging population is to measure the number of people age sixty-five and older relative to those age twenty to sixty-four—those of prime working age who generate the bulk of national income (and pay most taxes) needed to support public programs for the aged. In the United States in 2000, this dependency ratio was 21.1 percent, compared to 27.5 percent in France, and 27.9 percent in Japan. By 2040, this ratio will rise to 37.9 percent in the United States but will grow to 50 percent in France, 54.5 percent in Germany, and 59.9 percent in Japan. This will place intense pressure on government's ability to finance long-term care.

4. By comparison, in the United States, the combined payroll tax rate for most workers (for Medicaid and Medicare) is 15.3 percent—half paid by employees and half by employers.

5. $1,000 is 1.7 percent of about $59,000.

6. Letter from Emperor William I to Parliament, 1881, cited in the Social Security Administration History Archives, http://www.ssa.gov/history/ottob.html.

7. A description of the German system is available through the Federal Ministry of Health and Social Security, at http://www.bmg.bund.de/DE/Service/Suche/Fehler/fehler_node.htm.

8. Mary Jo Gibson and Donald Redfoot, "Comparing Long-Term Care in Germany and the United States: What Can We Learn from Each Other?" AARP Public Policy Institute, 2007.

9. In Germany, of course, they'd be getting benefits in euros, not dollars. Based on the exchange rates in May 2008, the benefit of €1,432 for approved home care was equal to about $2,200. The cash benefit of €665 was equal to about $1,030. The dementia payment of €460 was equal to about $750.

10. In Germany, as in the United States, need is measured by the ability to perform activities of daily living (ADLs), such as eating, bathing, getting in and out of bed, or going to the bathroom without assistance. The minimum requirement for receiving benefits in the German system is needing help with at least two ADLs; http://www.bmg.bund.de/DE/Service/Suche/Fehler/fehler_node.htm.

11. Melanie Arntz, "The German Social Long-Term Care Insurance: Structure and Reform Options," Centre for European Economic Research, 2007.

12. M. von Schwanenflugel, Directorate of Long-Term Care Insurance, Federal Ministry of Health, 2006; available at www.bmg.bund.de.

13. Ibid.; available at http://www.bmg.bund.de/DE/Service/Suche/Fehler/fehler_node.htm.

14. German Ministry of Health and Social Security, 2006.

15. Melanie Arntz, Ralf Sacchetto, Alexander Spermann, et al., "The German Long-Term Care Insurance: Structure and Reform Options," Institute for the Study of Labor, 2007.

16. J. Hacker and B. Raffelhuschen, 2004, cited in Arntz, et al., "German Social Long-Term Care."

17. Gibson and Redfoot, "Comparing Long-Term Care."

18. Olivia Mitchell, John Piggott, and Satoshi Shimizutani, "Aged-Care Support in Japan: Perspectives and Challenges," NBER, Boston, Mass., 2004.

19. John Creighton Campbell and Naoki Ikegami, "Long-Term Care Insurance Comes to Japan," *Health Affairs* 19, no. 3 (2000): 26–39.

20. Ibid.

21. Centers for Disease Control, Chartbook, 2007.

22. A description of the Japanese system is available through the Ministry of Health, Labor, and Welfare, at http://www.mhlw.go.jp/english/topics/elderly/care/index.html.

23. S. Shimizutani, "Japan's Long-Term Care Insurance Program: An Overview," *Schweizerische Zeitschrift für Volkswirtschaft und Statistik*, Sondernummer 2006: 23–28.

24. Benefits range from around ¥61,500 ($600) to ¥358,300 ($3500) a month based on the May 2008 exchange rate.

25. For an excellent description of the inner workings of the program, see Campbell and Ikegami, "Long-Term Care Insurance."

26. All-Japan Federation of National Health Insurance Organizations, 2003, cited in Mitchell, et al., "Aged-Care Support."

27. Speech by Dr. Naoki Ikegami to AARP Global Aging Program Idea Exchange, April 19, 2006. Summary available at http://www.aarp.org/research/international/events/apr19_06_ikegami.html.

28. Mitchell, Piggott, and Shimituzani, "Aged-Care Support." Their estimate assumes that the number of users and the price of home care continue to rise at historical rates, but that both use and costs of institutional care are frozen. In the more likely event that they continue to rise as well, long-term-care costs could be substantially higher.

29. Ibid.

30. Mark Merlis and Paul N. Van de Water, "Long-Term Care Financing: Models from Abroad," Washington, D.C., National Academy of Social Insurance, 2005.

31. *International Reform Monitor*, Bertelsmann Stiftung, 2007. Available on the Web at http://www.bertelsmann-stiftung.de/cps/rde/xchg/SID-0A000F0A-E41F3F3F/bst_engl/hs.xsl/54224_54228.htm?reform.id=65196.xml&rm.show=reform.

32. Nathalie Morel, "Providing Coverage Against New Social Risks in Bismarkian Welfare States: The Case of Long-Term Care," Paris, France, Université Paris I,

Pantheon-Sorbonne. This paper also provides a good history of the political environment in both Germany and France as these countries reformed their long-term-care programs.

33. Ibid.

34. OECD, 2005.

35. Ruth Hancock, Raphael Wittenberg, Linda Pickard, et al., "Paying for Long-Term Care for Older People in the UK: Modeling the Costs and Distributional Effects of a Range of Options," London School of Economics and Political Science, London, 2006.

36. For a basic description of benefits and means testing, see http://www.kingsfund .org.uk/publications/briefings/longterm_care.html.

37. OECD, "Long-Term Care for Older People," Paris, France, 2005.

38. Royal Commission on Long-Term Care, 1999.

39. Joseph Rowntree Foundation, 2006, "Paying for Long-Term Care: Moving Forward," London, 2006; available at www.jrf.org.uk.

40. Derek Wanless, King's Fund, London, 2006; available at http://www .kingsfund.org.uk/resources/publications/securing_good.html.

41. Wanless, King's Fund..

42. Joshua Wiener, Jane Tilly, and Alison Evans Cuellar, "Consumer-Directed Home Care in the Netherlands, England, and Germany," Washington, D.C., AARP, 2003. Also Mary Jo Gibson, Consumer-Directed Home Care in the Netherlands, England, and Germany, Washington, D.C., AARP Public Policy Institute brief, 2003.

THIRTEEN

Solutions

1. American Association of People with Disabilities, "Section 811 Supportive Housing for Persons with Disabilities 2006 HUD Budget Proposal," 2006.

2. Joanne Lynn, Barry M. Straube, Karen M. Bell, Stephen F. Jencks, and Robert Kambic, "Using Population Segmentation to Provide Better Health Care for All: The 'Bridges to Health' Model," *The Milbank Quarterly* 85, no. 2 (2007).

3. Joanne Lynn, "Living Long in Fragile Health: The New Demographics Shape End-of-Life Care," Hastings Center Report, 2005.

4. American Association of Homes and Services for the Aging, "Financing Long-Term Care: A Framework for America," 2006.

5. A summary of the bill is available at http://kennedy.senate.gov/newsroom/press_ release.cfm?id=ff644903-1844-4478-b53a-5cfb712a5850.

6. The Moran Company, "Modeling a New Long-Term Care Financing Plan," 2007.

7. Christine Bishop, "A Federal Catastrophic Long-Term Care Insurance Program," Working Paper No. 5, Georgetown University Long-Term Care Financing Project, 2007.

8. Anne Tumlinson and Jeanne Lambrew, "Linking Medicare and Private Health Insurance for Long-Term Care," Working Paper No. 6, Georgetown University Long-Term Care Financing Project, 2007. In this plan, those with lower incomes would pay less out of pocket.

9. William Galston, "Reviving the Social Contract: Economic Strategies to Promote Health Insurance and Long-Term Care," Opportunity 08, The Brookings Institution, 2007.

10. All premium estimates provided by The Moran Co. Projections for the AAHSA plan are at The Moran Company, "Modeling a New Long-Term Care Financing Plan," 2007. Estimates of the five-year plan were computed at the author's request. Premiums for both plans assume a cash benefit and a five-year vesting period. The cost of low-income subsidies is built into premium costs, and the plans would pay for themselves over seventy-five years. Premiums for a service, rather than a cash, benefit, would be significantly lower.

11. Credit for this idea belongs to Donald Redfoot of AARP.

12. Amy Finkelstein, "The Aggregate Effects of Health Insurance: Evidence from the Introduction of Medicare," *Quarterly Journal of Economics* 122, no. 1 (2007): 1–37. Finkelstein found that such a steady revenue stream through Medicare drove up prices of health care providers.

13. Voltaire, *La Bégueule*, 1772, cited in Wikipedia at http://en.wikiquote.org/wiki/Voltaire.

FOURTEEN
Dorothy

1. Robert Alter, *The Five Books of Moses*, New York; W. W. Norton and Co., 2004: 1017.

Where You Can Find Help

There are hundreds of Web-based resources for those who are caring for family members or friends. Here are some of the best:

AARP: www.aarp.org. AARP is an advocacy and marketing juggernaut, but its Web site includes lots of practical information about finances, housing, health care, and aging.

Alzheimer's Association: www.alz.org. Not just for Alzheimer's. This site has information about all dementias, as well as good tips for caregivers. Most other diseases also have associations with their own Web sites.

Area Agencies on Aging: These government-funded organizations can guide you to helpful services in your community. To find one closest to you, go to www.elder care.gov or call 1-800-677-1116.

Caring From a Distance: www.cfad.org. Guidance for those who face the special challenges of long-distance caregiving.

Family Caregiver Alliance: www.caregiver.org. Practical advice about all facets of caregiving.

Home Health Compare: www.medicare.gov/HHCompare. A government Web site where you can research home health agencies.

Medicare Rights Center: www.medicarerights.org. Everything you need to know about Medicare from an independent advocacy group.

National Academy of Elder Law Attorneys: www.naela.org. A helpful guide to lawyers who specialize in elder care and disability issues.

National Association of Insurance Commissioners: www.naic.org. Click on the long-term-care link for consumer information on long-term-care insurance.

National Association of Professional Geriatric Care Managers: www.caremanager .org. If you need more hands-on assistance, this site will help you find a care manager.

National Family Caregivers Association: www.nfcacares.org. Resources and advocacy for family caregivers, as well as links to dozens of other helpful sites.

Nursing Home Compare: www.medicare.gov. This government Web site lets you compare the quality of nursing homes. But these measures should be only the start of your search.

Index

government, U.S. *(continued)*
reverse mortgage insurance by,
141–42
Social Security program by, 25, 34,
48, 81, 133, 140, 151, 164,
208–10, 211, 213, 224, 241
spending, on Medicaid, by, 19,
89–90, 131, 148–49, 151, 156,
160–64, 166–70, 211, 244, 246,
270*n*28, 270*n*31, 275*n*3, 284*n*4
spending, on Medicare, by, 34, 164,
210, 246, 284*n*4
spending, on Social Security, by,
164, 211, 213
Green Houses (group homes), 77,
101–4, 106, 114, 160
solutions, long-term-care, and,
236–37
viability of, 105
Greer, David, 28
group homes
for disabled, non-elderly, 71–72
for elderly, 29–30, 92, 160
Green House concept of, 77, 101–6,
114, 160, 236–37

Haldol, 87
Hanna, Richard, 32–33, 259
health aides
abuse by, 31, 53–54
in assisted-living facilities, 98–99
case studies with, 4–5, 7–8, 11–16,
49–50, 158–61
companions as, 64, 159–61
cost of/salaries of, x, 12–13, 23, 29,
32–33, 44–45, 51, 53, 64, 85,
102, 105, 112, 132, 189, 201,
237
demographics of, 52–53, 55, 65,
201
future of, 201
home care by, x, 4–5, 7–8, 11–16,
49–55, 111, 112–17, 158–61,
201, 233–34, 237

insurance benefits for, 51–53
insurance, private, coverage of,
12–13, 135
international care systems and, 220
Medicare coverage of, 5, 176
medication dispensed by, 51,
113–14
new institutional models and, 98–99,
102–6
in nursing homes, 75–77, 85–87,
201, 237
training/skills of, 50–51, 64, 113–17,
233–34, 237
working conditions for, 51, 85–86
health care, general. *See also* insurance,
health; long-term care; Medicare
advancements in, 23–25, 30, 60
cost estimates on, 34, 208, 282*n*32,
283*n*37
geriatric medicine in, 27–28, 91,
202, 237, 289
insurance coverage of, x–xi, 19, 28,
34, 51–53, 81, 133, 134, 205–6,
208, 217, 273*n*4, 282*n*34
resources for, 289
HECM. *See* Home Equity Conversion
Mortgage
Hemphill, Ayars, 159–61, 258
HMOs, 128
home care, long-term. *See also*
caregivers, family; health aides
adult day centers supporting, 29, 52,
126–27, 164–68, 169, 234, 239
caregiver demographics related to,
2, 3, 18, 28, 40, 52–53, 200–201,
265*n*2
case studies featuring, 8–18, 39–50,
51–53, 158–61
co-housing in, 29, 124–26
cost of, 36–37, 112
for disabled, non-elderly, 23–24,
57–67, 232–33
by families, 3, 8–18, 28, 31, 36–37,
39–55, 107–30, 134–35, 265*n*2